The Transformation of Freemasonry

'The Revolution of the World!'

David Harrison

D1612596

Published 2010 by arima publishing

www.arimapublishing.com

ISBN 978 1 84549 437 7

© David Harrison 2010

Printed and bound in the United Kingdom

Typeset in Garamond 12/14

arima publishing
ASK House, Northgate Avenue
Bury St Edmunds, Suffolk IP32 6BB
t: (+44) 01284 700321
www.arimapublishing.com

Acknowledgements

In researching and writing this work I would like to thank a host of people for their assistance: John Belton for his help in co-writing Chapter Three and assembling the tables and graphs, supplying information on numerous lodges and participating in proofreading the book, Mr. G. A. Gerrard for supplying information on The Merchants Lodge No. 241 in Liverpool and giving access to his private library, Tony Stringer for supplying information regarding the Ellesmere Lodge No. 758 in Runcorn, Diane Clements, librarian at the United Grand Lodge of England for her help on membership lists and lodge histories, The Rev. Neville Cryer for supplying documents relating to 'The Wigan Grand Lodge', Stanley Churm of The Lodge of Lights No. 148, Warrington, for supplying access to the lodge documents and the Masonic library, the United Grand Lodge of England, and Dr. William Ashworth of the University of Liverpool who supervised my PhD and various papers. Special thanks to arima Publishing for their support and patience. All photographs taken by Marie Shaw except were indicated.

Contents

Foreword

I first met David Harrison in 2005 at the second of Prof Andrew Prescott's Conferences at the Centre for Research into Freemasonry. This was one of those very rare occasions when researchers into Freemasonry got together to listen to each other's work and generally chew the fat over meals or a beer. David is a professional historian who is also a Freemason; I am a Freemason who is also interested in history. I had had a long interest in the causes of the current Masonic decline and while I had dabbled in analyzing lodge data I had done nothing serious about it. David had been working on the Lodge of Lights in Warrington and we got together and looked at what was happening in some lodges in the Industrial North West of England – and this is in Chapter 3 of this book.

There is a general view held by Freemasons that Freemasonry has marched ever onwards from strength to strength and will do so forever. The period since 1950 has given us ever fewer initiates each year, the number of masons in England and Wales has probably halved and the number of lodges increased by around thirty percent. With a calculator one can work out that an average lodge probably had around 70 members and that has now fallen to under 30. And of course it is not only Freemasonry that has struggled with membership, so have many other organizations. The fact is simple; Freemasonry is part of the society of the day and its members are subject to the same information, the same stresses, the same worries over jobs, income, family. That is as true today as it was two hundred years ago.

David has set about trying to paint a picture of Freemasonry in the first half of the nineteenth century, and chose to do so not at the Grand and formal level but at a lodge and individual brother level. He has chosen to do so fairly much in the context of the Industrial North West of England and to explore a little some of the Masonic connections that took place with international trade. This part of Britain is where we both live and the past is there to be seen whether in the form of the grand buildings in the centre of Liverpool and Manchester or the weirs and mill races on the rivers and the remains of the stone walls of long gone mills.

The first half of the nineteenth century were hard times and the rate and pace of change fast, uncontrolled and chaotic (the pace of change today being probably equally fast and furious). Fortunes were made and almost as easily fortunes lost, build a mill using the current technology and if you were unlucky and the next development came early and allowed a ten-fold increase in production speed – then your investment was never going to show a decent return. For the working man who had emigrated from country to industrial town, life was hard and housing conditions truly awful. This brought with it ill health, and epidemics of diseases such as cholera, all made worse by the gross overcrowding.

Representation in Parliament was still, and until the Reform Bill of 1832, unaddressed especially as far as the new industrial cities were concerned. Even after this Act the working classes were still in ferment and an air of 'radicalism' abroad. For example at a meeting in Manchester to inaugurate the Anti Corn Law League were present Richard Cobden (cotton merchant and internationalist), John Bright (a Quaker carpet manufacturer from Rochdale and James Wilson (Scottish journalist and founder of *The Economist*). The Chartist Movement was active from 1838 to 1842 and it was also around this time that Karl Marx traveled round greater Manchester and as a result of what he saw came to the conclusion that revolution by the masses was inevitable.

However events like the large cholera epidemic of 1832 also helped Britain to reach a realization that the general unsanitary conditions were not only bad for the populace but that a healthier workforce would be more productive, and maybe to thus able to consume more. All this led to the appearance of gas lighting, sewers which took the soil away underground, clean water piped into towns (which of course helped industry because it too needed water).

By about 1860 conditions were generally more acceptable, reforms in many areas of society had taken place, and revolution now seemed a much more distant prospect. This general air of prosperity allowed a burgeoning middle class to appear – a more complex industry needed a greater range and number of professionals and managers. These were men who could afford to house their family in a newly built villa and for whom the more rough and ready style of Freemasonry in the room above the tavern was perhaps no longer so socially acceptable. And thus started the era of purpose built Masonic halls. The values of Freemasonry and its newly acquired social graces were still desirable and it prospered as did many other fraternal organizations like the Oddfellows and Independent Order of Rechabites.

That is the backdrop to the themes of this book. Hopefully it paints a picture of the world ones great grandfather would have known and if a Freemason some of the events that might have trickled down through the grapevine and the Masonic press.

John Belton
January 2010

Introduction

'The Revolution of the World!'

Thomas Paine replying to the standing ovation given to him after a dinner at the London Revolutionary Society in 1791, when a song was composed in his honor, heralding Paine as the great reformer.[1]

'The key is the symbol of the first ripe fruits of American principles translated into Europe'.

Thomas Paine speaking after he was handed the key of the Bastille by the Marquis de Lafayette, which was to be delivered to George Washington, both of whom were Freemasons.[2]

'The first of these conspiracies was that of those men called Philosophers. The second that of the Philosophers united with the Occult Lodges of the Freemasons. The third was that of the Philosophers and the Occult-Masons coalesced with the Illumines, who generated the Jacobins.'

Abbé Augustin Barruel, *Memoirs Illustrating the History of Jacobinism*, 1799.[3]

In my previous work *The Genesis of Freemasonry*, I charted the history of English Freemasonry from its early beginnings as a society in the seventeenth century, through its development in the eighteenth, examining three transitions of the Craft; the change from 'Operative' Masonry to a 'Speculative' society, the foundation of the 'Premier/Modern' Grand Lodge in London in 1717 and the birth of the Modern ritual by leading Freemason and natural philosopher Dr. John Theophilus Desaguliers. The subsequent rebellions within the Craft were also discussed, especially in York and with the foundation of the Antients, culminating in the Union of 1813 which brought the Moderns and the Antients back together. This new work will act as a companion to that

---

[1] J. Dos Passos, (ed.), *The Living Thoughts of Tom Paine*, (London, 1946), p.27.
[2] Ibid., pp.24-5.
[3] Abbé Barruel, *Memoirs Illustrating the History of Jacobinism Part I – Vol. I. The Antichristian Conspiracy*, (London: Hudson & Goodwin, 1799), p.iv.

book, a sequel of sorts, looking at how Freemasonry transformed itself once more as a result of a number of political and social changes which affected the Craft, particularly the Unlawful Societies Act of 1799. Freemasonry adapted and transformed itself to adjust to an ever changing society.

The closing years of the eighteenth century in Great Britain were swathed in a climate of fear, with the Tory government of William Pitt the younger suffering the angst of revolution, rebellion and riot. The French Revolution in 1789, the subsequent Bloody Terror and the rise of Napoleon had cast a shadow of dread and paranoia over Great Britain.[4] This anxiety had been compounded by rebellion in Ireland in 1798 and frequent riots and protests by the working classes, with groups of factory workers combining to form seemingly ever more aggressive 'trade unions'. Radical societies such as the 'United Irishmen' and the 'London Corresponding Society' were singled out as extremist and treasonous, and the growing fear that revolution could spread to Britain was very real.

The alarm of secret gatherings of men swearing oaths to solidify their united cause created a powerful image of the haunting spectre of Jacobinism, and Freemasonry - both 'Antient' and 'Modern', was to be associated with these societies in the over fretful minds of the government. When the Unlawful Societies Act was passed in July 1799, Freemasonry was unavoidably affected, the Craft having to adapt to what many saw as an oppressive legislation. The original proposal of the bill would have completely banned Freemasonry along with other secret societies, but the Earl of Moira and other leading Freemasons from both the 'Moderns', the 'Antients' and the Scottish Grand Lodge prevailed upon Pitt to amend it by exempting Masonic lodges *'sitting by the precise authorization of a Grand Lodge and under its direct superintendence'*. This however would have destroyed the independent Scottish lodges like Lodge Kilwinning, so, aided by their Scottish MP William Fullerton who was acquainted with Pitt, a further alteration on behalf of the lodge was obtained. The bill in its final form stated that *'all Lodges declaring upon oath before a Justice of the Peace that they were Freemasons'* were exempt from its provisions.[5]

---

[4] See John Barrell, *The Spirit of Despotism*, (Oxford: Oxford University Press, 2006). Barrell puts forward that the fear of the French Revolution spreading across the channel created a culture of suspicion and surveillance, effecting how people behaved in all aspects of their lives. See also David Worrall, *Theatric Revolution*, (Oxford: Oxford University Press, 2008). Worrall deals with stage censorship during the sensitive period between 1773-1832.

[5] See L.A. Seemungal, 'The Edinburgh Rebellion 1808-1813', *AQC*, Vol. 86, (York: Ben Johnson & Co. Ltd.,1973), pp.322-325.

Thus, Freemasonry managed to escape the Act by agreeing to submit annual returns of lists of members and lodge meetings which could be inspected by the appropriate authorities. Masonry would henceforth have an element of transparency, but did Freemasons in general feel comfortable with this new declaration? And how did the general public feel about Freemasonry during this atmosphere of political anxiety? Answers to these questions can be found at local level, were the individual lodges showed signs of change and transition, especially in the industrial heartland of England where radicalism amongst the working classes was most associated.

An example of changes in the character of lodges at local level can be found with the 'Modern' Lodge of Lights, which was based in the industrial town of Warrington in the north-west of England – a lodge that will be explored in more depth. This lodge made a special mention in its minutes of August 1799 that, in accordance to the recent Unlawful Societies Act, it would hereafter submit a list of its members every March.[6] The lodge subsequently underwent a transition, reflected in the incoming occupations of the new members, revealing more men extracted from the laboring trades. Other lodges in industrial areas in England and Wales, such as Oldham, Stockport, Merthyr Tydfil, and the mining communities of Cornwall, also reveal an influx of laboring tradesmen during this period, and this impact on localized Freemasonry will be discussed.

All the lodges studied from this period revealed low membership and financial problems; some lodges survived, others became extinct. Indeed, the immediate years following the Act saw fewer 'Modern' lodges being founded and the 'Antient' lodges recycling existing lodge numbers which had become defunct rather than issue new warrants. This was a result of the 'Antients' having imposed emergency measures on themselves after their meeting with Pitt, stating that they would *'suppress and suspend all masonic meetings, except upon the regular stated lodge meetings'*, a declaration which enforced that only their current lodges at the time of the bill would operate, the Grand Lodge refusing to issue new warrants. The 'Antients' may have done this because of their close relationship with Irish Freemasonry, or perhaps because of the large number of lodges under their jurisdiction within the industrial north-west of England. They were seen by the 'Moderns' as a secessionist Grand Lodge, a view which was

---

[6] The list of the membership of the Lodge of Lights No. 148 date from the lodge's consecration in 1765, the surviving minute books however date from the 1790s.

dangerous during this time of paranoia. The Antients, founded in 1751, held different ritualistic and administrative practices that conflicted with the 'Moderns', the feud becoming increasingly bitter as the eighteenth century progressed.

It seems that during the eighteenth century, whenever there was a Revolution, Freemasons were not far away. The American Revolution had many Masons leading the cause, such as Benjamin Franklin, George Washington, John Hancock, James Monroe and James Otis to name but a few. With the outbreak of the French Revolution in 1789, Freemasons were again involved in the leadership of various revolutionary factions, with Louis Philippe II, Duke of Orleans, the Grand Master of the Grand Orient being prominent, along with the Marquis de Lafayette and a host of others, some, such as Jean Paul Marat, being revolutionaries, but were against fellow Freemasons like Lafayette.[7] Four brothers of Napoleon Bonaparte were also Freemasons, Napoleon placing them in important positions; Joseph Bonaparte was made Grand Master of the Grand Orient of France, Louis the Deputy Grand Master, Lucian also became a member of the Grand Orient, and Jerome was made Grand Master of the Grand Orient of Westphalia. With the Bonaparte's firmly linked to Freemasonry, it is not surprising that, especially to people who did not understand Masonry, the Craft became tinted with revolution.[8]

Freemasons were certainly accused of influencing the French Revolution at the time, most notably by the French Jesuit Abbé Augustin Barruel, who wrote vehemently about a Masonic conspiracy to overthrow the monarchy and aristocracy of Europe in his work *Memoirs Illustrating the History of Jacobinism*. His work, though unfounded, became very popular, with editions being printed in England and the United States.[9] Freemasons in certain parts Europe had also suffered persecution, most famously with Count Cagliostro who was imprisoned in Rome and charged with being a Freemason in 1789 – a crime for which he was sentenced to death.[10]

---

[7] See Stanley J. Idzerda (ed.), *Lafayette in the Age of the American Revolution: Selected Letters and Papers 1776-1790*, Vol.I, December 7, 1776-March 30, 1778, (New York: Cornell University Press, 1983).

[8] See David Harrison, 'Freemasonry and Revolution', in *Freemasonry Today*, Issue 49, (Grand Lodge Publications, summer 2009), pp.26-28.

[9] Abbé Barruel, *Memoirs Illustrating the History of Jacobinism Part I – Vol. I. The Antichristian Conspiracy*, (London: Hudson & Goodwin, 1799), p.iv.

[10] See Philippa Faulks and Robert L.D. Cooper, *The Masonic Magician; The Life and Death of Count Cagliostro and his Egyptian Rite*, (London: Watkins, 2008).

Masonic symbolism featured prominently in Revolutionary propaganda and in official pamphlets for the French Revolutionary governments; symbols such as the All Seeing Eye and the Plumb-Rule were commonly being used to portray the supposed Enlightenment and justice brought about by the Revolution. The Enlightenment itself, brought to prominence by writers like the Freemason Voltaire, had an engaging influence on the origins of the Revolution, with works such as *The Rights of Man* by Thomas Paine, who had also been linked to Freemasonry, being written in support of the Revolution. The Revolution however, descended into violence and political turmoil, the enlightened road of liberty being a long and blood stained one, with an estimated 15,000-40,000 people being guillotined.[11] The guillotine was named after Dr. Joseph-Ignace Guillotine, physician, Assembly member and Freemason. Freemasonry had thus been tinted with the blood of Revolution and this did not help its position in Britain. The Painite radical Richard Carlile commented on the public perceptions of the Craft in his *Manual of Freemasonry*, observing that:

'All the particulars of Freemasonry being now laid before the public eye, there remains not the shadow of an excuse or reason why it should be continued as a secret association.' He then remarked on the Act saying *'the legislature being about to deal with other secret societies, would do well now not again to make an exception of Masonry'*.

Carlile realized that the Craft had escaped a period of persecution.[12] Freemasonry and Revolution became further entwined during the first part of the nineteenth century, with the Freemason Simon Bolivar being involved in the revolutionary struggle of South America[13] and Freemasons becoming involved in the wave of Revolutions that swept through Europe in 1848.[14]

Because Freemasonry had adapted in response to the threat of the Unlawful Societies Act, it survived, but still suffered from the combination of the effects of the Act and the social issues of the period. In industrial towns like Warrington, Wigan, Stockport and Oldham,

---

[11] See Peter Jones, (ed.), *The French Revolution in Social & Political Perspective*, (London: Arnold, 1996), pp.192-199.

[12] Richard Carlile, *Manual of Freemasonry*, (Croydon: New Temple Press, 1912), p.86.

[13] See J.B. Trend, *Bolivar and the Independence of Spanish America*, (London: The English Universities Press, 1946), pp.168-169.

[14] See Peter Jones, *The 1848 Revolutions*, (London: Longman, 1991), and Mike Rapport, *1848: Year of Revolution*, (London: Abacus, 2009).

laboring tradesmen joined the lodges, mixing with industrialists and professional men, though membership numbers dwindled in the wake of the Act. However, Freemasonry in these areas eventually revived; the society expanding after the mid-nineteenth century with the make-up of the membership changing, becoming far more consistent - the lodge membership lists revealing an array of wealthy industrialists, merchants, professionals and local gentry. This work will explore the revival and expansion of Freemasonry in the later nineteenth century and will attempt to explain why this happened.

Despite these changes within Freemasonry, education and charity were still essential features of the Craft. Ever since the foundation of the 'Premier' or 'Modern' Grand Lodge in London in 1717, these features became entwined with the ethos of the Craft. Morality, brotherly love, relief and truth, became vital components to the practice of Masonry, and various lectures were given within lodges to remind the Mason of his duty to his fellow brethren and the community. Indeed, these themes are entwined throughout the ritual, constantly reminding Freemasons of the importance of charity. Dr. John Theophilus Desaguliers, an exponent of Newtonian philosophy, and a leading Freemason of the time, argued for the importance of the central control of a Masonic charity as early as 1730, and constantly promoted the teaching of natural philosophy. Freemasonry certainly led the way when, in 1788, a charity was formed to look after the daughters of deceased Freemasons, which would supply a home and an education. In 1798, a similar fund was set up for the sons of Freemasons. Besides these central charities within Freemasonry, local lodges also demonstrated methods of self support, providing claims for relief and burial.

The ethos of education within Freemasonry can also be seen clearly at local level, with local lodges such as the Lodge of Lights in Warrington and the Lodge of Friendship in Oldham supporting local educational institutions and learned societies during the eighteenth and nineteenth centuries. An example of this was the radical Warrington Academy, which was a progressive centre of learning for young male dissenters founded in 1757. The Academy had a number of tutors that were Freemasons, while other tutors who were not Freemasons, clearly mixed in Masonic circles. The Academy was an influential radical and cultural centre, and some of its tutors and students openly supported both the American and French Revolutions. Despite closing in 1786, the spirit of education was kept alive by certain members of the local Lodge of Lights, with many schoolmasters joining the lodge. The wealthy industrialists and professionals of the town who later joined the lodge praised the memory of the Academy and founded a diverse number of learned societies and as we shall see, funded other local educational centres.

A similar occurrence can be seen in Oldham, with members of the Lodge of Friendship supporting the Oldham Lyceum. In the Lodge of Friendship, there were members who valued the promotion of education, such as James Butterworth who became a local school teacher and writer, publishing books on Masonic symbolism, poetry and local history. This work will also look at other lodges in other industrial towns throughout England and Wales, and will present a view of how local Freemasonry supported and promoted education and charity, assisting in the development of industrialised areas during the later eighteenth and nineteenth centuries, helping to form a cultural identity within the particular town. Networking was also an important feature of Freemasonry during this period, the society creating an opportunity of interweaving business contacts and relationships that equally spread ideas of civic improvement.

During the later eighteenth and early nineteenth centuries, Masonic lodges were intricately linked to the social, economic and industrial identity of their locality. The membership of Liverpool lodges, like its neighbouring towns, reflected the local industry, with many merchants being members. The port of Liverpool had around ten lodges operating during this period, both Antient and Modern, and the role of individual Freemasons within the slave trade and within the abolition movement will be discussed. The cotton trade with the Southern States of America was vitally important for Liverpool, and along with other trades, such as tobacco, the intricate networking links between Liverpool and the USA will be examined, Freemasonry, as we shall see, playing a vital role.

The discontent that led to the infamous Masonic Rebellion in Liverpool will also be discussed, some Liverpool Freemasons deciding to create their own Grand Lodge, effectively resurrecting the Antients ten years after it had so ceremoniously merged with the 'Moderns' in the Union of 1813. As in other industrial towns, the Liverpool Freemasons supported local charities and local education, and a philanthropic zeal can be seen taking place. With the Liverpool Masonic Rebellion and the subsequent founding of the Wigan Grand Lodge, an example of a cultural identity developed in the locality, with Freemasonry being a central part of the social nexus within the community.

Freemasonry underwent a transformation in the nineteenth century that would ultimately lead to the expansion of the society, the Craft maturing, becoming extremely successful and highly respectable. Aspects of this change can be seen with the ever-growing interest in other Masonic Orders such as the Royal Arch and Mark Masonry, and the networking culture of clubs and secret societies in Victorian England will be examined. Freemasons during this period were still searching for hidden knowledge, exploring the mystical nature of the Craft, leading some Masons to delve into the more magical elements of ritual, creating new independent Orders. Certain Freemasons eagerly explored the 'occult sciences' using Freemasonry as an influence, the Craft attracting intellectuals and writers who went on to establish the Hermetic Order of the Golden Dawn.

The expansion of Freemasonry during the later nineteenth century can be seen in the rapid creation of new lodges and the building of Masonic Halls throughout the country. Freemasonry thus became more respectable and recognisable as a society for the wealthy and affluent industrialists and professional classes. This work will explain these developments, and will also express how the society still retained its educational and charitable ethos, both remaining central to the Craft. The transformation of Freemasonry during the nineteenth century was a difficult one; the Unlawful Societies Act, the effects of the Napoleonic war, the social upheaval caused by industrialisation, and reaction and change caused by the Union of 1813, all played a part in the development of the society during this period. This book will explore this development, and will examine the reasons for the transformation of Freemasonry.

Chapter 1

The Warrington Academy; Freemasonry, Education and Charity[15]

Warrington, the seat of an Academy destined to give the town in the eighteenth century the proud title of the "Athens of the North".[16]

I feel a high responsibility resting with me, not only that the religious duties to be performed with regularity and zeal, but also that the morals of the people be carefully guarded and advanced, both by precept and example, to the highest degree of excellence of which they are capable.'
Freemason Dr. George Oliver discussing his ideas for improving education in Wolverhampton [17]

The schools of the Greeks were schools of science and philosophy, and not of languages; and it is in the knowledge of the things that science and philosophy teach that learning consists.'
Thomas Paine, *The Age of Reason,* 1794[18]

The Warrington Dissenting Academy had an excellent location, its elegant Georgian building, situated on the banks of the River Mersey dominated the entrance to the historical market town of Warrington, which lay in-between the major port of Liverpool and the growing textile centre of Manchester. The location of the Academy was chosen mainly due to these reasons, yet Warrington had a long tradition of dissenting activity, and the proposed institute had support from the town, support that was drawn from several influential Freemasons. The town also had a

---

[15] Part of the content of this chapter was presented at the International History of Freemasonry Conference, Edinburgh, on the 29th of May, 2009.
[16] .H. McLachlan, *Warrington Academy, Its History And Influence,* (Manchester: Chetham Society, 1943), p.1.
[17] George Oliver, *Hints for Improving the Societies and Institutions Connected with Education and Science in the Town of Wolverhampton,* in R.S.E Sandbach, *Priest and Freemason: The Life of George Oliver,* (Northamptonshire: The Aquarian Press, 1988), pp.72-4.
[18] Thomas Paine, *The Age of Reason: Being an Investigation of True and Fabulous Theology, Part First,* (Boston: Josiah P. Mendum, 1852), p.42.

history of Freemasonry, Warrington being the place where Elias Ashmole was made a Freemason in October 1646.

There had been many Dissenting Academies in existence throughout England and Wales during the early part of the eighteenth century, such as in Abergavenny, Tewksbury and in Kendal - where the industrialist John 'Iron-Mad' Wilkinson had been a student, though many of these had been short lived. The first Dissenting Academy opened in Warrington was in 1697, being situated in Sankey Street. This survived until 1746, and was the forerunner of the new Warrington Academy, which was opened in 1757. The Lodge of Lights, a 'Modern' Masonic Lodge was founded in Warrington in 1765, and soon included various professionals, merchants, craftsmen, and local gentry, many of whom were leaders of the local community. A number of Freemasons appeared to be sympathetic with the values of the dissenters, and would be linked to the Academy from the outset. A founder of the Lodge of Lights, Benjamin Yoxall, who was also a schoolmaster,[19] had previously assisted in the foundation of the Warrington Circulating Library in 1758, along with the Rev. John Seddon, businessmen Thomas & Samuel Gaskell, and local printer and bookseller, William Eyres.[20] The Rev. John Seddon was the founder and spiritual leader of the Warrington Academy, and local support from the prominent townsmen was vital.

Independent Academies had been founded during the earlier eighteenth century by Freemasons, such as Martin Clare, a Fellow of the Royal Society and an active Freemason in the 'Premier/Modern' Grand Lodge, who had founded the Soho Academy in London in about 1718.[21] Another Freemason who had founded an Academy at Little Tower Street in London in the early eighteenth century was Thomas Watts. Watts was a Whig MP and teacher of mathematics who was also involved in the early insurance industry, becoming a member of the Court of Assistants of the Sun Fire.[22] The ethos of education within the Craft certainly inspired individuals to create independent institutions of learning.

By the mid eighteenth century, many non-conformist families were involved in industry, such as Josiah Wedgwood, whose son, John, attended the Warrington Academy. John 'Iron-Mad' Wilkinson was also

19 *List of Members of the Lodge of Lights no.148, Warrington, 8th of November, 1765.* Warrington Masonic Hall. Not listed. Benjamin Yoxall is also mentioned in local land leases in the *Patten Deeds,* Warrington Library, reference MS1216.
20 A.M. Crowe, *Warrington, Ancient and Modern,* (Warrington: Beamont Press, 1947), p.171.
21 Larry Stewart, *Rise of Public Science,* (Cambridge: Cambridge University Press, 1992), pp.134-6.
22 P.J. Wallis, 'Thomas Watts. Academy Master, Freemason, Insurance Pioneer, MP', *History of Education Society Bulletin,* Vol.XXXII, (1983), pp.51-3.

a supporter of the Academy, his daughter Mary, marrying Academy tutor Joseph Priestley,[23] and his son, William, also attended the Academy. Wedgwood was linked to Freemasonry,[24] and, along with Priestley, he was also linked to the Birmingham based Lunar Society, a society which actively promoted natural philosophy. The Freemason Erasmus Darwin was another celebrated member of the Lunar Society.[25]

Joseph Priestley was a dissenting minister, philosopher, groundbreaking scientist, Academy tutor, and a supporter of the American and French Revolutions. There is no evidence to suggest that he was a Freemason, but he certainly mixed in Masonic circles. Like his friend and fellow dissenter Richard Price, he also believed that in the French Revolution, he was witnessing the turmoil before the dawning of God's everlasting kingdom, the peace that would occur in the millennium.[26]

Laced with radicalism, the late eighteenth century was a period of political pamphleteering and republican ideology which exploded into revolution for the American Colonies and for France. Leading

---

[23] P. O'Brien, *Warrington Academy 1757-86, Its Predecessors & Successors,* (Wigan: Owl Books, 1989), p.21.

[24] A lodge named after Josiah Wedgwood (No. 2214) was founded in 1887 in Stoke-on-Trent. Josiah Wedgwood's son, Josiah Wedgwood II (1769-1843), was a member of the Etruscan Lodge, which met at the Old Bridge Inn at Etruria on the Wedgewood estate. Wedgwood's business partner William Greatbatch was also a Freemason and was also a member of the Etruscan Lodge. Greatbatch was responsible for designing Masonic artwork on some pottery (see V. Greenwald, 'Researching the Decoration on a Greatbatch Teapot', in *The American Wedgwoodian,* December 1979, (The Potteries Museum, Stoke-on-Trent). This particular Etruscan Lodge closed around 1847, though another lodge with the same name surfaced shortly afterwards. Freemasonry in the Staffordshire area has continued links with the Wedgwood family, and as recently as 1971, two direct descendants of Josiah Wedgwood; brothers Josiah and William Wedgwood, attended the Josiah Wedgwood Lodge in Stoke.

[25] Erasmus Darwin joined the St. David's Lodge, No. 36, in Edinburgh in 1754. He was also a member of the renowned Canongate Kilwinning Lodge No. 2.

[26] See J. Fruchtman, 'The Apocalyptic Politics of Richard Price & Joseph Priestley: a study in late eighteenth century English republican millenialism', in *Philadelphia American Philosophical Society,* (1983). For Price's Masonic career, see Jenkins, *History Of Modern Wales,* p.176, in which he states that Price was Master of a lodge in Bridgend in 1777. The lodge that Jenkins refers to belonged to the 'Antients' (no. 33b) and met in the Bear Inn, Dunraven Place, Bridgend during 1777. Price had used the Bear Inn to present lectures, though his leadership of the lodge appears to have been short lived as it lapsed the same year due to a misunderstanding amongst the leading brethren. Correspondence between local Freemasons and the Grand Secretary, first in October, 1803 and then in May the following year, shows an effort to revive the erased warrant of Lodge no. 33b. This brief correspondence exists in the United Grand Lodge records, Ref: GBR 1991 AR/621/1 & 2. Price is also referred to as a Freemason in John Money, 'The Masonic Moment; Or Ritual, Replica, and Credit: John Wilkes, the Macaroni Parson, and the Making of the Middle-Class Mind', in *The Journal of British Studies,* Vol. 32, No. 4, (October, 1993), pp.358-95.

intellectual figures and natural philosophers Dr. Richard Price and
Benjamin Franklin were both Freemasons, and they both influenced Dr.
Joseph Priestley in his work while he taught at the Warrington Academy,
which, from 1757-1786, became Britain's most progressive learning
centre. Creating an intellectual nexus, the Academy became an
exceptional and desirable location for students, Priestley expressing its
ideology and ethos in his memoirs:

> *'..the Academy was in a state peculiarly favourable to serious pursuit of truth, as
> the students were about equally divided upon every question of much importance, such
> as Liberty and Necessity, the sleep of the soul, and all the articles of theological
> orthodoxy and heresy ; in consequence of which all these topics were the subject of
> continual discussion.*[27]

Religious freedom was also part of the ethos of Freemasonry during
this period. After the civil war, anti-Puritan feeling caused a public
backlash against non-conformists, leading to their exclusion from the
English Universities of Oxford and Cambridge, due to the Test Acts.
After the Revolution of 1688, a Toleration Act was passed, which
removed a lot of the hatred away from non-conformists over to the
Catholics. This gave 'dissenters' slightly more freedom, and new
Academies, such as the one situated in Warrington began to flourish,
attracting many radical free-thinkers.

Tutors such as Priestley, who became a tutor at the Academy in 1761,
John Reinhold Forster, John Aikin, his son John Aikin jnr, William
Enfield, Gilbert Wakefield, George Walker and Jacob Bright, all had
excellent reputations, the Academy's status growing as a result. It was
during his time at Warrington that Priestley traveled to London,
becoming friends with Benjamin Franklin and Richard Price. The Royal
Society would also become an influence on Priestley, when he became a
Fellow in 1766 on the merit of his work on electricity. Richard Price and
Benjamin Franklin had both recommended Priestley, and his *History and
Present State of Electricity* had been written while he was at Warrington after
being encouraged by Franklin to conduct his own experiments.[28] The
links between Freemasonry and the Royal Society were still strong at this
time, the scientific mind of the eighteenth century being attracted to the
expressive ideals of natural philosophy which were apparent in both

---

[27] Joseph Priestley, *Memoirs of Joseph Priestley*, (Allenson, 1904), p.11.
[28] See Joseph Priestley, *The History and Present State of Electricity*, (London: Printed for J. Dodsley,
J. Johnson and T. Cadell, 1767).

societies. Priestley finally left the Warrington Academy in 1767, and had applied to accompany Captain Cook on his second voyage to the Pacific, but was stopped by the Board of Longitude, which, being mainly made up of the established Anglican Clergy, took offence to Priestley's extreme religious views.

Academy tutor John Reinhold Forster, who had befriended Joseph Banks, the botanist who had accompanied Cook on the first voyage, was offered the position on the second voyage instead of Priestley. Forster was a botanist who had joined the Academy as a tutor in 1768, his son, George, who accompanied his father on the voyage, had been a student there. On his return, Forster became resentful towards the Admiralty, who had forbid him to write about the voyage, so he gave the task to his son, who published his findings in the much criticized book *A Voyage Around The World*. Forster continuously wrote to Banks, who became President of the Royal Society in 1778, indicating that he had been mistreated, and had not been paid in full.[29] Banks responded to the letters by supplying a loan to Forster, which was never repaid.[30] When Forster died in 1799, Banks cancelled the debt after Forster's widow wrote to him expressing her impoverished state.[31]

Forster was one of the two recorded Academy tutors who were Freemasons, being initiated into the Lodge of Lights in Warrington in the same year he came to England, in the December of 1766.[32] Forster later joined the Zu den drei Degan Lodge in Halle, were he worked as a professor of Natural History and Mineralogy after returning from the Cook voyage. He served as orator and warden, though he had to leave the Lodge when he fell into 'adverse circumstances'.[33] His son George, who taught Natural History at Cassel, was also a Freemason, and in 1784, the Zur Wahren Eintracht Lodge in Viena, held a Lodge of Festivity in honour of his presence there. This Lodge also boasts a variety of other prominent figures of the time, such as Haydn, Alxinger, Denis, Born, Eckhel, and Sonnenfels.[34] Forster was always the net-worker, and while he was based in Warrington he became close to the Blackburne family, who were none other than the Lords of the Manor of Warrington,

---

[29] Correspondence between Banks and Forster quoted in H.C. Cameron, *Sir Joseph Banks*, (Angus and Robertson, 1966), pp.110-1.
[30] Ibid.
[31] Ibid.
[32] *List of Members of the Lodge of Lights no.148, Warrington, 27th of December, 1766.* Warrington Masonic Hall. Not listed.
[33] A.F.A., Woodford, *Kennings Cyclopaedia of Freemasonry*, (London: Kenning, 1878), p.228.
[34] Ibid.

Forster naming a genus of plants he had discovered on Cook's voyage after Anne Blackburne. It is also interesting to note that like Forster, Joseph Banks was also a Freemason.[35]

Banks, unlike his fellow Freemasons, Price, Franklin, and Forster, was neither a radical nor a dissenter. He was also far removed from that other radical Fellow of the Royal Society, Joseph Priestley. Priestley was a republican and outspoken dissenter; Banks on the other hand, seemed to be a firm supporter of the establishment, having attended Eton and Oxford, coming from a wealthy landed family. Banks was much respected as the President of the Royal Society, being a formidable figure in science and discovery. It is this zeal that makes a firm connection with Freemasonry, his ambition and scientific mind blending with the educational ethos of the Craft. He may have been made of different material than Priestley, Price and Franklin, but his respect for men of science seemed to rise above political and religious differences. In 1780, a Copley medal was sent from the Royal Society to Benjamin Franklin, despite his involvement in the American Revolution. Banks wrote to Franklin:

'In testimony how truly they respect those liberal sentiments of general philosophy which induced you to issue your orders to such American cruisers as were then under your direction to abstain from molesting that great navigator.[36]

Banks seemed to have respected Franklin's liberal attitude, and when Britain was at war with France, Banks managed to gain a number of concessions from both Governments.[37] Banks also held much respect for Priestley, and was sympathetic when Priestley was rejected from accompanying Cook on his second voyage. He stated his disgust in a letter, saying that he thought the appointment was a matter of philosophy and not of divinity.[38] In 1790, Priestley wrote to Banks to complain of the rejection of a colleague who wished to become a Fellow of the Royal Society. This colleague, a certain Mr. Cooper, was an open republican, and Banks wrote back to Priestley, urging him that in no way was the

---

[35] Joseph Banks is recorded in the Grand Lodge Registers as having been a member of the Old Horn Lodge (now the Royal Somerset House and Inverness Lodge No. 4), London "previous to 1768". The Lodge's Minutes for the period have not survived, so there are no means of telling whether he was initiated in the Lodge or was a joining member of it.

[36] Banks' letter to Franklin, 1780, quoted in Cameron, *Sir Joseph Banks*, p.151.

[37] Ibid.

[38] Ibid., correspondence between Banks and Priestley, 1772, p.47.

decision to reject Cooper based on religious or political prejudice.[39] Banks' response to these incidents also reflects the ethos of political and religious harmony within Freemasonry, Banks putting science above the discriminations and intolerance of eighteenth century bigotry. Banks also corresponded with Matthew Boulton, who, like Priestley, was also a member of the Lunar Society.[40]

Jacob Bright was the second recorded Academy tutor to have been a member of the Lodge of Lights, entering the lodge some five months before Forster in the July of 1766.[41] Bright played quite an active part in the lodge, becoming Worshipful Master in 1771-2.[42] Yet, despite teaching for twenty years at the Academy, from 1763-1783, being one of the longest serving tutors there, Bright has been rather neglected by many historians. His occupation is listed in the Lodge of Lights as schoolmaster,[43] and his credits at the Academy include the teaching of writing, shorthand, drawing, book-keeping and surveying. No published material has yet come to light by Bright, though he seems to have been a popular tutor, unlike Forster who became disliked due to his over zealous attitude and over spending, as a result of which, he stayed only two years at the Academy.

The Academy became a fashionable and popular centre for study, attracting young male students from all over Britain, the West Indies and the American Colonies. However, despite the ethos of free thought, liberty and equality, it was still only the sons of wealthy industrialists, professionals and landowners that attended the Academy, though it did accepted students from all denominations, receiving sons from both Anglican and Dissenting clergy. Differences in class, race, and of course the exclusion of women was still very much apparent regarding further education in Britain during the eighteenth century, and in this, the Dissenting Academies were no different from England's two established Universities, Oxford, and, as Priestley put it, the *'Stagnant pool'* of Cambridge.[44]

---

[39] Ibid., correspondence between Banks to Priestley, April 1790, pp.159-61.
[40] Banks' letter to Boulton in J. Harris, *Industrial Espionage and Technological Transfer: Britain and France in the eighteenth century*, (Aldershot: Ashgate, 1998), p.498.
[41] *List of Members of the Lodge of Lights no.148, Warrington, 28th of July, 1766*. Warrington Masonic Hall. Not listed.
[42] Ibid.
[43] Ibid.
[44] See David L. Wykes, 'The Contribution of the Dissenting academy to the emergence of Rational Dissent', in *Enlightenment and Religion: Rational Dissent in Eighteenth Century Britain*, (Cambridge: Cambridge University Press, 2008), pp.99-139, on p.108, in which Wykes discusses a noted decline in teaching at the established Universities of Oxford and Cambridge.

Despite this, fundamental views in religious freedom and greater political expression were present at the Academy, and the American and French revolutions affected both tutor and student. It has even been suggested that the Freemason and French Revolutionary, Jean Paul Marat, taught at the Academy.[45] Many students actually lived with their tutors, and their strong radical nature was described by the early Academy historian Henry Bright:

'the politics of the students were no less inconvenient than their flirtations. Strong Whigs, and something more, as the tutors themselves were, they were alarmed and terrified at the anti-English zeal, which, during the American War, was displayed by several of the students. One of them, who boarded at Dr. Enfield's house, insisted on his right to illuminate his own windows for an American victory; but this the Doctor refused to allow, as it committed himself, the master of the house.[46]

Another example of the modern outlook of the tutors and the expression of liberty and democracy was the Widow's Fund Association, which was set up with the assistance of Warrington Academy tutors such as Priestley, Seddon, Enfield, Holt and Aikin, all of whom were involved in the early stages of the Academy. The use of ballot for Widow's Fund elections, represents the democratic ideals of the Warrington tutors, and also testifies to the nature and culture of Freemasonry, especially the approach to self help and support. Reports concerning the Widow's Fund and local charitable societies were duly printed by the Warrington based Eyres' Press.[47] There is further evidence in other developing industrial areas for links between local Freemasonry and charitable institutions at this time, such as in Sheffield, where, in 1797, the opening of the general infirmary was celebrated by a Masonic procession which included Freemasons from various lodges situated all over the north of

---

[45] McLachlan, *Warrington Academy*, pp.78-9. It was first revealed by William Turner in 1813, that a certain Frenchman named 'Mara' was mentioned as a teacher in the minutes of the Academy. Marat was a physician who had visited England in the early 1770s and it was during this visit that he was made a Freemason in London, with a Grand Lodge certificate of his membership being issued on the 15th of July, 1774.

[46] Henry Bright (1858) quoted in O'Brien, *Warrington Academy 1757-86*, p.93.

[47] P. O'Brien, *Eyres' Press 1756-1803, An Embryo University Press*, (Wigan: Owl Books, 1993), pp.108-9. Sermons on local charity were regularly printed by Eyres, such as *A Sermon: opening of a Charity School in Warrington for clothing, supporting & instructing Poor Children, Preached on Sunday February 3rd, 1782 by Edward Owen MA, Rector of the Parish*, (Warrington: Printed by W. Eyre. To Mr. Watkins & Mr. Dannett, Trustees, Charity School in Warrington, 1782).

England. The procession included the local clergy and a host of Sick Club's and Friendly Societies.[48]

The Eyres' Press, which was based in Horsemarket Street, worked with many of the Academy tutors, printing some of the most radical work at the time, and many free thinkers found a voice through this small printing press in Warrington, which was one of the first in Lancashire. Paine's *The Age of Reason* was reputed to have been printed by Eyres,[49] and John Howard, also a Fellow of the Royal Society, had his work on penal reform *The State of the Prisons* printed, after being introduced to Eyres by John Aikin. John's daughter, Anna Laetitia Aikin, also supported William Wilberforce's work on the abolition of the slave trade.[50] The London book seller Joseph Johnson, based in St. Paul's Churchyard, sold work printed by Eyres, and Johnson actively promoted women authors, being a mentor to the feminist Mary Wollstonecraft. Other pioneering works of the period printed by Eyres include Thomas Pennant's *Tour in Scotland* and *British Zoology*. Pennant was also a Fellow of the Royal Society, and a close friend of Banks, who had also contributed to the *Tour in Scotland*. John Reinhold Forster also had his work on mineralogy printed by Eyres, and the Rev. James Glazebrook, grandfather of Peter Rylands, also had work printed. Many of these books were to be found in the Circulating Library, supplying books for local readers and Academy tutors and students.[51]

The Social and Intellectual Scene created by the Academy

We owe much about what we know about the Academy to Anna Laetitia Aikin, and her niece, Lucy Aikin, who, in a world which denied them access to further education, were still highly active in the intellectual social scene in Warrington, becoming writers themselves and recording many aspects of life at the Academy. Anna Laetitia Aikin was rumored to have

---

[48] See Andrew Prescott, 'Freemasonry and the Problem of Britain', the Inaugural Lecture to mark the launch of the University of Sheffield's Centre for Research into Freemasonry, 5th of March, 2001, http://www.southchurch.mesh4us.org.uk/pdf/contemporary/freemasons-problem-sheffield.pdf [accessed 3rd of August, 2009]

[49] O'Brien, *Eyres' Press 1756-1803*, p.102.

[50] Ibid., p.56.

[51] Many of the books from the Circulating Library can still be seen in the Warrington Library archives. A collection of work published by William Eyres can be accessed online as part of the University of Wisconsin-Milwaukee special collection under the section titled 'Unitarians and Other Dissenters': http://www.uwm.edu/Library/special/exhibits/18thcent/18thcent_unitarians2.htm [accessed 10th of August, 2009]

become romantically involved with Jean Paul Marat, before marrying Rochemont Barbauld, a student at the Academy, and the descendant of French Huguenot refugees. Encouraged to write by Joseph Priestley, Anna Laetitia Barbauld's poetry was acclaimed by the likes of Wordsworth and Coleridge, but her later work, such as the radical *Eighteen Hundred And Eleven*, a poem criticizing Britain's involvement in the Napoleonic Wars, brought criticism and condemnation.[52] Barbauld had previously showed support for events in France with her poem *On the Expected General Rising of the French Nation in 1792*, were she urged France to *'Rise, mighty nation, in thy strength'*.[53] Despite falling out of favor, her work survived, and went on to influence many female writers, such as the local Unitarian writer and reformer Elizabeth Gaskell.[54]

The poet and writer Leigh Hunt even gave Anna Laetitia Barbauld a mention, albeit a critical one, in his poem *Blue-Stocking Revels; or, The feast of the violets*, in which he commented on the Blue-Stockings, a movement which advocated social and educational advancement for women, of which Barbauld was involved:

> *'Then Barbauld, fine teacher, correcting impatience,*
> *or mounting the stars in divine meditations'*.[55]

Both women seemed to have been influenced by the Academy and the radical, educational and literary culture surrounding it, Lucy Aikin writing of her experiences at Warrington:

> *'My youth was spent among the disciples or fellow-labourers of Price and Priestley, the descendants of John Taylor, the Arian, or in the society of that amiable of men, Dr. Enfield.*[56]

---

[52] For a discussion on Barbauld's poetry see Christine Gerrard, *A Companion to Eighteenth Century Poetry*, (Oxford: Wiley-Blackwell, 2006), pp.121-122. A contemporary critique of Barbauld's poem 'Eighteen Hundred And Eleven' can be seen in *The Quarterly Review: March & June, 1812, Vol. VII*, (London: C. Roworth, 1812), pp.309-313.

[53] Anna Laetitia Barbauld, 'On the Expected General Rising of the French Nation in 1792', in *The Works of Anna Laetitia Barbauld With a Memoir by Lucy Aikin*, (Boston: David Reed, 1826), pp.133-134.

[54] See Elizabeth Gaskell, *North And South*, (London: Penguin, 1994), p.85, where Gaskell begins Chapter IX with a verse from the Barbauld poem 'Groans of the Tankard', see Anna Laetitia Barbauld, *Poems by Anna Laetitia Barbauld*, (Boston: Wells and Lilly, 1820), pp.19-23. A branch of the Gaskell family resided in Warrington, being local businessmen, and, like Barbauld, attended the Cairo Street Unitarian Chapel during the same period.

[55] Leigh Hunt, *The Poetical Works of Leigh Hunt and edited by his son Thornton Hunt*, (London: George Routledge and Sons, 1860), p.217.

[56] Letter from Lucy Aikin to Dr. E. Channing transcribed in O'Brien, *Warrington Academy*, p.66.

There was a 'literary society' associated with some of the Academy tutors, with Dr. John Aikin and Dr. William Enfield being involved, the society discussing poetry and philosophy.[57] Lucy Aikin reminisced further in her memoir for Anna Laetitia Barbauld's collective works:

Warrington academy included among its tutors, names eminent both in science and in literature: with several of these, and especially with Dr. Priestley and Dr. Enfield and their families, she (Mrs. Barbauld) formed sincere and lasting friendships. The elder and more accomplished among the students composed an agreeable part of the same society: and its animation was increased by a mixture of young ladies, either residents in the town or occasional visitors, several of whom were equally distinguished for personal charms, for amiable manners, and cultivated minds. The rising institution, which flourished for several years in high reputation, diffused a classic air over all connected with it. [58]

However, Price and Priestley were not held in such high esteem by everyone at the time. The Freemason Edmund Burke in replying to Price's radical sermon (given to the Revolution Society) in his *Reflections on the Revolution in France* in 1790, commented on:

'the polluted nonsense of their most licentious and giddy coffee-houses[59], adding that *'the leaders of the legislative clubs and coffee-houses'* were *'intoxicated with admiration at their own wisdom and ability'*, calling the so called philosophers *'quackish'.*[60]

---

[57] McLachlan, *Warrington Academy*, pp.86-7.

[58] Anna Laetitia Barbauld, *The Works of Anna Laetitia Barbauld With a Memoir by Lucy Aikin*, (Boston: David Reed, 1826), pp.xi-xii.

[59] Edmund Burke, 'Reflections on the Revolution in France, and on the proceedings in certain societies in London relative to that event: In a letter intended to have been sent to a gentleman in Paris', in *The Works of The Right Honorable Edmund Burke, Revised Edition, Vol. III*, (Boston: Little, Brown, and Company, 1865), p.321. Burke, Whig politician and supporter of the American Revolution and Abolition, was also a Freemason; being associated with the London based Jerusalem Lodge No. 44 (erased), which was sometimes referred to as 'Burke's Lodge'. This lodge, which had also initiated the politician John Wilkes while he was in prison, had listed in its registers the signature 'Burke', which has been seen as evidence of his connection to the Craft. He was also a member of numerous London based gentlemen's clubs. Burke's support for America and his stance on anti-slavery, echo the ethos reflected in the political thoughts of both Paine and Price, but it was Burke's views on the French Revolution which would launch Paine's groundbreaking response in the *Rights of Man*, creating a pamphleteer war. The feminist and philosopher Mary Wollstonecraft also responded to Burke by writing *A Vindication of The Rights of Men*, published by Joseph Johnson.

[60] Ibid., pp.408-9.

Burke had been referring to the clubs and coffeehouses of Paris, but he may well have been discussing the radical clubs that were becoming so popular in Britain. Burke further admonished other institutions for stirring up trouble, stating:

> '*nor is it in these clubs alone that the public measures are deformed into monsters. They undergo a previous distortion in academies, intended as so many seminaries for these clubs, which are set up in all the places of public resort.*'[61]

Burke's harsh response to Price's sermon reflected his fears of France falling into chaos as a result of the Revolution, a view which was to fuel the paranoia of the British government of Pitt the Younger, leading to the Unlawful Society Act and the Combination Acts.[62]

Entwined with science, politics, religion, literature and radical thought, the progressive Warrington Academy can be seen as producing a modern intellectual movement in the town, yet one that worked on an international basis. New teaching methods in various subjects, such as natural philosophy, mathematics, languages, history and the classics, all helped to establish Warrington as a progressive centre for education at the time, representing ideals of self help, education and charity, ideas which can also seen in Masonry at the time. The town had developed into a cultural centre, with the Academy as a focus of independent learning. The town also became a rapidly growing centre for industry and trade. Many prominent local businessmen became members of the Lodge of Lights, such as the watchmaker Edward Harrison who joined on the 27th of December 1766, the same day as Academy tutor John Reinhold Forster.[63] Fashionable social circles would have intermingled, and the social scene of the burgeoning industrial town included a number of clubs and societies which began to meet in the coffee houses and inns of the town, such as the Lodge of Lights.

The most popular occupation in the lodge was that of innkeeper, a total of eight being members from 1765-1799.[64] Warrington had always been a busy commercial market town, and as a result, there were many inns and taverns. When the Academy was open, the taverns and inn's of

---

[61] Ibid., p.321.
[62] See P. O'Brien M.D., *Debate Aborted: Burke, Priestley, Paine & The Revolution in France 1789-91*, (Durham: Pentland Press, 1996), pp.261-263.
[63] *List of Members of the Lodge of Lights no.148, Warrington, 27th of December, 1766.* Warrington Masonic Hall. Not listed.
[64] Ibid.

the town became a focal point for the students, their unruly behavior being noted at the time.[65] The lodge actually met at numerous taverns during the late eighteenth century, first meeting at the Golden Fleece, moving next to the fashionable Lingham's Coffee House in Horsemarket Street, then, in 1770, the lodge settled at the Woolpack, where it met for sixteen years. It then moved to the Swan Inn, before returning to the Golden Fleece in 1797.[66]

Lingham's Coffee House was a popular gathering place for industrialists and professionals during this period, and was also the meeting place for the Amicable Club, which met there from 1788. This club included an array of local industrialists and dignitaries, such as soap factory owner George Crosfield, banker Thomas Lyon esq., Mr. Greenall and Mr. Orrett, partners of the local Greenall Brewery, and Mr. Beamont, who was the father of Warrington's first Mayor, William Beamont. Another prominent member was local gentleman William Leigh, and though the club, according to the minute books, seemed to be an innocent dining club with a rather large alcohol bill, the meeting of these local 'giants' may have led to some interesting discussions concerning local affairs.[67] Another popular club that met in Warrington between the years 1812-1829 was the patriotic Pitt Club, which met at the Nag's Head and The George Inn.[68] A further dining club was the Eagle & Child Club, which operated from 1781-1785, and included among its members the Academy tutor John Aikin jnr. Other members of the club included such prominent locals as the Lord of the Manor of Warrington John Blackburne, Rob Hesketh Esq., the Rev. W. Owen, Capt. Baldwin, and a certain Capt. James. Only the minute book survives which lists the members present, but unfortunately, does not record the discussions that took place.[69]

The end of the Academy

The Academy had been moved to larger premises in 1762, in the area of what is now Academy Street in Warrington, due to the growth of the institute, yet by 1786, it was all over. Financial support disappeared, and

---

[65] McLachlan, *Warrington Academy*, pp.94-5.
[66] *List of places and dates of meetings of The Lodge of Lights, no.148, 1765-1938, compiled by Herbert Woods & James Armstrong,* (1938).
[67] *Minute Book of the Amicable Cub, Warrington, 1788-1802,* Warrington Library, reference MS13.
[68] Crowe, *Warrington Ancient and Modern*, p.177.
[69] *Minute Book of the Eagle & Child Club, Warrington, 1781-1785*, Warrington Library, reference MS14.

student numbers fell, caused perhaps by a lack of student discipline and poor management.[70] Yet, the influence of the Warrington Academy continued well into the nineteenth century, and its radical culture effected many leading free thinkers and political reformers. The larger Academy building was used to house the Mechanics Institute and later, the Warrington Guardian.

Many of the students from the Academy had entered into politics, law, medicine, local industry, and some had become involved in promoting education themselves, such as Dr. Thomas Percival, a Fellow of the Royal Society, and friend of Benjamin Franklin, who became President of the Manchester Academy and founder member of the Manchester Literary and Philosophical Society. Percival's highly influential work *Medical Ethics*, published in an expanded version in 1803, became a code for medical physicians and institutions, his pioneering work with the Manchester Infirmary leading him to advocate the need for professional care and conduct.[71] Percival's friend Franklin had also founded an American Philosophical Society, and during his time as a printer, had founded the first American subscribing Library.[72] The Manchester Academy, founded after the closure of the Warrington Academy, became the home for the Warrington Academy's library and archive.

William Turner, another ex-student, eventually wrote the first history of the Academy, also becoming a Fellow of the Royal Society, and Thomas Malthus FRS, author of the controversial *An Essay on the Principle of Population* also attended the Academy.[73] Another famous ex-student was John Goodricke, who despite having a hearing disability, went on to become an excellent chemist, mathematician, and astronomer, being awarded the Copley Medal by the Royal Society. Goodricke was from an influential York family who had connections to prominent local Freemasons.[74] John Aikin jnr became a literary critic as well as teaching at the Academy himself for a while.[75]

---

[70] McLachlan, *Warrington Academy*, p.105.

[71] Thomas Percival, *Medical Ethics; or, A Code of Institutes and Precepts adapted to the Professional Conduct of Physicians and Surgeons*, (Oxford: John Henry Parker, mdcccxlix), pp.13-16. See also Lisbeth Haakonssen, *Medicine and Morals in the Enlightenment: John Gregory, Thomas Percival and Benjamin Rush*, (Amsterdam: Rodopi, 1997), pp.113-120.

[72] See Benjamin Franklin, *The Autobiography of Benjamin Franklin*, (New York: Courier Dover Publications, 1996).

[73] See Thomas Malthus, *An Essay on the Principle of Population as it Affects the Future Improvement of Society*, (London: Printed for J. Johnson, 1798).

[74] John Goodricke was a member of the Goodricke Baronet family of Ribston, Yorkshire. See T.B. Whytehead, 'The Relics of the Grand Lodge at York', *AQC*, Vol.XIII, p.95, in which Whytehead refers to Sir Henry Goodricke who married the daughter of 'York Grand Lodge'

Joseph Priestley eventually settled in the USA in 1794, after his house and property in Birmingham were destroyed by an anti-dissenter mob three years earlier. Priestley had turned to Joseph Banks for help:

'I shall be obliged to you if you will mention my situation to any of your friends whose laboratories are furnished and who may have anything to spare to set up a broken philosopher.'[76]

Like fellow radical Thomas Paine, Priestley seemed to have found some peace in the USA in his final years, his friend President Thomas Jefferson stated that Priestley was *'one of the few lives precious to mankind.'*[77] Priestley died in 1804, and as a victim of religious intolerance, seems to stand out in late eighteenth century radical, ant-establishment politics, whose work as a natural philosopher and as a tutor in Warrington reached far into the nineteenth century, his work on electricity being an influence on the work of Michael Faraday and William Herschel.[78]

The Warrington Dissenting Academy had opened as a reaction to the religious intolerance of the day and has been described as *'the earliest and most important institutional style academy in England'*,[79] attracting many leading intellectual figures of the age, making the town an extremely vibrant centre for progressive education. Recently the historian David L. Wykes has indicated that the Warrington Academy *'has acquired a reputation as the greatest of the non-conformist academies, indeed, as one of the leading educational establishments of the eighteenth century'* and that its reputation as the 'Athens of the North' remains intact.[80]

The ideals of Freemasonry were certainly entwined with the modern educational ethos of the dissenters, and it would have been only natural for the Freemasons from the local lodge to be present in the same social circles as the teachers from the Academy, especially as the lodge included

---

member Tobias Jenkyns, who served as Mayor twice in 1701 and 1720, and also served as MP for York in 1715.

[75] John Aikin jnr wrote many critiques for a number of popular poetical and literary works of the period, including *Aikin's British Poets (X Volumes)*, (London: Longman, Hurst, Rees, Orme & Brown, 1821), and William Somerville, *The Chace*, (London: T. Cadell & W. Davies, 1796).

[76] Letter from Priestley to Banks quoted in Cameron, *Sir Joseph Banks*, p.161.

[77] See B. Willey, *The Eighteenth Century Background*, (Chatto & Windus, 1946), p.204.

[78] See William J. Ashworth, 'Memory, Efficiency, and Symbolic Analysis: Charles Babbage, John Herschel, and the Industrial Mind', *ISIS*, Vol.87, No.4, USA, (1996), pp.629-653.

[79] Haakonssen, *Medicine and Morals in the Enlightenment*, p.97.

[80] David L. Wykes, 'The Contribution of the Dissenting academy to the emergence of Rational Dissent', in *Enlightenment and Religion: Rational Dissent in Eighteenth Century Britain*, (Cambridge: Cambridge University Press, 2008), pp.99-139, on p.132.

two Academy tutors. Many of the leading tutors, students and members of their 'intellectual circle' were only in Warrington for a short period of time, but this collective group of radical thinkers shared many of the same views, inspiring each other to teach, write and publish innovative topics, such as new teaching methods as seen in Priestley's *Lectures on History and General Policy*,[81] and influential views supporting the abolition of slavery and women's rights, such as Anna Laetitia Barbauld's poem *Epistle to William Wilberforce on the Rejection of the Bill for Abolishing the Slave Trade*,[82] and her powerful *The Rights of Woman*.[83] The Aikin family became involved in the abolition movement and prison reform, becoming central in the fashionable wave of radicalism that swept through the dissenting and intellectual circles in Warrington during this time.

John Seddon, the driving force behind the Academy, had founded the Circulating Library with Benjamin Yoxall, a schoolmaster and founder member of the Lodge of Lights, giving evidence of early friendships and the mutual like-mindedness in establishing and promoting local outlets for education. Priestley was certainly close to Freemasons Richard Price and Benjamin Franklin during his time in Warrington, and their ideas blended to form a focused desire for the research and experimentation of natural philosophy, which echoed the embodiment of the Craft. John Reinhold Forster became a member of the Lodge of Lights almost immediately after his arrival in the country, and would have met his future colleague, Academy tutor Jacob Bright at the lodge. This connection may have assisted Forsters' appointment at the Academy in 1768, revealing the networking aspects of Freemasonry. Through Forster's friendship with another fellow Freemason, Joseph Banks, he became a Fellow of the Royal Society in 1772, joining the ranks of Priestley, Percival, Price, and Franklin, and this friendship certainly assisted in gaining future financial assistance.

The social aspects of joining a fashionable society are also evident here, with Priestley's links to the Revolutionary Society in London and

---

[81] See Joseph Priestley, *Lectures on History and General Policy*, (Dublin: P. Byrne, 1788), in which Priestley presented a series of lectures given to Academy students at Warrington which encompass a wide assortment of topics such as law, agriculture, art, taxation and war, Priestley putting forward that the study of history allows the students to participate in the progress of mankind, enabling them to comprehend the natural laws of God. The *Lectures* became highly regarded in many educational institutions such as Cambridge.

[82] Anna Laetitia Barbauld, 'Epistle to William Wilberforce on the Rejection of the Bill for Abolishing the Slave Trade, 1791', in *The Works of Anna Laetitia Barbauld With a Memoir by Lucy Aikin*, (Boston: David Reed, 1826), pp.128-132.

[83] Ibid., pp.136-137.

the Birmingham based Lunar Society, ultimately leading to links with Freemasonry, and in turn, connecting to other influential societies, such as the Royal Society. Price and Paine were both involved in the Revolutionary Society, and were also close to major figures in the new American Government. With many social circles blending together, like circular ripples merging in water after the stones of discontent have been throne, it is easy to see how the famous Warrington Academy can easily be considered as a centre of radicalism and Masonic ideals. Not so much a hotbed of revolution, but certainly an influential, progressive, educational centre, which had links to Freemasonry, and certainly expressed elements of its ethos, which ultimately manifested itself through many prominent individuals of the time.

The 1760s witnessed the height of the Academy, and it is interesting to see that Warrington's Masonic lodge began in the same decade, attracting many prominent local professionals and industrialists. The Eyres' Press was also entwined with this intellectual and radical ethos, printing many works on science, literature, and politics by the Academy tutors and local writers, the Circulating Library also playing a role in the educational development of the town, distributing the new groundbreaking work. The establishment of the Widow's Fund, with its democratic approach, also represents the ideals and ethos of the Warrington Academy tutors. Networking and the introduction to social circles may have played a part in becoming a member of the lodge, but the community certainly benefited due to the meeting of a collective body of prominent local men; with charity donations, and business contacts being made between the members, new friendships being forged, and Jacob Bright would have been a constant link between the lodge and the Academy. Freemasonry in the town certainly advocated the ethos of self-help, charity and education, ideals that were embedded within the Warrington Academy.

The Warrington Circulating Library had found a natural home at the Eyres' Press, which continued to operate until 1803. The press was then taken over by the Haddock family, who ran the service well into the nineteenth century, dominating printing in the town until the introduction of the Warrington Guardian in 1853. Peter Cartwright Haddock, who owned the Exchange News Room, which was situated near to Haddock's Press, joined the Lodge of Lights in 1846.[84] Thomas and John Haddock joined the lodge in 1851, with George Haddock, a stationer, joining the

---

[84] *List of Members of the Lodge of Lights no.148, Warrington, 1765-1981,* Not listed. Haddock is also listed in *Slaters' Trade Directory of Warrington, 1848.*

following year.[85]   The Circulating Library eventually merged with the Natural History Society, which was founded in 1837, two of the pioneers of the society being Peter Rylands and Joseph Stubs, two local industrialists and prominent members of the Lodge of Lights.[86]

The lodge continued to operate successfully through the 1780s and the 1790s, attracting members from various occupations, yet in 1799, with the introduction of the Unlawful Societies Act, the lodge began to undergo a transitional period.   The transformation was to almost destroy the lodge, affecting the public image of Freemasonry in the town, and it would be a number of decades before it fully recovered.

---

[85] *List of Members of the Lodge of Lights no.148, Masonic Hall, Warrington, 3rd of February, 1851 and 30th of November, 1852.* Not Listed.
[86] Ibid., also see *the Minutes of the general meetings of the Natural History Society, 1837-53,* Warrington Library, reference MS22.

Chapter 2

Freemasonry after the Unlawful Societies Act – labouring men and self help[87]

'I went in quest of the manifold object which Nature had scattered throughout the land.'
Freemason and Warrington Academy student George Forster, *A Voyage Round the World*, 1777[88]

'Such is the state of things which I wish to take place in the united American states. In order to introduce and perpetuate it, and at the same time to give it the greatest effect on the improvement of the world, nothing is more necessary than the establishment of a wise and liberal plan of Education.'
Freemason Dr. Richard Price, 1785[89]

'Who would have expected to have seen this favourite child of freedom leagued with the oppressor of the world? She who, twenty years ago, shed her blood for independence – She that, ever since that time, has boasted of the superiority of her citizens above all the nations of the globe – She that, watched over in her infancy by Great Britain, with parental tenderness and anxiety, nursed in the very lap of liberty, and educated in the school of republicanism, is now seen truckling to France'.
Freemason George Canning on the War with America, 1813[90]

---

[87] The author has previously written on this particular subject in a paper presented at the Conference on the History of Voluntary Action, University of Liverpool, 11-13 September 2001, and published as David Harrison, 'Freemasonry, Industry and Charity: The Local Community and the Working Man', in *The Journal of the Institute of Volunteering Research*, Volume 5, Number 1, Winter, 2002, pp.33-45. Other contents from the chapter were presented as 'Working Men within Masonic Lodges in the North West Towns of Industrial England' at the Freemasonry in Radical and Social Movements 1700-2000 Conference for the Centre for the Research into Freemasonry, University of Sheffield, on the 19th of November, 2004, and as 'Transition and Change: Working Men and Masonic Lodges in Industrial Towns in the Northwest of England', at the Post Graduate Seminar for the University of Sheffield, United Grand Lodge of England, London, on the 27th of May, 2005.
[88] See George Forster, *A Voyage Round the World, Vol. I.*, (London, 1777).
[89] Richard Price, 'Observations on the Importance of the American Revolution and The Means of making it a Benefit to the World', (1785), in David Oswald Thomas, (ed.), *Political Writings by Richard Price*, (Cambridge. Cambridge University Press, 1991), p.137.
[90] George Canning, 'Address Respecting the War with America, February 18th, 1813', in Robert Walsh (ed.), *Select Speeches of the Right Honourable George Canning with a Preliminary Biographical Sketch, and an Appendix of Extracts From His Writings and Speeches*, (Philadelphia: Crissy & Markley, 1850), p.224.

Focusing on the educational and charitable aspects of Freemasonry at the local level in the industrial north-west of England, this chapter will discuss the ways in which Freemasons became involved in, and supported local benevolent and learning organisations in the late eighteenth and early nineteenth centuries. The Unlawful Societies Act of 1799, introduced by Pitt the Younger amid the fear caused by the French Revolution, changed Freemasonry, and in certain industrial areas, such as Warrington, Oldham and Wigan, the Craft witnessed an influx of men extracted from the labouring trades. These labouring men entered a society which was suffering from low membership, debt and an amount of instability, but some, as we shall see, found a society which provided a sense of security, some men claiming relief for themselves and their families. Links between local Freemasonry and other local benevolent clubs and Friendly Societies will be discussed, as will Masonic donations to local charities, such as the Bluecoat School in Warrington, and the interests of Freemasons in the development of those local learned societies crucial to the delivery of education to the labouring men of the town. Finally, Masonic links to the Unitarian Church will be explored, again focussing on connections to local education and to local charity.

In accordance with the Unlawful Societies Act of 1799, the Lodge of Lights in Warrington began to submit a list of its members to the local Magistrates every March.[91] The membership of the lodge suffered during this period, becoming alarmingly low, and the new and joining members reveal an influx of more labouring tradesmen, even though a number of local industrialists were still evident. One of these local industrialists was Thomas Kirkland Glazebrook, a glass manufacturer who entered the lodge in 1802.[92] He was Worshipful Master for two years running, though, after only five years in the lodge, he departed.[93] In the next few decades, many local manufacturers joined the lodge, and seemed to have been accompanied by some of their workers.

There were five weavers in the lodge between the years 1810-1830,[94] and though weavers were linked at this time with radicalism, especially with the Lancashire weavers' strike and the Luddites, in this lodge they

---

[91] *Minutes of the Lodge of Lights, No.148, Masonic Hall, Warrington, August, 1799.* Not listed.

[92] *List of Members of the Lodge of Lights, No.148, Masonic Hall, Warrington, 29th of March, 1802.* Not listed.

[93] *Minutes of the Lodge of Lights, No.148, Masonic Hall, Warrington, 1802-1807.* Not listed. See also *Warrington Trade Directories, 1792-1855*, Warrington Library, reference S10121, Thomas K. Glazebrook is mentioned as a glass manufacturer, residing in Fennel Street, Warrington in 1824.

[94] *List of Members of the Lodge of Lights, No.148, Masonic Hall, Warrington, 1810-1830.* Not listed.

are brushing shoulders with many local cotton manufacturers.[95]   For example, in 1830, William Bullough, a local weaver, joined the lodge as a member from the local Lodge of St. John, only one month after Thomas Eskrigge joined from the same lodge, Eskrigge being a local cotton manufacturer.[96] This occurrence had been seen before in the lodge, when in 1810, James Knott, another local cotton manufacturer, entered as a joining member from another lodge, and was quickly followed by Richard Pearson, a weaver who originated from the same lodge as Mr. Knott.[97] The coincidence certainly suggests that in both cases, the men knew each other.

There were weavers entering lodges in other industrial towns which were associated with cotton manufacturing during this period, such as Wigan, where weaver Joshua Wood joined the Antient Lodge of Antiquity No. 178 in 1803, becoming Worshipful Master three years later.[98]   Across the county border in Yorkshire, the Royal Yorkshire Lodge No. 265, based in the industrial mill town of Keighley, also had a number of weavers joining the lodge from the 1790s. Other labouring trades also appeared, such as tinner, joiner, blacksmith and whitesmith, all joining the lodge in the first part of the nineteenth century.[99]

Three fustian cutters joined the Lodge of Lights in the years 1814-1834. Fustian cutting was a successful local industry involved in the making of sail cloth. Two cordwainers also became members during this period, one of them, William Evans, actually becoming Worshipful Master.[100] There were also plumbers, factory workers, joiners, builders, painters, plasterers, machine makers and tin plate workers, all mixing with industrialists, professionals, excise officers, and businessmen.[101] A good mix of labouring tradesmen had entered the lodge, perhaps attracted to its benevolent-society aspects, or possibly its educational ethos.

---

[95] See Appendix 1 which further discusses the occupational categories included in this and subsequent chapters.
[96] *List of Members of the Lodge of Lights, No.148, Masonic Hall, Warrington, 29th of March & 26th of April, 1830.* For Thomas Eskrigge also see Anon., *Warrington in 1824,* (Warrington: Mackie & Co. Ld., Guardian Office, 1906), p.43, and *Warrington Trade Directories, 1792-1855,* Warrington Library, reference S10121. The Lodge of St. John was originally warranted in Manchester in 1769 and moved to Warrington in 1817.
[97] *List of Members of the Lodge of Lights, No.148, Masonic Hall, Warrington, 30th of July & 24th of September, 1810.* Not listed.
[98] *List of Members of the Lodge of Antiquity, No.178, Masonic Hall, Wigan, 1803-1806.* Not listed.
[99] *List of Members of the Royal Yorkshire Lodge No. 265* in J. Ramsden Riley, *The History of the Royal Yorkshire Lodge,* (Yorkshire, 1889), pp.79-87.
[100] *List of Members of the Lodge of Lights, No.148, Masonic Hall, Warrington, 1814-1834.* Cordwaining – shoemaking with soft leather - appears to have been declining during this period.
[101] Ibid., *1814-1850.*

Membership Decline, Public Prejudice and the Desire to be Respectable

John Evans, who was a writing master, joined the Lodge of Lights in 1794 and served as Worshipful Master nine times in all, being a very charismatic and intellectual figure. In doing so he certainly seemed to hold the lodge together during its difficult period in the opening years of the nineteenth century.[102] Evans gave numerous lectures during his time as Master of the lodge, including two lectures on astronomy. Indeed, they became so popular that a non-Mason attended one of the lectures at the invitation of a member of the lodge, resulting in the Mason who invited him being suspended![103] Evans also promoted the teaching of *'Masonic science'* and had a book-lending system in the lodge where the brethren could borrow Masonic literature, which included many mysterious works on Masonic history, all of which have now been lost, along with other early documents of the lodge including the original Warrant.[104] Certainly the educational aspect of the lodge was still very much in existence, an aspect which dated back to the days of the Warrington Academy.

The Lodge of Lights also exhibited links with the local militia. In 1798, for example, with the war with France escalating, many local Freemasons seemed anxious to become involved in the local militia, nicknamed the 'Bluebacks' due to the colour of their uniform. Many of the brethren joined, and one particular lodge night in 1798 had to be cancelled because of commitments to this local volunteer force.[105] In 1802, the important Masonic festival of St. John the Baptist had to be cancelled because so many members of the lodge were serving in the Volunteers, the proposed meeting clashing with their duties.[106] In May 1808, many members were again excused from being present because of their commitments to the Volunteers. In November 1809, during a period which saw special Masonic Jubilee celebrations for George III, five Masons from the Royal Artillery were present.[107] This local lodge certainly reacted with change, and the members of the Lodge of Lights seem to reflect a deliberately stern patriotic stance. The lodge minutes also reflect a concerted effort to regain the membership of the local

---

[102] Ibid., *1794-1816*.
[103] *Minutes of the Lodge of Lights, No.148, Masonic Hall, Warrington, March, 1801*. Not Listed.
[104] J. Armstrong, *History of the Lodge of Lights, No.148*, (Warrington, 1898), p.37.
[105] *Minutes of the Lodge of Lights, No.148, Masonic Hall, Warrington, November, 1798*. Not listed.
[106] Ibid., *May, 1802*.
[107] Ibid., *November, 1809*.

gentry less than one year after the Unlawful Societies Act, the Secretary of the lodge writing in January 1800:

'I think there is a prospect of the Lodge being once more respectable as several Gentlemen have expressed their desire to become members'.[108]

Two prominent gentlemen, James and Charles Turner, did join in the October of that year, James being a Lieutenant in the Lancashire Militia, Charles being a cotton manufacturer,[109] bringing hopes that suspicions about the nature of the lodge could be dispelled.[110] For example, in 1802, during a funeral for Brother John Johnson, the minutes record that:

'It was asserted that the spectacle removed from the greater part of the onlookers and the public those prejudices which have so much prevailed against the Order especially in this place'.[111]

Nevertheless, the local public, perhaps in light of the Napoleonic Wars and the atmosphere of paranoia it had created, seemed to be suspicious of the lodge, and a notable low attendance rate is evident at this time. In 1806, the average attendance was only six to nine members, and by 1808, the membership was reduced to seven.[112] In January and February of 1809, only four members were present, and by March, there was a desperately low turnout of three.[113] A poor turnout of members continued, at least until the late 1840s.[114] In 1820, there were twelve members in total, yet in 1831, despite the recent amalgamation with the local Lodge of St. John; an average attendance of seven was recorded, being reduced to six in 1832.[115] During the early 1830s there was a severe outbreak of cholera in Warrington, and regular outbreaks of diseases during the early nineteenth century would affect the regular membership of certain lodges that met in densely populated industrial towns like Warrington and Liverpool. There were some years, such as in 1844,

---

[108] Ibid., *January, 1800.*
[109] *List of Members of the Lodge of Lights, No.148, Masonic Hall, Warrington, 15th & 27th of October, 1800.* Not listed.
[110] See John Barrell, *The Spirit of Despotism,* (Oxford: Oxford University Press, 2006).
[111] *Minutes of the Lodge of Lights, No.148, Masonic Hall, Warrington, 26th of January, 1802.* Not listed.
[112] Ibid., *1806-1808.*
[113] Ibid., *January, February & March, 1809.*
[114] Ibid., *1792-1850.*
[115] Ibid., *1820-1832.*

when the lodge did not meet at all, and a number of years would pass between new members entering the lodge.[116]

Even in Liverpool, lodges which had always attracted gentlemen and wealthy merchants also suffered from low attendance and low membership, such as the Merchants Lodge, which in 1812, during the year when the second American War had broken out disrupting trade, endured a particularly poor year.[117] Many Liverpool Freemasons went on to join the Liverpool Masonic Rebellion in the early 1820s, a revolt which, as we shall see, reflected the dissatisfaction with the ritualistic and administrative changes brought on by the recent Union of the Antients and the Moderns in 1813.

Other Liverpool lodges also suffered low membership and financial problems, such as the Ancient Union Lodge, which, like the Merchants Lodge, had members that openly joined the rebellion. The Ancient Union Lodge did survive, but only after experiencing years of fluctuating membership.[118] The Merchants Lodge went on to experience further trauma in the early 1830s, suffering debt and low membership, with the lodge having only 11 members in 1832, and only showed signs of recovery by 1850.[119] The Liverpool based Lodge of Harmony also suffered financial difficulties in the 1840s, some members being in regular arrears with their lodge fees.[120] Claims for relief by the brethren were also commonplace in these Liverpool lodges, the beneficial and 'self help' aspects of Freemasonry again being apparent during the bleak period of the early nineteenth century. This can be seen in the Lodge of Harmony in the 1840s when *'a collection of 12/8 was made for a Brother Howell who was in prison for debt'*.[121] Like Warrington, Liverpool suffered from constant visitations of disease, enduring outbreaks of cholera and Scarlet Fever throughout the 1830s and 1840s, which may have affected membership as most lodges during this period met in taverns in the centre of the port.

Freemasonry was also suffering in parts of the USA during this period, due in the main, to the fallout from the infamous Morgan Affair. William

---

[116] Ibid., *1844*. See also *List of Members of the Lodge of Lights, No.148, Masonic Hall, Warrington, 1800-1850*. Not listed.

[117] John Macnab, *History of The Merchants Lodge, No. 241, Liverpool, 1780-2004*, Second Edition, (Liverpool, 2004), p.36.

[118] *A List of the Members of the Ancient Union Lodge No. 203, 1792-1855, C.D. Rom: 139 GRA/ANT/UNI, The Library and Museum of Freemasonry, United Grand Lodge, Great Queen Street, London.*

[119] Macnab, *History of The Merchants Lodge*, pp.36-50.

[120] Anon. *The History of The Lodge of Harmony No. 220*, (Liverpool, 1948), p.10.

[121] Ibid.

Morgan had been rejected from a lodge in Batavia, New York, and subsequently declared his intention of publishing an exposé entitled *Illustrations of Masonry*. However, before the work was published, Morgan mysteriously disappeared, and a number of Freemasons were charged with his kidnapping. Morgan's disappearance and the intrigue surrounding the affair caused a public backlash against Freemasons in New York and neighbouring States, and the Ant-Masonic Political Party was founded, which ran a candidate opposing the Freemason Andrew Jackson in the 1828 election. Freemasonry was openly criticised as a result and many lodges in the New York area endured low membership with some lodges closing. The English radical writer Richard Carlile who had published his own exposé slightly earlier, claimed to be an influence on Morgan's work, and sensationally stated that Morgan had been murdered by Masons – a theory that had quickly took hold soon after Morgan's disappearance and fuelled ant-Masonic opinions.[122]

In England, certain elements of society would have become more wary of Freemasonry after the Unlawful Societies Act of 1799, and the fear of association with a secret society that had been linked to radicalism and revolution would certainly be more apparent in industrial areas. The lodges of certain industrial areas such as Warrington, Oldham, Stockport and Liverpool, suffered greatly with low attendance and certainly began to struggle, but the period was one of social upheaval, and these industrial towns witnessed periods of high unemployment, strikes and insurrections, outbreaks of disease, and, as the labour historian Hobsbawn puts forward, a dramatic decline in the standard of living between 1790-1850.[123]

For any man joining Freemasonry during this period, education was an attraction, and a man could join a lodge and become learned in social etiquette and conduct, especially in the art of socialising and dining. There are a lot of fines for drunkenness, swearing, and general coarse conduct during this period in the Lodge of Lights, social etiquette and politeness being important in the running of the lodge. In 1792, a certain Bro. T. B. was expelled from the lodge for his unacceptable behaviour, in which he was:

---

[122] See William Morgan, *Illustrations of Masonry By One Of The Fraternity Who has Devoted Thirty Years to the Subject*, (Batavia, New York: David C. Miller, 1827). Also see Carlile, *Manual of Freemasonry*, p.87.

[123] E.J. Hobsbawm, *Labouring Men*, (London: Weidenfeld and Nicolson, 1986), pp.64-104.

'..setting off his apron and damning the whole Lodge without any cause or provocation.'[124]

In May, 1795:

Bro. G. was appointed J.W. - he was later fined for swearing.[125]

And in July 1797:

Mr. S. D. of Burtonwood was initiated into the first degree of Masonry. He was much intoxicated and counselled to come no more in that condition.[126]

In May, 1798, two brethren were again charged for the use of improper and insulting language, and the drunkenness of the brethren was again evident during the September meeting in 1801. The misuse of drink was apparent again in the March of 1803 when:

Bro. H., who had been initiated three years before, took the chair because the W.M. (J. Evans) came intoxicated - the W.M. was suspended till May.[127]

The drunken behaviour continued in the September of 1804, when, a certain Bro. J.H. was fined for entering the lodge intoxicated, and in 1805, Joseph Leather was forever expelled from the lodge for his ever increasing drunkenness and offensive behaviour.[128] In 1806, another member had *'nine times violated the rules of Masonry'* by swearing and becoming extremely drunk.[129]

Freemasonry, Friendly Societies and Trade Unions

With the Union of the Antients and the Moderns in 1813, the ritual was re-examined, lodges were re-numbered, and new rules were applied. This transformation seemed to have taken decades to be fully implemented. It was only natural for existing members to have been stuck in their ways, and it was not until the older generation of members gave way to the

---

[124] *Minutes of the Lodge of Lights, No.148, Masonic Hall, Warrington, 1792.* Not listed.
[125] Ibid., *May, 1795.*
[126] Ibid., *July, 1797.*
[127] Ibid., *March 1803.*
[128] Ibid., *1804-1805.*
[129] Ibid., *1806.*

new, that changes occur. By the 1840s, less of the labouring tradesmen appear in the membership records, and a steady influx of industrialists and professionals appear. This change coincides with the growing success of Friendly Societies such as the Oddfellows and Foresters, especially in industrial areas. Trade Unionism also flourished after this period, and the political climate began to change as the fear of revolution gradually subsided.[130]

Trade Unions and Friendly Societies may have eventually attracted the labouring tradesmen away from Freemasonry, especially in industrial areas, offering various benefits for sickness, burial and also family support. Trade Unions and other Friendly Societies like the Oddfellows and the Foresters met in lodges and used very similar regalia and displayed similar symbolism to Freemasonry; from the banners and marches of Trade Unions, to the aprons, medals and sashes of the Oddfellows. Ritual had also played a large part in the early development of the Oddfellows and Foresters, and for all these movements, balloting and oaths were taken. There was certainly a relationship between Freemasonry and Friendly Societies such as the Oddfellows, with members joining both and enjoying the benefit of dual membership.[131] The Oddfellows also met in lodges and, like Freemasonry, built Halls for the purpose of lodge meetings, such as the magnificent Oddfellows Hall in Chester.

The Oddfellows certainly had many elements of Freemasonry, and in the early decades of the 1800s, the Oddfellows kept in close contact with Masonry. For example, an article in the *Oddfellow's Magazine* in 1829 declares how the society was originally instituted on Masonic principles, commenting on moral codes of brotherly love which were strong features of Freemasonry.[132] Another example of this close link is seen when a prospective Oddfellow member was turned down after the society had sought advice from the Masonic Grand Lodge[133]. The Oddfellows and Foresters were extremely popular in Lancashire and Cheshire, having the

---

[130] See John Halstead and Andrew Prescott, 'Breaking The Barriers: Masonry, Fraternity And Labour', in *Labour History Review*, Vol. 71, No. 1, April 2006, pp.3-8.

[131] See P.H.J.H. Gosden, *The Friendly Societies In England 1815-1875*, (Manchester: Manchester University Press, 1961). See also Andrew Prescott, 'The Spirit of Association: Freemasonry and Early Trade Unions', A Paper Presented at the Canonbury Masonic Research Centre, 30 May 2001, *CRF*, University of Sheffield, http://freemasonry.dept.shef.ac.uk/index.php?lang=0&type=page&level0=243&level1=387&level2=394&op=387 [accessed 15th of May, 2009]

[132] Gosden, *The Friendly Societies in England*, p.127.

[133] Ibid., taken from the Minutes and Documents of the Grand Committees of the Manchester Unity of Oddfellows, 15th March, 1815.

largest number of lodges there in England during the first half of the nineteenth century.

The Friendly Society Act of 1793 gave Friendly Societies legal status and protection of their funds, and importantly, gave them a reprieve from the Combination Acts of 1799 and 1800. The legal protection of their funds, used to support working men and their families for sickness and burial, was thought to reduce the demand for poor relief, and the Act of 1793 was an attempt to regulate the many Friendly Societies that were being founded all over England and Wales.

Because of this, many illegal radical gatherings subsequently took the guise of Friendly Societies; groups of labouring men being driven underground by the Combination Acts to meet in private to discuss their grievances. A famous example of this was the formation of the 'Agricultural Labourers Friendly Society' by six Dorset farm labourers in March 1834, otherwise known as the Tolpuddle Martyrs. The Agricultural Labourers Friendly Society which was effectively a Trade Union, had an initiation ritual which included the taking of an oath, and, reminiscent to the Craft rituals of Freemasonry, the initiate was led into the 'lodge' room blindfolded and then shown a picture of a skeleton. The Tolpuddle Martyrs were arrested for swearing illegal oaths, and sentenced to seven years transportation.

The 'Journeymen Steam Engine and Machine Makers Friendly Society' – or 'Old Mechanics' as they were known, was founded by the Manchester based John White, who had campaigned ardently for the society and had travelled to industrial towns like Stockport, Oldham and Bolton on Saturday nights to promote it, walking home on a Sunday and changing his lodgings every three or four weeks to avoid the constables. Though at the beginning, the 'Old Mechanics' used 'Friendly Society' in the title, it was evident that they were really a Trade Union.

When the society was well established, White acted as treasurer, and had to hide as much as £6000 up the chimney and in the cellar of his house, as Trade Unions had no legal security for their funds in the banks. The many branches of the society met in local public houses where the landlord held the box containing the funds, the rules of the society stating that:

'the box shall contain three different locks and keys outside also three different locks and keys for the cash drawer which shall be kept by the president and the two acting stewards.'

The 'Old Mechanics' had an initiation ceremony which had hints of the Masonic ritual, where, behind specially put up curtains in a room in a public house, a new member received a password and had to swear secrecy on the Bible. A pistol was pointed at him while he took his oath and a skull was revealed to remind the new member of what would become of him if he revealed the society's secrets.[134]

The 'Old Mechanics' became very successful due to their secrecy and by uniting the old and the new class of workmen; for example, bringing the older millwrights and the newer engineers together, and changing and adapting by amalgamating numerous societies to become a stronger 'Union'. By 1851 the 'Old Mechanics' and the newly amalgamated societies called themselves the 'Amalgamated Society of Engineers, Machinists, Smiths, Millwrights and Patternmakers', and by the end of the year had 10,841 members, having a new trade protection fund to provide strike pay, and covering benefits for unemployment, sickness, pension, accident and funeral, all for 1 s. per week.[135]

Another less radical example was the 'IOR Friendly Society' - the Independent Order of Rechabites, which was founded in Salford in 1835 to provide funeral and sickness benefits to members, drawn from the skilled working classes. The society also used Masonic-like regalia and initiation ceremonies, and worked to a strict moral code.[136] The IOR was formed as a Temperance society, and held its first meeting at the Salford Coffeehouse, but the society soon spread. Each branch of the IOR was called a 'tent' – each 'tent' being given names from the Bible to reflect morality. By 1843 there were over 1000 tents and nearly 30,000 members, the society becoming commonplace in industrial towns in South Wales and in the north-west of England such as Wigan and Skelmanthorpe.

Other Temperance 'self-help' societies also emerged with Masonic style oath taking, iconography and regalia, such as the International Organisation of Good Templars which was founded in the USA in 1851, but soon spread to Britain.[137] Many more of these 'Friendly Societies' were founded throughout the nineteenth century, all embracing a similar ethos; that together, people could work towards a better quality of life. They adopted Masonic style signs and handshakes of recognition, and,

---

[134] P.W. Kingsford, *Engineers, Inventors and Workers*, (London: Edward Arnold, 1973), pp.88-90.
[135] Ibid.
[136] See Jack S. Blocker, David M. Fahey, and Ian R. Tyrrell, *Alcohol and Temperance in Modern History*, (ABC-CLIO Ltd., 2003), p.513.
[137] Ibid, pp.320-321.

importantly, also took oaths, which, according to labour historian E.P. Thompson, formed a direct link with Freemasonry and the old guild organisations.[138]

Many of the labouring tradesmen who had joined the Lodge of Lights in the early decades of the nineteenth century had joined from other lodges, such as the aforementioned cotton manufacturer James Knott and weaver Richard Pearson, who had entered the Lodge of Lights from Lodge No. 279 in 1810. In 1820, weaver Henry Harrison and fustian cutter John Latham both joined the lodge as 'joining members'. Another weaver, William Halton, entered as a joining member from Lodge No. 120 in 1829, and machine maker Robert Hughes also entered as a joining member in 1820. Charles Wainwright, a dyer, was a member of a lodge in Manchester, but had been born in Warrington and chose to be buried there, his grave – which is adorned with an array of Masonic symbols – can be found nearby various other Masonic gravestones belonging to members of the Lodge of Lights.[139]

Besides the labouring tradesmen joining from other lodges, there were soldiers who also entered as joining members from other lodges, along with men of more professional occupations, such as excise officers, and schoolmasters.[140] Local lodges were certainly not isolated, and were aware of, and in regular contact with other lodges in other towns, Freemasonry being used as an excellent social networking system, allowing the members to visit and join other lodges in other areas. This interweaving between lodges created a larger social interaction, and workers and professionals alike could move around the country, settle where the work was and freely join another lodge, making new social and business contacts. This social web was also apparent in the Friendly Societies and Trade Unions, allowing workers to join other 'lodges' or branches if they moved location, automatically giving them social connections.

---

[138] E.P. Thompson, *The Making of the English Working Class*, (Pelican, 1970), pp.676-9.

[139] 1841 Census for Worsley, Manchester Library, ref: HO107/543/13 AND 1851 Census for Levenshulme, Manchester Library, ref: HO107/2219. The Masonic gravestone of Charles Wainwright is located in the churchyard of St. Elphin's, Warrington, a photograph of which can be seen in David Harrison, *The Genesis of Freemasonry*, (Hersham: Lewis Masonic, 2009).

[140] *List of Members of the Lodge of Lights, No.148, Masonic Hall, Warrington, 1800-1850*. Not listed.

Claims for Relief: Self Help within Freemasonry

The benevolent features of joining a Masonic lodge were still apparent during this period. For example, the Masonic Benefit Society attracted a number of members from the Lodge of Lights in 1799,[141] and there seems to be a relationship between the lodge and the White Hart Benefit Society, members of which were present at the funeral of the aforementioned Brother Johnson in 1802.[142] In the February of 1802, a collection was made in the lodge on behalf of a certain Brother George Phillips, who was a prisoner for debt in Lancaster Castle.[143] Though a Mason, he was not a member of the Lodge of Lights, but he was seen as a brother in need of help. A similar case featured in the minutes of the lodge in 1812, when Brother Charles Tatlock, a Mason from a Leigh based lodge, who was also a prisoner in Lancaster Castle, had an application for relief made on his behalf.[144] Charity for a distressed brother featured again in 1805, when Brother Glazebrook applied to Grand Lodge for relief for Brother James Fletcher, who subsequently received the princely sum of £5.00.[145] The cultivation of self help during this period would certainly have made Freemasonry appealing, and there is ample evidence that the lodges studied here had beneficent and benevolent features. This is a view which has been developed in recent years within the study of Freemasonry, which can *'be set firmly alongside friendly societies and other voluntary benevolent organisation in promoting principles of collaboration between self-determining citizens in pursuit of specific goals and interests'.*[146]

The Lodge of Friendship in Oldham, Lancashire, had, like the Lodge of Lights in Warrington, a list of initiates revealing weavers, joiners, turners, blacksmiths and cordwainers, dominating the lodge during the period 1789-1840. There are also claims for relief mentioned in the minutes, such as in 1792, when a Brother was granted 5/- on the grounds that his wife had been ill for some time, and in 1804, when a gift of 10s.

---

[141] *Minutes of the Lodge of Lights, No.148, Masonic Hall, Warrington, August, 1799.* Not listed.

[142] Ibid, *26th of January, 1802.*

[143] Ibid., *22nd of February, 1802.*

[144] Ibid., *25th of My, 1812.*

[145] Ibid., *25th of November, 1805.*

[146] See Roger Burt, 'Fraternity and Business Networking in the British Non-ferrous Metal Mining Industry in the Eighteenth and Nineteenth Centuries', (University of Exeter), p.13, referencing John Money quoting Margaret Jacob in, 'The Masonic Moment: Or Ritual, Replica and Credit: John Wilkes, the Macaroni Parson, and the Making of the Middle-Class Mind', *Journal of British Studies*, 32 (1993), p.372. Also see Roger Burt, 'Industrial Relations In The British Non-Ferrous Mining Industry in the Nineteenth Century', in *Labour History Review*, Vol. 71, No. 1, (April 2006), pp.57-79.

6d. was given to Brothers who were prisoners in Lancaster Castle. Relief of 6s. was also given to three sailors in 1810, and in 1852, a large sum of £40 was given to victims of a burst reservoir at Holmfirth, with an additional £5 given to the victims of a local boiler explosion. A coffin was purchased by the lodge for the burial of a deceased brother in 1816, and a Benevolent Society was started in connection with the lodge in 1828, with a Sick Fund being founded the following year.[147]

In 1841, the Wigan Grand Lodge founded a Warrington lodge called the Lodge of Knowledge, which met at the Cock in Bridge Street. The lodge only survived for a short period, and there is no record of any interaction with the Lodge of Lights, the lodge remaining isolated. Despite its seclusion from the United Grand Lodge of England, the Wigan Grand Lodge also founded a funeral fund in 1839 which served its members. During the 'schism' of the eighteenth century, Antient Freemasons could enter the Modern Lodge of Lights, though a member of an Antient lodge had to swear allegiance to the Modern Grand Lodge of England, and had to pay a higher fee. The Antients had broken away from the Moderns in 1751, alarmed at what they saw as the modernisation of Freemasonry, and wanted to retain what they saw as the Antient landmarks of the Craft.[148]

Other industrial towns located in Cheshire also had Masonic lodges which witnessed an influx of labouring tradesmen as members from the 1790s to the 1840s. Strong evidence for labouring tradesmen joining Freemasonry appears in a lodge in the industrial town of Nantwich, which had the rather loyal name of the King's Friends Lodge. The lodge was constituted in Chester in 1793, and in 1808, the minutes reveal that a number of the brethren of the lodge were of a lesser *'social standing'*, being described as *'artizans'*, having occupations such as joiner, gardener, locksmith, haymaker, cordwainer, ropemaker, skinner, and miller.[149] A Lodge named 'Beneficient', opened in 1789 in Macclesfield, and a Lodge of 'Benevolence' was founded in Stockport, which had originally started as an Antients lodge in 1759. This Lodge of Benevolence also had brethren from mixed social backgrounds, and has evidence for claims for relief, such as in 1774, when the burial of two deceased brethren was paid for by the lodge. One particularly interesting claim for relief on the 7th of

---

[147] *Minutes of the Lodge of Friendship, No.277, Masonic Hall, Oldham, 1789-1852.* Not listed.

[148] See David Harrison, *The Genesis of Freemasonry*, (Hersham: Lewis Masonic, 2009), pp.190-198.

[149] Extracts of the Minutes of the Kings Friend's Lodge No.293, Nantwich, 1798-1831, copied in J. Armstrong, *A History of Freemasonry in* Cheshire, (Kenning, 1901), pp.315-22.

February 1774 concerned a travelling Mason who appeared to be commuting from lodge to lodge, perhaps searching for work:

'Agreed to give a distress'd Bro. that applies for Relief 1d. per mile, if on horseback 2d. per mile for every mile he goes to another Lodge.[150]

A lodge in Knutsford called the Lodge of Harmony, was founded in 1818, many of the founders being members of the Lodge of Lights.[151] William Evans, who was Worshipful Master of the Lodge of Lights at the time, gave a lecture to the Knutsford lodge in 1821,[152] giving evidence for a continuing close relationship between the two lodges. The Knutsford lodge was however, quite short lived, and after declining attendance, the lodge was closed in 1839.[153] A note after the minutes of the last meeting, written by the last Worshipful Master of the lodge, Brother Peter Richardson, reads:

The rich in and about Knutsford take little notice of Freemasonry, the industrious and middle classes very naturally enquire what benefit is there in joining, when explained, they join other societies where they are insured a direct benefit.....if something of this kind was established (a weekly payment in case of sickness and funeral expenses in case of death) in connection with this Lodge it would flourish.[154]

Transformation of Freemasonry and Participation in Public Ceremonies

Freemasonry began to be much more open during this period, with the Lodge of Lights participating in many public events. One such event was a procession by all the Warrington clubs, celebrating the coronation of George IV in the July of 1821. The minutes of the lodge describe a lively meeting held before the procession,[155] and a local poster from the period, now on public display in the Warrington Parish Church, lists the local

---

[150] Ibid. Extracts from the Lodge of Benevolence No. 83, Stockport, pp.282-284.

[151] *Extracts of the Minutes of the Lodge of Harmony, No.705, Knutsford, 1818-1839*, copied in Armstrong, *A History of Freemasonry in Cheshire*, pp.339-44.

[152] Ibid.

[153] Ibid.

[154] Ibid. A photograph of the Masonic gravestone of Peter Richardson appears in Harrison, *Genesis of Freemasonry.*

[155] *Minutes of the Lodge of Lights, No.148, Masonic Hall, Warrington, 19th of July, 1821.* Not listed. Also see the photograph of the poster advertising the Coronation procession of George IV in July 1821, held in St. Elphin's Church, Warrington.

Freemasons leading a march of nineteen local clubs through the streets of the town. These clubs included many friendly societies and trade clubs such as the Union Club, the Union Coffee House Club, and the Subscription Club, all representing their respective taverns and coffee houses. Another established society, the Amicable Club, also made an appearance. Local trades were also represented, such as the spinners, pin makers, tin-plate makers and glass makers, all marching behind the Freemasons – symbolising the hierarchy of societies in the town.

Though the Lodge of Lights celebrated the coronation of George IV, it did not proceed with a proposed procession for the coronation of William IV ten years later, which was probably due to the poor attendance and the small amount of members for 1831, as other clubs and societies did take part in a procession in Warrington to celebrate the coronation, the Oddfellows taking a prominent role.[156] The lodge also failed to celebrate the coronation of Victoria, though this may have been a wise decision in the light of Victoria's dislike for the Craft. George IV had been Grand Master of the Moderns, and his brother, William IV had also been a high ranking Freemason. Their continued links to the Craft made both of their coronations a cause for celebration in many lodges in towns throughout England and Wales, and a procession by Freemasons did take place in Manchester in honour of the new King William IV, with lodges from Liverpool also taking part as well as the '*Union of Odd Fellows*' and the '*Royal Foresters*'.[157]

On the 22nd of December, 1836, the Lodge of Lights did hold a lavish ceremony for the laying of the keystone of a new bridge over the Mersey, leaving a number of offerings, including a Masonic glass box, showing the set square and compass, and a number of coins. The son of the architect of the bridge, George Gamon of Knutsford, was specially made a Freemason just so he could participate in the ceremony. A procession had taken place from the Market Hall to the bridge, and boys from the Bluecoat School also took part in the procession, along with local Constables and Churchwardens. Money was collected to give the

---

[156] Ibid., *1831*. Also see the photograph advertising the Coronation procession of William IV, held in St. Elphin's Church, Warrington.

[157] Anon., *The History of The Lodge of Harmony No. 220*, (Liverpool, 1948), p.9. See also Andy Durr, 'Chicken and Egg – the Emblem Book and Freemasonry: the Visual and Material Culture of Associated Life', in *AQC*, Vol. 118, (2006), pp.20-36, in which Durr discusses the procession to celebrate the coronation of William IV in Manchester, and how the various Associations involved (Freemason's, the Independent Odd Fellows and the various Trade Societies for example) used similar styles of regalia and used similar symbolism and iconography on their banners, certificates and commemorative jugs.

Bluecoat boys a meal, and other Lancashire lodges attended the ceremony, such as the Lodge of Harmony from Liverpool.[158]

A sense of Freemasonry becoming more 'people friendly' and trying to become more open to society was taking place. An effort to be less secretive and more public, becoming involved with local charities and education and building up a relationship with the authorities and the local gentry were all part of this. By taking part in marches and public celebrations, Freemasonry was promoting itself in the town, and thus attracting new members. The benevolent aspects of Freemasonry were still apparent in the lodge, for example, in 1831, 8s.10d. was issued by the lodge for relief, and petitions were quite common, being put forward on a regular basis during this period.[159] In 1845, there were a number of petitions for relief by the brethren,[160] yet, by the late 1840s, changes began to appear in the lodge makeup, and claims for relief became rarer.

Perhaps because of the rise of the Oddfellows and Foresters in the town[161] or because of Trade Union developments, the Lodge of Lights had less and less labouring tradesmen joining by the 1840s.[162] More industrialists joined the lodge, such as the charismatic Sir Gilbert Greenall, a local brewer, who, when he joined in 1850, was the Conservative MP for Warrington.[163] Shaw Thewlis, a local file manufacturer, joined in 1846, and many other professional gentlemen entered the lodge, such as local surgeon William Hunt, solicitor James Bayley, and James Jones the Deputy Constable.[164] The Academy, which had closed in 1786, was still very much remembered, and the charitable ethos of Freemasonry filtered into the ideals of the industrialists and professionals of Warrington.

As will be explored in a later chapter, the local industrialists re-shaped the town, becoming involved in local politics and gradual social reform. Many of these factory owners, such as the Stubs, Rylands and Greenall families, became involved in local Freemasonry,[165] and they also played a

---

[158] *Minutes of the Lodge of Lights, No.148, Masonic Hall, Warrington, 22nd of December, 1836.* Not listed. The items are now on display at the Warrington Museum. See also Anon., *The History of The Lodge of Harmony No. 220*, (Liverpool, 1948), p.9.
[159] *Minutes of the Lodge of Lights, No.148, Masonic Hall, Warrington, August, 1831.* Not Listed.
[160] Ibid., *1845*.
[161] *Oddfellows Contribution Book, Loyal Orange Lodge, No.143, 1835-42*, Warrington Library, reference MS280 & *Foresters Laws & Regulations, Warrington, 1842*, Warrington Library, reference p1423.
[162] *List of Members of the Lodge of Lights, No.148, Masonic Hall, Warrington, 1840-1850.* Not listed.
[163] Ibid., *28th of June, 1850*.
[164] Ibid., *1837-1850*. Also see *Warrington Trade Directories, 1792-1855*, Warrington Library, reference S10121.
[165] *List of Members of the Lodge of Lights, No.148, Masonic Hall, Warrington, 1837-1865.* Not listed.

major role in the learned societies that evolved in the nineteenth century. They helped to maintain the Masonic ethos of education by supporting the establishment of civic centres such as the Warrington Library and Museum, the Art College, and the School of Science, echoing the involvement of early Masons in local educational pursuits such as Benjamin Yoxall. Many of the learned societies supported by local Freemasons met in the old Academy buildings, such as the Mechanics Institute, and the Lodge of Lights were present during the ceremony for the laying of the foundation stone for the Library and Museum in 1855.

Many other local Freemasons became involved in these local learned societies, such as George Hughes, and Thomas Morris, both being Curators of the Natural History Society.[166] Two of the pioneers of the society were Peter Rylands and Joseph Stubs, both local industrialists and members of the Lodge of Lights.[167] Stubs extended his involvement in local charity by being on the committee for the Warrington Dispensary and Infirmary. The local Unitarian Chapel had held Sunday school classes since the early 1800s, and had been involved in welfare work, forming a sick club and clothing club. In 1862, the local Unitarian Minister, J. Nixon Porter, became a Freemason and continued a link that had existed between the Lodge of Lights and the Unitarian Ministry that had started with John Seddon, the founder of the Academy.[168]

The Royal Yorkshire Lodge in Keighley, Yorkshire, which had also witnessed many labouring tradesmen enter the lodge from the 1790s, also began to have an increased influx of professionals, industrialists, and business men (including men from the 'High Street' such as Butchers and Grocers) after the 1840s. Labouring tradesmen appeared less and less and by the 1840s the transformation of the membership is evident, with the lodge being filled with local Gentlemen, Schoolmasters and local manufacturers.[169]

Why did this change take place? The social historian Eric J. Evans has discussed that a greater divide between the 'working classes' and 'middle classes' occurred after the Reform Act of 1832, the old collaborations between these middle and working classes disintegrated after what he termed the *'middle-class betrayal of 1832'*. Evans also examined how in the

---

[166] Ibid., *1837-1865*. Also see *Minutes of General Meetings of the Natural History Society, 1837-53*, Warrington Library, reference MS22.
[167] Ibid.
[168] *List of Members of the Lodge of Lights, No.148, Masonic Hall, Warrington, 28th of July, 1862*. Not listed.
[169] *List of Members of the Royal Yorkshire Lodge No. 265* in J. Ramsden Riley, *The History of the Royal Yorkshire Lodge*, (Yorkshire, 1889), pp.79-87.

industrial cotton producing towns of Lancashire, there was a *'greater distance observed between the master and the spinner'.*[170] As a class conscience developed, and Freemasonry became increasingly attractive to the professionals, businessmen and industrialists, the labouring tradesmen that had shared the lodges with them in various industrial towns in the first half of the nineteenth century were not replaced, the younger labouring tradesmen and semi-skilled factory workers finding other social activities and joining other clubs and societies. More organised and legal Trade Unions[171], and the increasing popularity of the Oddfellows and Foresters and other 'ritualistic' Friendly Societies such as the IOR, which from about 1841 started to introduce medical benefits,[172] attracted more working men (and in some Friendly Societies such as the IOR – they also began to accept women as members), and thus Freemasonry in the industrial towns featured less and less of the labouring tradesmen and factory workers.

During the troubled period of the early nineteenth century, the local gentry seemed to have still been ever present in the lodges in the Provincial centre of Chester. However, the satellite lodges of the provinces, situated in more industrialised areas such as lodges in Nantwich, Knutsford, Warrington, Oldham and Wigan, had an influx of labouring tradesmen balancing the membership with the local industrialists and professionals. Chester continued to be the Provincial centre for Freemasonry in Cheshire, with Provincial Grand Lodge meeting regularly there until the 1830s.[173] Charity was always an important feature of the Provincial Grand Lodge meetings, such as when it met at Crewe in 1851 and collected £12. 10s. 10d. for the Provincial Fund of Benevolence.[174] Local newspaper accounts of a meeting in Chester in 1867, reported that £20 was collected, to be divided between

[170] E. J. Evans, *The Forging of the Modern State: Early Industrial Britain 1783-1870*, (London: Longman, 1992), pp.172-173.

[171] The Combination Acts were finally repealed in 1824, but an amended Combination Act was passed the following year, which permitted Trade Unions but restricted their activity, and secret oath-taking still concerned the authorities. Despite the Tolpuddle Martyrs and the collapse of Robert Owen's 'Grand National Consolidated Trades Union' in 1834, the more organised skilled trades unions flourished, such as the aforementioned 'Old Mechanics' and the 'Amalgamated Society of Carpenters and Joiners'. In 1867, there was a Royal Commission set up into Trade Unions which eventually led to the Trade Union Act of 1871 which secured the legal status of Trade Unions and protected their funds.

[172] Jack S. Blocker, David M. Fahey, and Ian R. Tyrrell, *Alcohol and Temperance in Modern History*, (ABC-CLIO Ltd., 2003), p.513.

[173] Armstrong, *A History of Freemasonry in Cheshire*, pp.62-96.

[174] Ibid., p.126.

the restoration of St. John's Church and the Chester Infirmary. Another Provincial Grand Lodge meeting, held in Birkenhead two years later, discussed financial reports from the committee of the fund of benevolence, recommending that the most deserving candidate for admission to the Masonic School for Boys be nominated. Other evidence of Masonic charity and its links to local education was indicated by funds given to the Cheshire Education Institution.[175] The local gentry and wealthy industrialists were also consistently present in the prestigious Hope and Anchor Lodge No. 37 in Bolton, a lodge which supplied a number of Provincial Grand Master's for Lancashire.

A transformation in localised Freemasonry can be seen in the Lodge of Lights from the 1790s to the 1840s. The wars with France and the Unlawful Societies Act may have been responsible for the departure of many of the more affluent men from the lodge, especially as local paranoia and suspicion against Freemasonry was well documented in the minutes of the Lodge of Lights. Certainly, there is evidence of the lodge desperately trying to recruit local *'Gentlemen'* in an effort to regain local credibility and to shake off suspicion, and the minutes hint at a public discord with Freemasonry. In Chester, many of the high ranking local gentry remained in the Craft, seemingly unaffected by the public opinion of Freemasonry. This shows how different localities may have had different attitudes to Freemasonry, creating an uneven picture within the national framework of the Craft. Perhaps because the Chester lodges were close to Provincial control, the high ranking local gentry had nothing to fear from public attitudes. Chester was also not as heavily industrialised as Warrington.

In Chester, Freemasonry had always remained in the hands of the local gentry. As the centre of the Province of Cheshire, a certain exclusiveness and 'snobbery' seemed to prevail, even during the sensitive years after the Unlawful Societies Act. The Royal Chester Lodge for example, during the late eighteenth and early nineteenth centuries, had boasted the membership of Sir Watkin Williams Wynn MP, Sir John Grey Egerton MP, and Thomas Cholmondeley MP. However, by the 1820s, despite having such a distinguished membership, the lodge suffered from low attendance, and finally closed in 1829.[176] Other Chester lodges also suffered financial problems during the early part of the nineteenth century and it had been stated by Masonic historian John Armstrong that

---

[175] *Various Collected Newspaper Reports of Provincial Grand Lodge Meetings, Warrington Masonic Hall, 1867 and 1869.* Not listed.
[176] Armstrong, *A History of Freemasonry of Cheshire*, p.262.

Sir John Grey Egerton, the Provincial Grand Master of Cheshire from 1810-1825, had greatly neglected his duties, which had led to certain problems.[177] Lodges in Liverpool were also not immune to the effects of the period, such as the prestigious Merchants Lodge and the Lodge of Harmony, which also suffered periods of low membership and dept, the strain of which led to involvement in the Liverpool Masonic Rebellion.

Labouring tradesmen may have been attracted to certain lodges in industrial towns, such as the Lodge of Lights in Warrington, the Lodge of Friendship in Oldham and the King's Friends Lodge in Nantwich, because they recognised, in part, the educational and charitable aspects of Freemasonry. There are a number of petitions for relief in the Lodge of Lights during this time, and the educational value of Freemasonry was apparent, with lectures being given. Industrialists and professionals were also still involved in the lodge, such as the cotton manufacturer James Knott and glass manufacturer Thomas Kirkland Glazebrook, but with overall membership down, labouring tradesmen such as weaver Henry Harrison could enter the lodge and take an active role, and freely mix with men of a higher social standing.

The benevolent values of Freemasonry were evident throughout in the late eighteenth and early nineteenth centuries, with support for widows and children of deceased brethren, funerals being taken care of, and support for members who were in debt. This would make joining a lodge a very attractive proposition for a labouring tradesman, and would be extremely advantageous to his family. The amount of labouring men that entered local lodges became fewer, and this coincided with the development of more organised legal Trade Unions, and especially the development of Friendly Societies such as the Oddfellows and Foresters. The introduction of more organised Burial Societies such as the 'Liverpool Independent Legal Victoria Burial Society', founded in 1843,[178] and Benefit Societies like the 'Benefit Building Society' established in Liverpool in 1865, would have also attracted specifically the working classes that were interested in burial cover.[179] Freemasonry seemed to

---

[177] Ibid., p.90.

[178] The Liverpool Independent Legal Victoria Burial Society, founded in 1843 in Liverpool, accepted a premium of ½ d. or 1 d. per week to cover funeral costs. It became known as the Liverpool Victoria Friendly Society in 1893.

[179] *Rules of The Clarence Street Permanent Benefit Building Society, Established at Liverpool, May 3, 1865*, (Liverpool: Thomas Walmsley, 1868). Countless 'Assurance' and 'Benefit' companies were founded at this time, all targeting the 'working classes', for example, in *The Warrington Guardian, Saturday 9ᵗʰ of April, 1853*, the front page was mainly taken up with adverts for Assurance

become more elitist as more local industrialists, businessmen and professionals joined, but support for local charity and education was still as strong as ever, and local Freemasons continued to forge a local and cultural identity.

---

companies such as 'The Tines Life Assurance and Guarantee Company' and 'The English Widows Fund and General Life Assurance Association'.

Chapter 3

The Rise of the Middle Class within Freemasonry in the industrial north-west of England[180]

'...for it has oftener happened that men have been too passive than too unruly, and the rebellion of Kings against their people has been more common and done more mischief than the rebellion of people against their Kings.'

Freemason Dr. Richard Price, 1789[181]

'But what is liberty without wisdom and without virtue? It is the greatest of all possible evils; for it is folly, vice and madness, without tuition or restraint.'

Freemason Edmund Burke, 1790[182]

'Not sufficiently content with abusing the National Assembly, a great part of his work is taken up with abusing Dr. Price (one of the best-hearted men that lives), and the two societies in England known by the name of the Revolution Society, and the Society for Constitutional Information.'

Thomas Paine, responding to Edmund Burke's attack on Price's speech, 1791[183]

---

[180] Special thanks to John Belton who co-wrote this chapter and compiled the data for the Lodge of St. John No. 104 and Anchor and Hope No. 37, assembling the tables and creating the graphs. Part of the content of this chapter was presented to the Centre for Research into Freemasonry Seminar, at the Douglas Knoop Centre, University of Sheffield, on the 24th of October, 2006, as 'Freemasonry in Flux, a study of membership trends in Masonic lodges in the north west of England in the first half of the 19th century'. The paper was duly published, see David Harrison and John Belton, 'Society in Flux' in *Researching British Freemasonry 1717-2017: The Journal for the Centre of Research into Freemasonry and Fraternalism*, Vol. 3, (Sheffield: University of Sheffield, 2010), pp.71-99.

[181] Richard Price, 'A Discourse on the Love of our Country, delivered on Nov. 4, 1789, at the Meeting-House in the Old Jewry, to the Society for Commemorating the Revolution in Great Britain', in David Oswald Thomas, (ed.), *Political Writings by Richard Price*, (Cambridge: Cambridge University Press, 1991), p.185.

[182] Edmund Burke, 'Reflections on the Revolution in France, and on the proceedings in certain societies in London relative to that event: In a letter intended to have been sent to a gentleman in Paris', in *The Works of The Right Honorable Edmund Burke, Revised Edition, Vol. III*, (Boston: Little, Brown, and Company, 1865), p.559.

[183] Thomas Paine, *Rights of Man: Being An Answer to Mr. Burke's Attack on The French Revolution*, (London: Holyoake and Co., 1856), p.5. His *Rights of Man*, which was a response to Burke's *Reflections on the Revolution in France*, became an enormous influence on the many Corresponding Societies that emerged in the 1790s.

'It is impossible but that, in the very great political convulsion which has recently shaken Europe, our society must have been materially affected. This I know, that, in the unhappy country where the shock has been the greatest, the brethren of the social band have not been able to assemble according to their order without a dread of the Revolutionary Tribunal.'

Dr. Watkins, *A Charge Delivered to a Society of Free Masons, The Freemasons' Magazine*, January 1796[184]

The chapter will examine the early nineteenth century membership of four masonic lodges in four industrial towns in the county of Lancashire, north-west England, following the wake of the Unlawful Societies Act of 1799. The lodges will be presented as a case study, showing fluctuations in membership and changes in character. The chapter will present reasons for the transformation in the composition of the lodges, from a 'working-class' membership to a more 'middle-class' makeup. While Masonic associationalism prospered in the later years of the century it had seriously declined in the period from 1820 to 1860. By the time the Lancashire 'Cotton Famine' had run its course, all the lodges had begun to grow in size and prosperity under new lodge leadership. The paper will also examine the role of these charismatic individuals who became local Masonic leaders and turned their individual lodges around.

Recent work on fraternal networking within working class communities in the eighteenth and nineteenth centuries, such as Tim Newton's work which focussed on assessing previous studies on organisations and employee subjectivity,[185] and Roger Burt's work on the Cornish mining industry, has demonstrated how in certain industrial areas during this period, businessmen and professionals constructed *'webs of affiliation'*, Freemasonry creating business networks, assisting in bringing together like-minded men in pursuit of similar interests.[186]

Other research conducted by Andrew Prescott has encompassed similar themes, and compounded the view that Masonic lodges were important to the development of their surrounding community, especially

---

184 *The Freemasons' Magazine: And Cabinet of Universal Literature For January 1796*, p.6.
185 Tim Newton, 'From Freemasons to the Employee: Organization, History and Subjectivity', *Organization Studies*, 25 (8): pp.1363-1387.
186 Roger Burt, 'Fraternity and Business Networking in the British Non-ferrous Metal Mining Industry in the Eighteenth and Nineteenth Centuries', (University of Exeter). Also see Roger Burt, 'Fraternity and Business Networking in City and Provinces in the Late Nineteenth and Early Twentieth Centuries', (University of Exeter).

in their influence of early Trade Union movements.[187] The relationship between the Masonic lodges and the socio-economic development of the surrounding area was one of intricacy and intimacy, the lodge reflecting its town's individual industrial development, and this can be seen in the work of Pam Davies, who commented on the connection between local Freemasonry and radicalism in the industrial town of Merthyr Tydfil, South Wales.[188] The study of the lodges discussed here reveals the importance of fraternalism (in the form of Freemasonry) within these communities, and the importance of how the lodges and their individual flux, acted as a reflector of the economic conditions and developments of the period, one of intense technological and social change.[189]

The Flux of Freemasonry

From the formation of the 'Premier/Modern' Grand Lodge in 1717, until 1751, there were only four lodges formed in the South Lancashire cotton belt.[190] The appearance of a rival 'Antients' Grand Lodge in 1751 brought competition and resulted in the founding of more lodges. Of those lodges in Lancashire, apart from some early examples, many survived well into the nineteenth century. This might lead one to think that Masonic fraternalism was a constant process of growth, both in the number of lodges and the number of members. However, during the early part of the nineteenth century, some lodges simply vanished forever, while others, like the Lodge of St. John in Stockport, stuttered for a time, struggling with perilously low membership and debt and then they would suddenly reappear to prosper. It also seems likely that in the early years, the Antients were less experienced and less particular who they issued Warrants to.

The membership data from the four lodges looked at here presented us with results that indicate this, though, considering their locations, the

---

[187] Andrew Prescott, 'The Spirit of Association: Freemasonry and Early Trade Unions', A Paper Presented at the Canonbury Masonic Research Centre, 30 May 2001, *CRF*, University of Sheffield, http://freemasonry.dept.shef.ac.uk/index.php?lang=0&type=page&level0=243&level1=387&level2=394&op=387 [accessed 15th of May, 2009]

[188] Pam Davies, 'Sir Josiah John Guest and the Merthyr Radicals: A Symbiotic Relationship', *CRF*, University of Sheffield, Seminars (2001-2007), http://freemasonry.dept.shef.ac.uk/index.php?lang=0&type=blog&level0=242&level1=263&level2=367&op=261 [accessed 15th of May, 2009]

[189] See Peter Clark, *British Clubs and Societies 1580-1800*, (Oxford: Oxford University Press, 2000), pp.313-319.

[190] See John Lane, *Masonic Records 1717–1886*, http://www.freemasonry.dept.shef.ac.uk/lane [accessed 15th of May, 2009]

peaks and troughs did not coincide exactly with the various problems in the cotton industry as a whole, but seemed to reflect more localised patterns. This might be because the factors influencing the decision to join the lodges were due to more local economic factors rather than those prevailing in either Lancashire or the country as a whole. The decades leading up to 1860 were characterised by repeated innovations in different parts of the cotton to cloth process. Thus in one year a mill could be exceptionally efficient and profitable, yet in the following years, the mill could be facing crisis because technological advances had rendered their machinery relatively inefficient and less profitable.

The Stockport, Warrington and Oldham lodges in particular show a relentless decline in new members from about 1820, this is followed by a notable peak in all four lodges examined around the 1850s–1860s, especially noticeable in the Lodge of St. John, the Lodge of Lights, and the Lodge of Friendship, which coincides with the popular and alluring leadership of the Rev. John Crennel, Sir Gilbert Greenall and Isaac Gaitskill respectively.[191] This sharp recovery around 1850-60, reveals something of an increased interest in fraternalism, especially Freemasonry, which continued for the rest of the nineteenth century.

The other part of the picture is the occupational groups of members and the foundation on which these lodges were built seems to have been those active in trade in the 'High Street' – the shopkeepers (grocers, butchers, bakers, watchmakers). In the first half of the century the balance of this sector was innkeepers and in the second half the number of merchants and agents rose sharply. It was equally noticeable that the number of industrialists and professionals (solicitors, doctors, clergy, public officials, engineers) rose very sharply in the 1850s marking a permanent change in the membership of these lodges. What was also noticeable was the decrease in importance of men following a trade. Included in this category would have been traditional manual tradesmen (joiners, farriers, smiths, cordwainers, building tradesmen), and of course cotton and cloth industry trades (weavers, spinners, fustian cutters).[192]

---

[191] Also see Stefan-Ludwig Hoffmann, *The Politics of Sociability: Freemasonry and German Civil Society, 1840-1918*, Translated by Tom Lampert, (University of Michigan Press, 2007), p.112. Stefan-Ludwig Hoffman discusses a surge of Masonic membership in Germany during the 1860s and 1870s, followed by stagnation in the following decades due to political and social factors.

[192] Indeterminate occupational descriptions given in lodge membership records made this group hard to split between tradesmen and manufacturers and is inevitably somewhat arbitrary. Where the word manufacturer is used all is clear. A single word e.g. weaver, printer, spinner was by our convention considered as a trade and phrases such as calico printer or cotton spinner were treated as manufacturers.

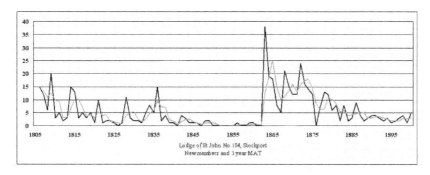

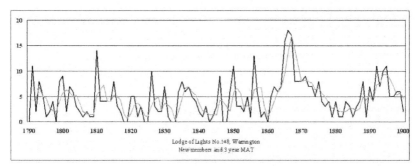

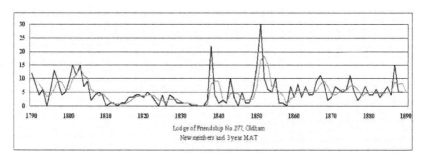

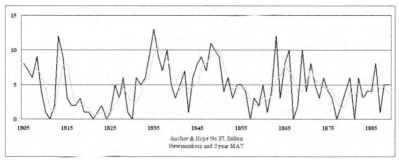

Four graphs showing the membership of the four lodges discussed. Notice the sudden peak indicating increased membership from 1850-1860 in the Stockport, Warrington and Oldham based lodges.

Table 1: Composite occupations of men becoming Masons by decade:

Occupation	1800 -09	1810 -19	1820 -29	1830 -39	1840 -49	1850 -59	1860 -69	1870 -79	1880 -89	1890 -99
Manufacturing	19	15	13	25	12	29	33	38	11	13
Professional	8	5	6	16	21	30	70	58	36	44
Sellers	34	25	20	20	32	43	84	77	50	45
Trades	82	34	29	52	18	20	22	18	14	14
Total	221	150	119	180	128	186	318	279	174	199

The totals figures clearly highlight the resurgence post 1860s which followed the leaner decades from 1820 to 1860. This resurgence also saw some decrease in the volatility of men becoming masons and was accompanied by a significant shift in the occupations.

The Lodge of St. John No. 104, Stockport

The Lodge of St. John was an 'Antient' lodge[193] founded in 1765 in Mottram in Longdendale in Cheshire. The lodge seemed to have floundered early on in its career, and the Warrant was transferred to Saddleworth in Yorkshire in 1775, where the lodge existed until 1784. After this date, the Warrant seemed to have been kept in the possession of one of its old members, who took it with him when he moved to Stockport, and, after getting it endorsed in London, started the lodge afresh in 1806. The lodge prospered, its membership being drawn from the local cotton industry, yet by the close of 1820s, the lodge began to enter a period of decline.

Stockport came early to the cotton industry and by 1814 was only surpassed by Manchester as a cotton-spinning centre.[194] Yet by 1825, Stockport had been completely overtaken by Manchester as the foremost centre of powerloom weaving while still containing more than a quarter of the nations power looms.[195] Stockport, like other cotton towns, experienced the frequent cycles of 'boom and bust' but the depression of 1837 was particularly extreme and there were no signs of a recovery until 1848. The cause of this stagnation was identified as the age of the factories in the town and a common sight were signs outside old mills

---

[193] See Appendix 2 for an explanation of terminology.
[194] P. Arrowsmith, *Stockport - a History*, (Stockport MBC, 1997), p.125.
[195] Ibid., p.154.

offering "a room with power – to let".[196]   The net result was that the
population of Stockport also became stagnant.

During this period, like other industrial towns during the first half of
the nineteenth century, Stockport suffered incidents of protest from its
cotton workers, such as in 1842 when there was a riot at the town
Workhouse.   This riot occurred during the General Strike of August
1842, a strike which was entwined with Chartist activity and radical
discontent amongst the cotton workers of Lancashire. Stockport suffered
high unemployment running at 50%, with the average weekly wage of
those fully employed being only 7s. 6½d.[197]   Stockport also witnessed a
serious riot in 1852, instigated by anti Catholic resentment, with the
sacking of a newly completed Catholic church. A quarter of Stockport's
population was Catholic,[198] and fears of a local labour market diluted with
unskilled Irish immigrants exasperated religious anger.   The 'born in
Ireland' proportion of the population of Stockport having doubled in the
decade between the 1841 and 1851 censuses.[199]

The cotton industry dominated the Manchester area, its surrounding
environs such as Stockport, Oldham and Salford developing at a rapid
pace during the close of the eighteenth century. The membership of the
Lodge of St. John reflected the industry of the town it was located in,
with weavers and cotton spinners initially dominating the lodge. It was
from this working class element that the 'Immortal Seven' were drawn,
seven members who kept the lodge alive during Stockport's, depressed
years, a deep depression which lasted until the early 1860s. These seven
men; George McAuley a dresser, William McAuley a weaver, John Perkin,
also a dresser, James Wood a shuttlemaker, William Gee a spinner,
Richard Jones a wheelwright, and John Oldham a bricklayer, were the
rump end of an older social structure that had clung on longer in
Stockport than elsewhere because of its older industrial legacy. The state
of the Lodge of St John is perhaps mirrored by that in the town in general
because in 1862 a Manchester business man who inspected a highly
suitable mill was reported to have:

*'declined the offer of the vendor ... because he had heard that the operatives were
apt to be troublesome'.*[200]

---

[196] Ibid., p.125.
[197] E. J. Hobsbawm, *Labouring Men*, (London: Weidenfeld and Nicolson, 1986), pp.75-6.
[198] E. J. Evans, *The Forging of the Modern State: Early Industrial Britain 1783-1870*, (London: Longman, 1992), pp.305-6.
[199] P. Arrowsmith, *Stockport - a History*, (Stockport MBC, 1997), p.216.
[200] N. Longmate, *The Hungry Mills*, (London: Temple Smith, 1978), p.54.

The lodge was only saved by the Rev. John Crennell MA joining the lodge in the December of 1859.[201] He was born in 1834 on the Isle of Man and in 1859 was a schoolmaster in Stockport. He eventually left Stockport in 1870 and in 1873 became Vicar of St. Andrews Church in Beamish and later Rector of Byers Green, Spennymore, in County Durham.

Four years before his death, the Rev. Crennell reminisced to fellow Freemason Herbert Finch on how he became acquainted with the lodge. Crennell's detailed memories offer not only a unique insight into freemasonry in Stockport at that time, but supply a glimpse into the state of the stagnant lodge:

'I had always (from being a boy) a great idea of becoming a Freemason, and when I went to Stockport, and got settled down, I turned my attention to joining the Craft". As to the state of Freemasonry in Stockport, the situation is clear: *"The working of Masonry at that time was at a low ebb; there were only two men in Stockport who could make any attempt at working Ceremonies, and it was almost painful to hear them. The members of St. John's, seeing what an interest I took in masonry, did all they could to help me, turning up regularly at the meetings, and we often followed up the little business we had to do in Lodge, by holding a Lodge of Instruction".* For the new and willing member there was little respite and *"I was made Warden a few months after being raised, and said to do my part better than any other officer. The next year I was made Master, and was said to do the work of the Chair creditably'.*[202]

Crennell served as Master for three periods of 6 months (then normal but it is now one year) stating that:

'The last evening I was in office (I was a year and a half in office) I had twelve Ceremonies - I think eight of them were Raisings, all done separately. I took the chair at 4.00pm and never left it until 11pm. I began office with eight members, and ended with 60 - a pretty good year's work, and I did every Ceremony. From that time better men took the helm and made the Lodge what it is. . . .'[203]

---

201 J. Armstrong, *A History of Freemasonry in Cheshire*, (Kenning, 1901), pp.305-307. *Lists of Membership of the Lodge of St. John, no.104, Stockport.* Not Listed.
202 C.A.A Ball, *Bi-centenary History of Lodge of St John 104 1806-2006*, in publication by the lodge. The authors are greatly indebted to a number of past and present members of St John's Lodge for the records they have kept, notably Herbert Finch in 1893 who wrote a lodge history as an appendix to the 1839 bye-laws and to Clive Ball the author of the 200th anniversary history.
203 Ibid.

Neither did he restrict his efforts to the Lodge of St John:

'The late Bro.Hy. Howard and myself worked up the Lodge of Concord. It had sunk very low, and we raised it to a high degree of efficiency and numbers. I had a Lodge of instruction for several years, both at St. John's and Concord. I was never a subscribing member of the Lodge of Concord but I was always treated as a member and when I left Stockport they made me an honorary member, which honour I hold to this day'.[204]

Crennell became the essential figure in turning the lodge's fortunes around. From a lodge which had witnessed a thriving membership mainly taken from the local cotton industry, the lodge had dwindled to a group of just seven, and it was literally Crennell's membership which became crucial to the lodge's new success. A schoolmaster who was entwined in the middle-class social nexus of Stockport, Crennell quickly became Worshipful Master in 1863, and subsequently initiated over fifty new members, breathing new life into the lodge, this time the membership being extracted from a more middle class background.

A similar occurrence can be seen in the industrial town of Neath in South Wales, with the Gnoll Lodge No. 506, named after the local industrialist and banker Sir Herbert Mackworth of Gnoll Castle, which was founded in 1777. Both Sir Herbert and later, his son, Sir Digby Mackworth had joined the lodge, but by 1800, Sir Digby had moved away and the lodge was struggling with low attendance. The lodge however was resurrected after the arrival of eight enthusiastic Masons who had been members of London lodges, but were residing in Swansea and wanted to found a new lodge there. They were informed that no new lodges were being warranted at the time due to the anxiety caused by the recent Unlawful Societies Act, and the eight Masons were referred to the struggling Gnoll lodge in Neath, which subsequently moved to Swansea. The lodge went on to become extremely successful in the following years, and was renamed and renumbered the Indefatigable Lodge No. 237.[205]

---

[204] Ibid.

[205] See 'The history of the Indefatigable Lodge No. 237' http://www.province.org.uk/Lodges/237.htm [accessed 1st of May, 2009]. Though Lane in his *Masonic Records 1717–1886* lists the Gnoll Lodge and the Indefatigable Lodge as two separate lodges, the lodge's centenary Warrant of 1877 recognises that the Indefatigable Lodge had worked continuously from 1777, the name being changed from Gnoll to Indefatigable in 1800. Many Masonic Halls have a wealth of hidden Masonic artefacts, and the Swansea Masonic Temple famously has on display a sword seized from the hands of a French sailor at Fishguard in 1797 during the last attempted invasion of Britain by a French led force, which landed in South Wales.

The Lodge of Lights No. 148, Warrington

A similar occurrence can be seen taking place in the Lodge of Lights, its membership, like that of the Lodge of St. John in Stockport, comprised mainly working class members during the early nineteenth century. The town itself, like Stockport, was undergoing a transition, with rapid industrial development and social change. Warrington, ideally placed on the River Mersey, attracted glass and soap manufacturing, weaving, various forms of metalworking, wire drawing and sail cloth manufacturing. This rapid industrial growth attracted workers, and Warrington had changed from a Lancashire market town to one of industry and trade. The population in 1801 was 10,567 and by 1851 it had almost doubled to 20,800. The lodge, like the town it was situated in, seemed to enter a transitional period, and the make-up of the lodge reflected an influx of working men into the town as it became more industrialised.

Yet, by the 1850s, a more middle class membership in the lodge became evident. A depression had effected certain industries in Warrington, such as Clare and Brownes glass works, which had stopped production in 1842[206] and the wire-drawing partnership of Greening and Rylands, formed about 1806, came to an end in 1843, the two families developing rival businesses in the town. The Rylands family had originally been involved in the linen business and sailcloth weaving, their diversity resulting in a successful stable industry in Warrington throughout the nineteenth century, Peter Rylands becoming a member of the Lodge of Lights in 1865.[207]

The industry in Warrington was so diverse that the town seemed to have avoided much of the disruption witnessed during the General Strike of 1842 in the cotton spinning towns of Stockport and Oldham. The glass industry was affected by the depression, and previously, there had been a number of lodge members that worked in the local glass industry, such as Thomas Crosier, a glass cutter who joined the lodge in 1815, and

---

According to the story, the French sailor was about to cut down an innocent civilian, but was slain himself, and on the 4th of June 1805, the sword was presented to the Tyler of the Indefatigable Lodge No. 237 by a certain Brother Mathias. See Andrew Prescott, 'Druidic Myths and Freemasonry', *CRF*, a lecture presented at the Masonic Weekend organised by the Lodge Hope of Kurrachee No. 337 at the Kirkcaldy Masonic Hall, 4th-6th of May, 2000, University of Sheffield, http://freemasonry.dept.shef.ac.uk/index.php?lang=3&type=page&level0=243&level1=387&leve l2=392&op=387 [accessed 1st of May, 2009]

[206] T.C. Barker, *Pilkington Brothers and the Glass Industry*, (London: George Allen & Unwin Ltd, 1960), p.119.

[207] *Minutes & Membership Lists of the Lodge of Lights No.148, Warrington, 1765-1900, 29th of December, 1865, Warrington Masonic Hall.* Not listed.

Joseph Perrin, a glass manufacturer who joined in 1827.[208] Perrin became an extremely active member of the lodge, serving as Master a mere four times, and resided in Fennel Street, which was also the location of Thomas Kirkland Glazebrook, another glass manufacturer and member of the Lodge of Lights who joined in 1802. The Lodge of Lights, like the Lodge of St. John in Stockport suffered low attendance, low membership, and also had a working-class content, but after 1850, the lodge increased its membership, and began to attract more industrialists, professionals and businessmen. This coincided with the appearance in the lodge of Sir Gilbert Greenall, a charismatic local industrialist and aspiring Conservative politician, who joined in 1850.[209]

Greenall's presence seemed to attract other industrialists from Warrington, swelling the numbers of the lodge, and like Crennell in the Lodge of St. John, his time as Worshipful Master (1865-1866) was one of the most successful years for incoming initiates. Indeed, the signs of the turnaround within the lodge had been reported in the *Freemason's Magazine and Masonic Mirror* in January, 1864, when, during the Festival of St. John the Evangelist, Bro. Shaw Lewis, another local industrialist, commented on how the lodge had undergone *'progressive improvement'* and *'prosperity'*. Greenall, who at the time was the Conservative MP for Warrington, also commented during the meeting, giving hints at the reasons why he joined Freemasonry and the networking that existed within the new middle class makeup of the lodge:

'here, as Masons, he must not, and dare not, enter on political topics, such being absolutely prohibited; he found the prohibition affording him an agreeable recreation after his ordinary experiences of the non-Masonic banquets. He had become a Mason on learning the disinterested and pure principles on which the Order is founded, and his experiences since having become a Mason, had corroborated and amplified his previous good opinions of the excellencies of the Institution. He had known (the Worshipful Master elect - John Bowes) intimately since he came into Warrington, now twelve years since... [210]

John Bowes, like Crennel from the Lodge of St. John, was a schoolmaster.[211] This turnaround in the lodge witnessed the end of

---

[208] Ibid.
[209] Ibid.
[210] *Freemasons Magazine and Masonic Mirror, Jan. 9, 1864, pp.24-6.*
[211] *Minutes & Membership Lists of the Lodge of Lights no.148, Warrington, 1765-1900, 30th of December, 1861, Warrington Masonic Hall.* Not listed.

'working class' membership, the lodge becoming filled with well connected middle class industrialists and businessmen.

The Lodge of Friendship No. 277, Oldham

The Lodge of Friendship, based in Oldham, was a 'Moderns' lodge founded in 1789, and again reveals a membership drawn from the local cotton spinning industry. Early members such as James Butterworth, reveal an element of social climbing, Butterworth for example being a weaver when he joined, but soon became a local teacher and bookshop owner, writing numerous works on local history and a book on Masonic symbolism in 1801. Like the aforementioned lodges, the Lodge of Friendship suffered a decline in membership and attendance during the early 1800s, its membership improving after 1850.[212] This 'revival' was witnessed in the lodge meeting on the 13th of November, 1850, when ten candidates were proposed and initiated in due course, eleven more candidates being accepted during the two subsequent lodge meetings. The years 1850-1851 became the most productive period for new initiates under the influence of schoolmaster Isaac Gaitskill, reflecting the 'rejuvenation' of the Lodge of Lights under Greenall and the Lodge of St. John under Crennell, who like Gaitskill, was also a schoolmaster. Gaitskill was presented with a gold watch, guard and ring for his services to the lodge in 1853, and was later considered to be the first in a long line of Masonic leaders in Oldham.[213]

Many workers from the cotton-spinning industry of Oldham were present at the infamous Peterloo Massacre in St. Peter's Fields, Manchester in the August of 1819. This reform meeting drew an immense crowd of around 60,000, the majority of which were workers from the cotton-spinning industrial towns surrounding Manchester. The meeting was stopped by the Manchester Yeomanry, and the crowd ruthlessly dispersed, causing eleven deaths and many hundreds injured. The events at Peterloo can be mirrored with the later insurrection which took place in the industrial town of Merthyr Tydfil, South Wales, in 1831, which, like Peterloo, resulted in many injuries after troops attempted to

---

[212] *Minutes of the Lodge of Friendship no.277, Oldham, 1789-1850, Oldham Masonic Hall.* Not listed. Also see David Harrison, 'Freemasonry, Industry and Charity: The Local Community and the Working Man'. *The Journal of the Institute of Volunteering Research*, Volume 5, Number 1, (Winter 2002), pp.33-45.
[213] *Minutes of the Lodge of Friendship no.277, Oldham, 13th of November, 1850, Oldham Masonic Hall.* Not listed. Also see B. Gee, *Lodge of Friendship no.277: History of the Lodge*, (Oldham, 1989), p.25.

dispel the rioters. The insurrection involved the town's ironstone miners, and many local Freemasons were involved in the organisation of gatherings, meetings and radical propaganda on the eve of the riots.[214]

John Lees from Oldham was one of those killed at Peterloo, and the minutes of the Lodge of Friendship refer to the incident rather casually on the 29th of September 1819, when they state that the lodge had to be adjourned as the *'room was engaged by the Coroner.*[215] The inquest was also mentioned in *The Globe*, on the 25th of September, concerning John Lees, who had died as a result of the wounds he received at Peterloo, the verdict being *null and void.*[216] There was a John Lees who joined the lodge in January 1817, but it is difficult to determine if he is one and the same as there is a lack of documentation.[217] Richard Carlile, the author of the *Manual of Freemasonry*, first published in 1825, witnessed the Peterloo Massacre, and was due to speak at the meeting, later publishing an account of the incident. Oldham was also tainted by the General Strike of 1842, though not as badly affected as Stockport, with Oldham suffering around 25% unemployment at the time.[218]

Anchor and Hope No. 37, Bolton

This extremely prestigious Lodge was founded in 1732 and occupied the position of being the oldest lodge in the Province of Lancashire since 1760, and indeed, is the oldest lodge outside London which has continued to meet in the same town.[219] The first Worship Master, Bro Edward Entwisle, mercer and member of a prominent local family, was the first Provincial Grand Master of Lancashire from 1734 until 1742. There was at that time only two other lodges in that area of Lancashire, No. 48 at Salford and No. 87 at Leigh. Sadly their records of members before 1765 no longer exist, and indeed those that exist were rescued from destruction when a clerk was discovered (inadvertently) burning the

---

[214] Pam Davies, 'Sir Josiah John Guest and the Merthyr Radicals: A Symbiotic Relationship', *CRF*, University of Sheffield, http://freemasonry.dept.shef.ac.uk/index.php?lang=0&type=blog&level0=242&level1=263&leve l2=367&op=261 [accessed 15th of May, 2009]

[215] *Minutes of the Lodge of Friendship no.277, Oldham, 29th of September 1819, Oldham Masonic Hall.* Not listed.

[216] *The Globe*, 25th of September, 1819. Private Collection, Not Listed.

[217] See Appendix 1 on the difficulties of cross referencing for the pre-census period.

[218] Hobsbawm, *Labouring Men*, p.75.

[219] David Hawkins, 'Membership of the Anchor and Hope Lodge, Bolton, 1732-1813', a paper presented at the ICHF, Freemasons' Hall, George Street, Edinburgh, 31st of May, 2009.

records, an incident that reminds the Masonic historian why complete lodge records are rare.

The Entwisle family were a well established family of minor gentry and it would seem that this got the membership of the lodge off to a broader based start for when records are available. The lodge certainly seems to have been more selective and prestigious than the Stockport based Lodge of St. John. Out of the 22 who joined the lodge in 1765 and 1766 there were three weavers, two 'Innkeepers & Parish Clerks', an engraver and a watchmaker, but from the professions also a schoolmaster, surgeon, attorney and doctor, giving the impression of a much more socially mixed lodge.

Freemasonry had clearly established itself within the community, for in 1809 on the occasion of the celebrations of the 50th anniversary of the reign of George III, a procession to the parish church was organised:

'the gentry marched thither, so did the boroughreeves and constables, the officers and men of the line then quesrtered in Bolton, also a number of verterans of the 72nd Regiment, Masonic brethren, Orangemen and Sunday School children'.[220]

This kind of public celebration was also seen in Warrington, where the Lodge of Lights also marched through the town to celebrate the coronation of George IV in 1821, though the lodge had a steady number of labouring tradesmen than the lodge in Bolton, the Lodge of Lights being accompanied by local trade organisations such as the spinners, pin makers, tin-plate makers and glass makers, and clubs associated with local pubs.[221]

Anchor and Hope lodge actually provided the Province with a second Provincial Grand Master, Stephen Blair. He was Master of Anchor and Hope from 1835–1844, Deputy Provincial Grand Master 1846–1855, Mayor of Bolton from 1848-1852, and then Provincial Grand Master from 1856 until his death in 1870. Stephen Blair and his brother Harrison (also a member of the lodge) were wealthy industrialists and philanthropists in Bolton. When Stephen Blair died in 1870 he left £30,000 for the construction of a hospital then known as 'The Blair Hospital'. The third was Lord Derby who was Provincial Grand Master

---

[220] J. C. Scholes, *History of Bolton*, (Bolton: The Daily Chronicle Office, 1892), p.438.
[221] *Minutes of the Lodge of Lights, no.148, Masonic Hall, Warrington, 19th of July, 1821.* Not listed. A local poster from the period, now on public display in the Warrington Parish Church, lists the local Freemasons leading a procession of nineteen local clubs through the streets of the town on this date.

from 1899–1948; a remarkable 49 years. Other early Mayors of Bolton who were also members of the lodge where Thomas Rodgeway Bridson and J. R. Wolfenden.

It is clear that Anchor and Hope got off to an auspicious start and maintained its propitious status throughout its life. The character and development of Bolton can perhaps shed some light on this. Bolton had its share of civil unrest, such as the Luddite machine-breaking riots in 1812. The riots were quashed with the help of the Bolton Light Horse Volunteers, the leader of the Volunteers being 'Major' John Pilkington, a member of the lodge and a much respected local merchant. The Magistrate and High Sheriff of the County at the time was William Hulton, and he was also a member of the lodge.[222] During the Chartist riots in 1839, the Parish Church was damaged and the Post Office attacked, and in 1842, the town witnessed the Plug Drawing Riots. However, despite this, the town also seemed to have a degree of early 'civicness' that was perhaps less notable in the other towns studied, and the lodge of Anchor and Hope certainly included the 'cream' of Bolton society.

In 1824 when canal charges rose there were proposals to build a railway to link with the Liverpool to Manchester line and this was opened four years later in 1828.[223] In the 1820s an industrial village was built at Barrow Bridge, creating a self-contained village with a school and social facilities for the factory workforce. An adequate water supply was created in 1824 by the construction of Belmont Reservoir, bought by the corporation in 1847, and expanded over the next century to a total of 11 reservoirs. The streets were lit by gas starting in 1819, and again bought by the corporation in 1872. The Bolton Improvement Act of 1850 compounded this sense of 'civicness', and the Anchor and Hope lodge seemed to reflect a more middle–class membership which fermented this ethos of social improvement at an earlier stage.

Bolton's cotton industry was biased towards weaving and in particular 'fine counts' – better quality products which were far less affected by the cotton famine of the early 1860s. For example, during the American Civil War when the cotton industry was under stress, in an 1863 report by H B Farnell on 'distressed Poor Law Unions' the percentages on relief were as follows; Ashton under Lyne 38.8%; Stockport 29.9%; Manchester 29.9%; Oldham 21.2% and Bolton 16.5%.[224]

---

[222] Hawkins, 'Membership of Anchor and Hope'.
[223] C. H. Saxelby (ed.), *Bolton Survey (County History Reprints)*, (Bolton: SR Publishers, 1971), p.71.
[224] N. Longmate, *The Hungry Mills*, (London: Longmans, 1978), p.103.

In conclusion, during the second half of the nineteenth century, Lancashire witnessed the appearance of a burgeoning professional middle class as the cotton industry matured. Evans discussed that in the cotton spinning towns of Lancashire, class-consciousness clearly developed, and a growing divide between working-classes and the middle-classes could be seen taking place, especially with the Chartist agitation in Oldham in 1842.[225]

In the first half of the nineteenth century, Oldham had felt the rippling effects of the Peterloo Massacre in 1819 and witnessed strike action in 1834 and 1842.[226] Stockport however, seemed to have suffered worse than Oldham during the General Strike of 1842 suffering stagnation, exemplified by a further riot in 1852 which was fuelled by increased anti-Catholic feeling due to the influx of unskilled Irish immigrants. The local Masonic lodges seemed to act as an indicator to the economic situations of the industrial cotton-spinning towns, with the Lodge of St. John in Stockport only showing signs of a recovery in the early 1860s, around the same time as the Lodge of Lights in Warrington, though ten years later than the Lodge of Friendship in Oldham.

The membership data shows that especially during the first half of the nineteenth century, an influx of men joining Freemasonry was greatly variable and erratic within the lodges in Stockport, Oldham and Warrington. This was the period when much of the membership was composed of working men, skilled labourers or owners in the smaller mills of the early part of the industrial revolution. A similar occurrence can also be seen in certain Manchester and Salford based lodges.[227] However the graphs do reveal a difference in the Bolton lodge, which seemed to be more stable and had a more regular 'middle-upper class' makeup.

There is also clear evidence that the membership of certain lodges included a significant proportion of Irish weavers. In the case of the Lancashire based 'Antient' Duke of Atholl Lodge, the nineteen founding members of 1795 all came from Ireland; sixteen were from what we would now call the 'Six Counties', two from County Monaghan and one from Dublin, and it is likely that they had left the linen trade for better

---

[225] See Evans, *The Forging of the Modern State: Early Industrial Britain 1783-1870*, p.172.

[226] Ibid.

[227] John Acaster, 'The composition of Masonic membership in Manchester and Salford during the period of early industrialisation before 1814', a paper presented to the ICHF, Freemasons' Hall, George Street, Edinburgh, 31st of May, 2009, and published in *Researching British Freemasonry 1717-2017: The Journal for the Centre of Research into Freemasonry and Fraternalism*, Vol. 3, (Sheffield: University of Sheffield, 2010), pp.41-55.

prospects in Lancashire.[228] This influx of Irish workers caused tensions in certain mill towns, an example of which can be seen in Elizabeth Gaskell's novel *North And South* published in 1854, where she wrote about the feelings of the mill workers of Manchester, being enraged at Irishmen taking their jobs while the workers were protesting for higher wages.[229]

Lancashire contained a good proportion of 'Antients' Lodges, that is lodges purporting to use an older more original ritual than their rivals dubbed 'The Moderns', and it is generally assumed among some Masonic historians that Antients lodges had a strong Irish bias both in membership and ritual and contained more members of a lower social status than Moderns lodges. However, the Masonic historian Gould writing in the late nineteenth century commented how 'Modern' and 'Antient' lodges could interact at local level,[230] and there is certainly evidence in the Lodge of Lights in Warrington that frequent interaction between 'Antient' and 'Modern' took place.[231]

Lancashire's cotton revolution saw an enormous influx or workers of whom the most enterprising developed their own businesses. The rate of technological change however was such that each new innovation required more capital, increased capacity, reduced unit costs and rendered older or smaller less efficient enterprises less profitable, a down skilled population experiencing a reduction of wage levels for those remaining. In a world with no social support, membership of freemasonry required employment to pay the dues. Thus, it was perhaps inevitable that less skilled trades should vanish from the membership lists.

The increase in wages and living standards after 1850 has been debated by Labour historians such as Hobsbawm, who questioned that a substantial and general rise in real wages had ever occurred in the 1850s and 1860s, and used the resignation statistics of the Oddfellows from 1864-1869 along with the tightening of the Poor Law administration in 1869-1871, to state that the working classes actually suffered a drop in standards during this period. The resignations within the Oddfellows began to fall in 1871 suggesting conditions had begun to improve.[232] E. J. Evans also debated the suggestion that wages and conditions began to rise after 1850, commenting that there was actually a decline in real wages

---

[228] Anon, *Duke of Athol Lodge Bi-Centenary*, published by the Lodge, (1995), p.4.

[229] Elizabeth Gaskell, *North And South*, (London: Penguin, 1994), pp.210-211.

[230] R.F. Gould, *The History of Freemasonry, Vol. I-VI*, (London, 1884-7), pp.435-49.

[231] *Minute Book of the Lodge of Lights, No.148, July, 1803*, Masonic Hall, Warrington. Not listed.

[232] Hobsbawm, *Labouring Men*, p.121-124, & p.135.

in the years in-between 1850-1858, with only a 15-20 % wage increase after 1862.[233] As Hobsbawm put it:

'There is plenty of evidence that the gap between the aristocrats and the lower strata widened in the middle decades of the century'.[234]

Financial difficulties certainly occurred in the Lodge of Lights and the Lodge of Friendship throughout the first half of the nineteenth century. The Lodge of Friendship had a discrepancy noted in the accounts book in August 1848, though this was rectified later.[235] The lodge fees for the Lodge of Friendship were raised in June 1851 to £5-5s. for initiation and £1-1s. for joining members. Annual subscription became £1-1s., a change from monthly to half yearly subscriptions.[236] This was in addition to the charitable expense, and the expense for Masonic festivities, such as the laying of the foundation stone of St. Mary's Church School in Oldham in April, 1843, where each member present had to pay 5s.[237] In the Lodge of Lights, the lodge subscription fee was raised to 18s. in 1852,[238] and in both lodges there was an ever increasing system of fines for non attendance and disorderly conduct.[239] This raising of fees in the early 1850s is in marked contrast to how the Lodge of Lights reduced fees in 1809 to attract new members, when it was officially agreed to reduce candidate admission rates from £3-8s /- to £2-7s.[240]

What is clear from the membership lists is that:-

a)   At some point between 1850 and 1860 the occupations of those becoming members changed to be more middle class and professional.

b)   There is clearly a key role played by charismatic individuals in lodges which seems to provide a focus for their growth and prosperity. This is probably paralleled by a similar economic role being played by individuals in the community as a whole. Putnam comments *'The more interesting question isn't*

---

[233] Evans, *The Forging of the Modern State 1783-1870*, p.150.

[234] Hobsbawm, *Labouring Men*, p.293.

[235] *Minutes of the Lodge of Friendship no.277, Oldham, 18th of August, 1848, Oldham Masonic Hall.* Not listed.

[236] Ibid., *11th of June, 1851.*

[237] Ibid., *17th of April, 1843.*

[238] *Minutes of the Lodge of Lights no.148, Warrington, 1852, Warrington Masonic Hall.* Not listed.

[239] For incidents of fines see the *Minutes of the Lodge of Lights no.148, Warrington, 24th of September, 1804, Warrington Masonic Hall.* Not listed, and the [239] *Minutes of the Lodge of Friendship no.277, Oldham, 27th of July, 1814, Oldham Masonic Hall.* Not listed.

[240] *Minutes of the Lodge of Lights no.148, Warrington, 1809, Warrington Masonic Hall.* Not listed.

whether leaders affect the stock of social capital, but rather what affects the stock of leaders.[241]

The point at which this transition takes place differs slightly according to the individual lodge, and is followed in the lodges studied by the large annual variations in the number of men becoming masons being less pronounced. In the case of the Lodge of St John, the only lodge for which we have full data on member's departure from freemasonry, it is clear that the duration of average membership in the nineteenth century was fairly short and only stabilised early in the twentieth century.

Freemasonry has been a part of many communities for some 300 years and throughout that time has been characterised by its use of ritual in 'making masons', and by social conviviality; both the above being conducted usually on the first floors of public houses until well into the twentieth century. There has also been a charitable element by which members who fall on hard times can obtain some financial support, although in principle a member is expected to continue to pay his subscription. Until the mid nineteenth century this came out of the funds of each individual lodge but thereafter national Masonic charities became more prominent. The first to be formed in 1842 was the Royal Masonic Benevolent Institution. Little else has changed to this day and the changes seen in lodge membership have to be largely a result of changes taking place in society, both local and national.

The development in class-consciousness, tied in with the evolution of an industrial society witnessed a change in living standards, unemployment and low wages during periods of recession, ultimately effecting disposable income.[242] One reason for working men being present in Masonic lodges during the first half of the 1800s could be that they found a social club with aspects of a benefit society.[243] While Marx in the 1840 recorded rampant capitalism and human misery and forecast revolution; the response to the 'Cotton Famine' was organised relief of starvation and through the decades that followed, improvement in public

---

[241] R.D. Putnam, *Democracies in Flux: The Evolution of Social Capital in Contemporary Society*, (New York: Oxford University Press 2002), p.17.

[242] See Evans, *The Forging of the Modern State: Early Industrial Britain 1783-1870*, p.151.

[243] Ibid. Evans discusses how the difficulty of finding pure water in industrial towns attracted the working man to the cosy public house, away from the damp and draughty cellar or tenement, which was his family home. The large sums spent on funerals by the workers of industrial Lancashire is also discussed, a 'proper send off' being preferable to the risk of community condemnation. Lodges in industrial towns such as Warrington, Oldham, and Stockport met at this time in local taverns, and the minutes of the Lodge of Lights in Warrington and the Lodge of Friendship in Oldham describes a number of Masonic funerals.

works to provide clean water, remove sewage and generally improve the urban environment – and generally to seek stability, gradually took place.

In this environment, charismatic personalities such as Crennell in the Lodge of St. John, Greenall in the Lodge of Lights, and Gaitskill in the Lodge of Friendship, all played a part in the 'revival' of their respective lodges, and the increased influx of professional men, industrialists and gentlemen. In short, after the mid nineteenth century, the growing middle-classes increasingly made freemasonry their preserve. These gentlemen recognised the ethos of education within the Craft, and with a philanthropic attitude, they would assist in founding learned societies, Freemasonry becoming an inspiration in the spread of local education and charity in the various towns. The professional classes used Freemasonry to elevate their position in local society, using the Craft for networking and to increase their status.

Chapter 4

Freemasonry, Industry and Charity: Industrialists, Education and the Local Community[244]

'I look to this and similar societies to keep the torch alight and hand on. It is well to be "the town of many industries". It was better to be "the Athens of England". And we may be that again.'
Alderman Bennett speaking in 1905 to the Literary and Philosophical Society about the Warrington Academy and his hopes that Warrington may once more become a cultural centre of learning.

'Schools of Industry...are of more actual service to the poor than schools of learning'.
Freemason Dr. George Oliver[245]

'but the multitude of this day is not strong of mind, and wants careful direction to abate its fears, to appease its alarms, and to unfold to its understanding the realities of past, present, and future. Let the Synagogue, the Church, and the Masonic Lodge, become schools for that purpose.'
Richard Carlile, *Manual of Freemasonry*[246]

This chapter will discuss the influence of Freemasonry on education at local level, looking at how the industrialists, businessmen and professionals who joined the local Masonic lodge at Warrington, used it for networking and to gain prestige within the local area. These men would also contribute to the development of local educational societies, forging a cultural identity in the later nineteenth century. Parallels will be presented with other lodges in industrial towns, such as in Oldham, Wigan and Liverpool, the philanthropic practices of the aspiring men of the lodges helping to make life better in their localities.

The local Dissenting Academy in Warrington, which had been such a centre for radical thought and had been linked to Masonic ideals of

---

[244] Part of the content of this chapter was presented at the Post Graduate Conference, University of Liverpool, on the 24th of May, 2002.

[245] George Oliver, *Hints for Improving the Societies and Institutions Connected with Education and Science in the Town of Wolverhampton*, in R.S.E Sandbach, *Priest and Freemason: The Life of George Oliver*, (Northamptonshire: The Aquarian Press, 1988), pp.72-4.

[246] Carlile, *Manual of Freemasonry*, p.97.

education and charity during the late eighteenth century, began to be romantically remembered during the nineteenth century, and many of the leading industrialists and professionals who were prominent Freemasons founded a variety of learned societies that were clearly influenced by the ethos of Masonry and the Academy. This philanthropic attitude created an educational drive in Warrington, and saw the foundation of civic buildings, places of worship and learned societies, with local Masons becoming directly involved with local politics, local publishing and local business.

These local Freemasons helped to re-shape Warrington, which witnessed gradual social reform during the Victorian era. Several of these charismatic industrialists, such as Joseph Stubs, Peter Rylands and Sir Gilbert Greenall, played a major role in the learned societies that evolved, the maintaining of the Masonic ethos of education being evident in their support for the establishment of educational centres such as the Warrington Library and Museum, the Warrington Art College, and the local School of Science, echoing the involvement of early Masons such as Benjamin Yoxall who had assisted in founding the circulating library in the eighteenth century.

In the Lodge of Lights itself, Masonic lectures were continually given, perhaps not as mysterious in nature as the subjects of 'Masonic science' and astronomy which had been given in the opening years of the century,[247] bit it was nonetheless a continuation of the promotion of education within the Craft. This promotion can also be seen in the Royal Lodge of Faith and Friendship, No. 270, which met in Berkeley, Gloucestershire, where natural philosopher Edward Jenner founded the Science Select Lodge; members of which had to produce a paper on a scientific subject.[248] Lectures of a more 'Victorian' nature were presented in certain lodges at this time, such as the Leigh based Marquis of Lorne Lodge No. 1354, when in 1881 *'a lecture on the Great Pyramids'* was given,[249] a rather topical subject which tapped into the popular heroic vision of the Victorian explorer and the interest in Egyptology.

Similar lectures were given in the Warrington Literary & Philosophical Society, such as paper presented in 1892 entitled *'What I Saw in Palestine'*, in which the lecturer vividly described his travels to Palestine and

[247] *Minutes of the Lodge of Lights no.148, Warrington, December, 1800 & May, 1802, Warrington Masonic Hall.* Not listed.

[248] *Minutes of the Royal Lodge of Faith and Friendship, No. 270, Berkeley, Gloucestershire.* Not Listed.

[249] P.G. Monk and F. Bent, *A History of the Marquis of Lorne Lodge No. 1354,* (Leigh: P.T.H. Brooks Ltd., 1971), p.15.

Egypt.[250]   This was a popular learned society which met in the lecture room of the Warrington Museum and included a number of local Freemasons.   As we shall see, local learned societies were commonly supported by Freemasons, as were local charitable education institutions, such as the Bluecoat school, something that can also be seen happening in lodges throughout the industrial north-west, in towns such as Warrington, Liverpool and Oldham.[251]

War Heroes and Charismatic Gentlemen within Freemasonry

High ranking charismatic figures became essential to Freemasonry, especially after the dark difficult years of the early nineteenth century that some lodges had experienced. These influential figures attracted aspiring social-climbing men to the lodges that they were associated with, playing a part in making the Craft popular again. One such charismatic figure was Viscount Combermere, who became Provincial Grand Master of Cheshire in 1830. Combermere developed into an active and extremely popular high ranking Freemason, following in the footsteps of his father Sir Robert S. Cotton, who had also served as Provincial Grand Master of Cheshire from 1785-1810.[252]   Stapleton Stapleton-Cotton, 1st Viscount Combermere was a war hero, having fought in the Peninsula Wars, and was a close friend of the Duke of Wellington, who was also a Freemason. He had served as commander of Wellington's cavalry, earning a reputation for fearless bravery and received the personal thanks from Wellington himself.

Combermere renovated his home at Combermere Abbey extensively and constructed the 'Wellington Wing' especially to commemorate the Duke's visit to the house in 1820.[253]   His popularity was evident when the Provincial Grand Lodge met in Macclesfield in 1852, where the procession route to the meeting place at the Macclesfield Arms Hotel was crammed with *'flags and banners'*, and in front of the Hotel *'a lofty triumphal arch of evergreens was erected, from which depended banners bearing 'Welcome*

---

250 Robert Garnett, J.P., 'What I Saw in Palestine', in *Proceedings of the Warrington Literary & Philosophical Society*, (Warrington: Printed at the Guardian Office, 1892), pp.1-81.
251 *Minutes of the Lodge of Lights no. 148, Warrington, 22nd of December, 1836 & 8th of November, 1865, Warrington Masonic Hall.* Not listed. *Minutes of the Lodge of Friendship no. 277, 20th of April, 1829, Oldham Masonic Hall.* Not listed. See also Anon., The History of The Lodge of Harmony No. 220, (Liverpool, 1948), p.9.
252 John Armstrong, *A History of Freemasonry in Cheshire*, (London: Kenning, 1901), pp.466-469.
253 The 'Wellington Wing' at Combermere Abbey was demolished in 1972.

Combermere' and *'Salamanca'.*[254] When the Provincial Grand Lodge met n Congleton in 1855, Combermere again received a rapturous hero's welcome, the public celebrations for the arrival of this *'Cheshire Hero'* being ecstatic:

> *'From early morn the bells of St. Peter's Church rang out their merry peals; from church tower, hall, public buildings, factories, and private dwellings waved innumerable flags...on small bannerets appeared the words 'Cheshire Hero,' 'Peninsula,' 'Bhurtpoor'.*[255]

Combermere's standing among the Masonic community of Cheshire was so great that he was toasted as *'The Hero of Cheshire'* at the Provincial Grand Lodge,[256] and his son Wellington Cotton, followed in his footsteps becoming a high ranking Mason within the Cheshire Province. On the death of the Duke of Wellington in 1852, Combermere gave a speech to the Provincial Grand Lodge, in which he said:

> *'He had been associated with him (Wellington) since 1793. Perhaps it was not generally known that the Duke was a Mason, he was made in Ireland, and often when in Spain, where Masonry was prohibited, in conversation with his Lordship, he regretted repeatedly how sorry he was that his military duties had prevented him taking the active part his feelings dictated, for it was his opinion that Masonry was a great and royal art, beneficial to the individual and to the community.*[257]

The Duke of Wellington's Masonic career had begun in 1790, when he entered into his family lodge in Ireland, but after 1795 he distanced himself from the Craft, and even opposed Masonic processions and meetings when in Lisbon, Portugal in 1810, realising it was sensitive to the local population. Despite this, as the speech by Combermere testified, Wellington's links to the Craft were well known, and in 1838, he was asked by his old lodge in Ireland for his permission to rename the lodge after him, though he declined to give it.[258]

---

[254] Armstrong, *A History of Freemasonry in Cheshire*, p.127.

[255] Ibid., p.138.

[256] Ibid., pp.97-99.

[257] Ibid., p.130.

[258] Arthur Wellesley (Wesley), the Duke of Wellington, was initiated into his family lodge Trim No. 494, in Ireland, on the 7th of December, 1790, his father and brother both serving as Worshipful Master of the lodge, and both serving as Grand Master of the Grand Lodge of Ireland. Wellington had been elected as MP for Trim that same year, and seemed to have abandoned

British war heroes became popular leaders of Freemasonry as the nineteenth century progressed, another example being the charismatic Troop Sergeant Major Richard Hall Williams who was one of the 'noble six hundred' in the infamous charge of the light brigade in 1854. Williams became a leading Freemason founding the Worsley Lodge No. 1814 in 1880 and served as its first Worshipful Master. Another Crimean war hero who became an influential Freemason was Sir Robert Loyd-Lindsay, 1st Baron Wantage, who was awarded the Victoria Cross and became involved in numerous lodges, Loyd-Lindsay going on to be a prominent figure within the United Grand Lodge of England. The importance of these war heroes within nineteenth century English Freemasonry suggests an arcane attraction to the enigmatic masculine figures of Empire; in drawing the celebrities of the period, be it aristocracy, war heroes or alluring local industrialists and professionals, Masonry would hold appeal to aspirant young men.

As discussed in the previous chapter, by 1850, the lodges in the north-west of England all started to attract more members, especially from the professional classes. These local industrialists and businessmen began to enter the lodges almost *en masse*, changing the overall make-up of the lodge. In the Lodge of Lights in Warrington, the town's only lodge during this period, a transformation took place, with a dramatic increase in membership which followed the arrival of industrialist Sir Gilbert Greenall.

The Lodge of Friendship in Oldham, like the Lodge of Lights, also witnessed an increase of industrialists and professionals joining during this time; with local factory owners, businessmen, solicitors, professors of music, and a number of schoolmasters, such as the Rev. Harry T. Sortwell, who was the governor of the local Bluecoat School.[259] There had been a good number of weavers and other labouring tradesmen in the lodge during the early part of the nineteenth century, but, like the Lodge of Lights, with the introduction of schoolmaster Isaac Gaitskill, a period of increased membership occurred.[260]

Freemasonry around 1795 after he had entered the military. See Yasha Beresiner, 'A Brother In Arms', in *MQ*, Grand Lodge Publications, Issue 9, April 2004.

[259] *List of Members & Minutes of the Lodge of Friendship no.277, 1789-1900*, Oldham Masonic Hall. Not listed.

[260] See B. Gee, *History of the Lodge of Friendship no.277*, (Oldham, 1989). Also see *List of Members & Minutes of the Lodge of Friendship no.277, 1789-1900*, Oldham Masonic Hall. Not listed.

Development of a Cultural Identity: Freemasons and the Promotion of Education and Charity

Back in Warrington, the industrialists and businessmen, perhaps feeling less culturally developed than the older, more established Warrington landowners, such as the Blackburne and the Leigh families, seemed to have felt the need to demonstrate their new status and civic duty. New industrialist dynasties such as the Greenall and Rylands family began to take over from the older established local gentry, becoming involved in Freemasonry and local politics, with the wire weaving factory owner Peter Rylands and brewer Edward Greenall jnr, both becoming prominent Freemasons[261] and both serving as Mayor.[262]

The Greenall and Rylands families, along with other new local dynasties such as the Stubs and the Crosfields families, became directly involved in many learned societies that developed during the nineteenth century, such as the Natural History Society, the Phrenological Society, the Botanical Society, the Warrington Lecture Society, and the all important Mechanic's Institution - which was specifically created to promote adult education for working men.[263] The Mechanic's Institution, with its small library and wide range of classes, served as an important outlet for the Masonic ideals of education and charity. However, during this time, as in the time of the Academy, divides in class and sex were still very apparent, and in some classes, a 'middle-class' exclusiveness did develop.

The Mechanic's Institution became famous for its 'cultural' impact on the town, and became extremely popular, attracting the ardent involvement of many local charismatic leading figures who were also Freemasons, such as wire manufacturer and one time Liberal MP for Warrington Peter Rylands[264], brewer and Conservative MP for Warrington Sir Gilbert Greenall,[265] and Alexander Mackie, the owner of

261 *List of Members of the Lodge of Lights no.148, Warrington, 1765-1981, Warrington Masonic Hall.* Not listed.

262 G.A. Carter, *Warrington Hundred*, Warrington, includes a transcribed list of Mayors of Warrington, 1847-1947, (Warrington, 1947), pp.65-69.

263 W.B. Stephens, *Adult Education And Society In An Industrial Town: Warrington 1800-1900*, (Exeter: University of Exeter, 1980), pp.37-38.

264 *List of Members of the Lodge of Lights no.148, Warrington, 29th of December, 1865, Warrington Masonic Hall.* Not listed.

265 Ibid., Sir Gilbert Greenall was initiated into the Lodge of Lights on the 28th of January, 1850, his son also Sir Gilbert Greenall became the first Lord Daresbury, and was initiated into the Lodge of Lights on the 26th of December, 1910. Sir Gilbert Greenall jnr was also a member of the musical Nobleman and Gentleman's Catch Club.

the *Warrington Guardian* Newspaper,[266] who also served as Mayor.[267] The Mechanic's Institution, which for a time, symbolically held its meetings in the second Academy building at Academy Place – a building which also housed a number of private tutors, held classes such as English language, geography, writing, arithmetic and history, and included a news and periodical room; the institution thus being vital in providing education to the local working classes.[268] Local support was essential, and a similar process can be seen in Wolverhampton, where leading Freemason Dr. George Oliver also became involved in the promotion of a Mechanic's Institute in the 1830s.[269]

In Liverpool, the Mechanic's Institute, based at Mount Street, became an extremely popular place for lectures, and with Liverpool's closeness to the USA, it attracted lecturers by American authors such as Ralph Waldo Emerson and the Freemason Mark Twain.[270] There was a Mechanic's Institute founded in most Industrial centres in the north-west of England, in Cheshire for example, there were many located at various towns, a relationship with local Freemasonry existing throughout the nineteenth century. This can be seen with the Cheshire Provincial Grand Lodge meeting on a number of occasions at various Mechanic's Institute's, such as at Crewe during September 1851, at the Institute at Hyde in 1875 and 1889, and in Stockport in 1879 and again in 1888 and 1890.[271]

Many of the Warrington learned societies, such as the Phrenological Society and some of the Musical Societies, were elective and catered for an exclusive audience, with rather high subscription fees and strict dress codes.[272] This would have certainly kept the membership selective, and would have promoted a high social conduct and etiquette. Despite this exclusiveness, these societies were seen as assisting to maintain

[266] *List of Members of the Lodge of Lights no.148, Warrington, 29th of April, 1878, Warrington Masonic Hall.* Not listed.

[267] G.A. Carter, *Warrington Hundred*, Warrington, list of Mayors of Warrington, 1847-1947, (Warrington, 1947), pp.65-69.

[268] *Slater's Trade Directory of Warrington, 1848,* Warrington Library, reference S10121. Also see *the Minute Books for the Mechanics Institute, 1838-1855,* Warrington Library, reference MS235.

[269] R.S.E Sandbach, *Priest and Freemason: The Life of George Oliver,* (Northamptonshire: The Aquarian Press, 1988), pp.74.

[270] Mark Twain was a member of Polar Star Lodge No. 79 A.F. & A.M. in St. Louis, being initiated as an Entered Apprentice on the 22nd of May, 1861, passed to the degree of Fellow Craft the following month on the 12th of June, and raised as a Master Mason on the 10th of July. Twain spoke at the Liverpool Institute on the 20th of October, 1873, but gave further speaches in Liverpool in January 1874 before returning to the USA. See Paul Fatout, *Mark Twain Speaking,* (Iowa: University of Iowa Press, 1978), pp.4-15.

[271] Armstrong, *A History of Freemasonry in Cheshire*, p.126-p.194.

[272] Stephens, *Adult Education And Society*, p.38-9.

Warrington as the *'Athens of the North*[273] and keeping the flame of the old Academy alight, the Academy being viewed as *'an intellectual lighthouse*[274] which guided the way for the further development of education in the town.

Lectures were given frequently by the societies, some of the societies using new buildings which had been constructed for a cultural and educational purpose, such as the Warrington Library and Museum, which had been built in 1855, the foundation stone laid with a Masonic ceremony.[275] A full page report of the procession through the town and the ceremony for laying the foundation stone appeared in Freemason Alexander Mackie's *Warrington Guardian*:

'Among the Freemasons we observed Gilbert Greenall, Esq., M.P., and others of our chief townsmen and neighbours.'

Future Freemason Peter Rylands Esq. was mentioned in the report as being chairman of the committee of the Museum, and the Mechanic's Institute were noted as following the Freemasons in the procession, who were in turn followed by the School of Art and other local schools. Local dignitary William Beamont gave a speech after the ceremony, which referred to the Warrington Academy, putting the town forward as a unique centre of education and culture.[276]

By 1857, the School of Art had opened in the Library and Museum building, eventually moving into its own building almost opposite the Museum, in 1884.[277] The Mechanic's Institution however, had closed by 1869 – just like the Academy before it, lack of funds and dwindling students bringing it to an end. The School of Art had originally developed from a drawing class in the Mechanic's Institution, and can be seen as a successful offshoot from the dying Institution.[278] Local industrialists had been involved in giving donations to start up the drawing class in 1853, Freemason Sir Gilbert Greenall personally contributing the sum of £5. Like the Institution, the School of Art also included the involvement of a number of local Freemasons, such as

---

273 See A. Bennet, *A Glance at some old Warrington Societies*, (Warrington: Mackie & Co. Ltd, 1906).
274 Canon Stevenson quoted in A.M. Crowe, *Warrington, Ancient and Modern*, (Warrington: Beamont Press, 1947), p.177.
275 *Minutes of the Lodge of Lights no.148, Warrington, 20th of September, 1855, Warrington Masonic Hall.* Not listed.
276 *The Warrington Guardian*, Saturday, September 22, 1855. Private Collection. Not Listed.
277 Stephens, *Adult Education And Society*, p.89 and p.94.
278 Ibid., p.79.

Chemist and town Mayor Samuel Mather Webster, who worked on the first committee for the School of Art.[279]

The classical sculptor John Warrington Wood was a member of the Lodge of Lights and had studied at the School of Art.[280] Wood had formerly been a student at the Manchester Academy, which had taken over from the Warrington Academy after its closure in 1786. He famously went on to make the statues and reliefs that adorn the front and side of the Neo-Classical Walker Art Gallery in Liverpool. Another student of the School of Art, Henry Woods, exhibited at the Royal Academy, his father, William Woods, also being a member of the Lodge of Lights.[281] Other influential and renowned students that had studied at the Warrington School of Art included Arthur Haywood and Oswald Garside, testifying to the quality of teaching.[282]

The Oldham based Lodge of Friendship also had a renowned local artist as a member; Charles Potter, who joined in December 1878. Potter had been a weaver on joining, but with the help of local dignitaries such as auctioneer William Henry Fletcher, who had been initiated into the same lodge in December 1849, he was given assistance and the opportunity to study art in Paris and to visit Italy.[283]

Other local professionals who became involved in educational developments and praised the old Academy included William Beamont and Dr. James Kendrick. Both local antiquaries, and both being close to local Freemasons, they held slightly romantic views on the history of Warrington, celebrating the town's Roman past, heralding the town as the *'Athens of the North'*. This was, in a sense, an excellent illustration of civic pride, one that could only help the progress of education in the town. However, some of the societies formed in Warrington at this time give an insight into the social life of the professional classes, such as the Orpheus Society for ladies and gentlemen, the Beautiful Warrington Society, the Philatelic and Polyglot Societies (both meeting at the old Academy) and The Field Naturalist Society.

---

[279] *List of Members of the Lodge of Lights no.148, Warrington, 28th of April, 1862, Warrington Masonic Hall.* Not listed. Also see the *School of Art Minute Book 1853-1893*, Warrington Library, reference MS1085.

[280] *List of Members of the Lodge of Lights no.148, Warrington, 27th of August, 1866. Warrington Masonic Hall.* Not listed. Also see the *School of Art Minute Book 1853-1893*, Warrington Library, reference MS1085.

[281] Ibid., *24th of November, 1862.*

[282] See the *School of Art Minute Book 1853-1893*, Warrington Library, reference MS1085.

[283] B. Gee, *History of the Lodge of Friendship no.277*, (Oldham, 1989), p.34-35. Also see *List of Members & Minutes of the Lodge of Friendship no.277, 1789-1900, Oldham Masonic Hall.* Not listed.

These societies catered for the middle-classes of the town, a social group that was already educated, had more free time and they could dress properly for the lectures and meetings and pay the high subscription fees. Indeed, the attitudes towards class can be seen in the comments of the Masonic writer Arthur Edward Waite on his visit to Kilmarnock, Scotland to receive the 'Early Grand Rite' in 1903, where he observed that the local brethren were of a more working class standing, stating that '*A considerable portion of them belonged to the mechanic order while one or two looked as if they were shepherds.*' After the meeting and the obligatory drinks and speeches that followed, Waite wrote how '*The whole experience was incredibly squalid...*'[284]

These new Warrington based societies certainly reveal a class divide, giving a somewhat patronising perspective on the development of the learned societies. Beamont and Kendrick, like the local industrialists, solicitors such as Percy Davies, who was also a Freemason,[285] and other members of the professional classes involved in these societies, were keen to provide education and act as philanthropists to an ever developing industrial town. But, it can also be seen that they had their own interests at heart; Gilbert Greenall and Peter Rylands were, after all, politicians, their involvement in local civil developments would have certainly gave them a good image to the ever growing electorate of Warrington.

There was also the issue of social control - during the nineteenth century, it was still seen to be dangerous to spread certain types of educational material to the labouring classes, material that may produce radical thought and eventual social disruption, and in Warrington, the committees for the Mechanic's Institution and certain learned societies were aware of this.

Certain books which were deemed to be associated with 'Owenism' were banned from the Institution's library in 1839, and the purchase of certain magazines which contained elements of radicalism were discontinued from time to time. The discussion of party politics was also forbidden in the Institution.[286] It thus seems the industrialists and professionals who were involved in the Mechanic's Institution wanted to censure and prevent the working-class members from being influenced by radical political views, and instead promote a spirit of harmony, which

---

[284] Taken from the diary of Arthur Edward Waite, 1902/3, and quoted in R.A. Gilbert, 'The Masonic Career of A.E. Waite', in *AQC*, Vol. 99, (London, 1986).
[285] *List of Members of the Lodge of Lights no.148, Warrington, 28th of February, 1887, Warrington Masonic Hall.* Not listed.
[286] Stephens, *Adult Education And Society*, p.54-5.

would remind one that the discussion of politics is disallowed in Masonic lodges.

In 1853 a 'discussion class' was established in the Mechanic's Institute which attempted to become an exclusive club, with new members having to be proposed by existing members, and were only accepted by a majority of them. The levels of debate in the class would have required quite a reasonable standard of education and was made up of middle-class males, thus going against the original ethos of the Mechanics Institute; to provide an inclusive education for working men. The 'discussion class' was eventually told to revise its rules, but even though it became inclusive, working-class men would have certainly found it difficult to fit in; the debates that took place in the classes being still intellectually demanding and requiring a high level of confidence to speak within a group.[287]

However, through the interaction of the local industrialists, professionals, Freemasons and reforming politicians of the town, education for the working-classes came closer to reality. There was a genuine belief at the time that education could improve society, a belief which was conveyed in *The Wigan Mirror* in June 1825, in which it put forward that the education of the mechanics class would result in *'general enlightenment'*.[288]

The early support for the Mechanic's Institution and the development of the Warrington People's College – which offered education to both sexes, were examples of how a permanent centre of education in Warrington was sought after. Finance was always a problem, and the ultimate failure of many of these societies, as in the case of the old Academy, came down to money. Some early learned societies, such as the Botanical Society (established 1808) and the Warrington Institution for the Cultivation of Science, Literature and Art (established 1811) were very short lived, yet seemed to influence other societies, seemingly passing on the torch of knowledge.

The interest in the foundation of learned societies in Warrington during the nineteenth century can be mirrored with other industrial towns in the north-west of England, such as Oldham, which witnessed the opening of its own Lyceum in 1839. The foundation of the Oldham Lyceum was linked to local Freemasonry, with members of the local

---

[287] Ibid., pp.81-82.
[288] Ibid., p.53.

Lodge of Friendship being directly involved, such as Thomas Bailey[289] who was the secretary of the Lyceum, and members such as William Bodden, who donated generously to both the Lyceum and the local Bluecoat School.[290]   Edwin Butterworth, the son of prominent local Freemason James Butterworth was also a founder member of the Lyceum.   Again, this involvement points to the ethos of education and charity within the Craft, and also points to a more local self supportive attitude.

The Lyceum held a library and a newsroom, and with a rapid increase in members, a new building was constructed, the foundation stone laid in 1855, the same year as the Warrington Library and Museum building. Like its counterpart in Warrington, the foundation stone was laid with Masonic honours, performed by the local Lodge of Friendship,[291] and the Lyceum was used for a meeting of the Provincial Grand Lodge in 1868.[292] The Lyceum held the School of Science and Art, the Literary Club, the School of Music, classes for machine construction and mechanical philosophy, and in 1864, in the tradition of Masonic architecture a dome was erected above the chemical laboratory for the purpose of creating an observatory.[293] A mining school in the nearby industrial town of Wigan was also founded, assisted by the interests of local Freemasons, and in nearby Earlestown, there were local Masonic interests in the Technical School there; the local Freemasons using the school as the starting place of a procession to lay the foundation stone of All Saints Church on the 10th July, 1913.   The ceremony was led by the Provincial Grand Master the Hon. Arthur Stanley.[294]

Civic pride in local society was also playing a major role in the Victorian development of Warrington.   Around fifteen members of the Lodge of Lights became Mayor of the town, and many more also played a part in local politics.   Many of the people involved in local education were Freemasons, with a total of thirteen schoolmasters joining the Lodge of Lights between 1845-1902, including John Bowes, the Master of the Bluecoat School.   A further four Professors of music joined the lodge during this time, including Thomas M. Patterson, who joined in 1868, and

---

[289] *List of Members & Minutes of the Lodge of Friendship no.277, February 1867, Oldham Masonic Hall.* Not listed.

[290] Ibid., *April, 1866.*

[291] *Minutes of the Lodge of Friendship no.277, 25th of June, 1855, Oldham Masonic Hall.* Not listed.

[292] *Minutes of the Lodge of Friendship no.277, 7th of May, 1868, Oldham Masonic Hall.* Not listed.

[293] See A. Tait, *History of the Oldham Lyceum 1839-1897,* (Oldham: H.C. Lee, 1897).

[294] W. L. Banks and R. F. Bullough, *Lodge of Faith No.484: History of the Lodge,* (1992).   United Grand Lodge Library, Call Number: BE 166 (484) BAN.

William Oakden, who joined in 1865 on the same day as Bookseller Percival Pearse. Patterson, Oakden and Pearse all became involved in the Warrington Musical Society soon after entering the lodge, joining the Greenall and Ryland families, who, being prominent members of the Musical Society, were also permanent members of most of the other Warrington learned societies.[295] Two Professors of languages also joined the lodge during this period.[296]

In 1848, a Provincial Grand Lodge meeting held at the Adelphi Hotel in Liverpool had education high on the agenda, when it was put forward that each lodge in the Province *'shall contribute five shillings per member to a fund for the purpose of education and advancement of children of Masons…'* This was followed by a Masonic Ball held in Liverpool in 1850 *'to assist the Educational Fund…'* The Ball became a regular occurrence in Liverpool in support of the fund.[297]

The social nexus within Warrington also involved the local religious community, with the Unitarian Minister James Nixon Porter[298] and J. D. Massingham, the vicar of St. Paul's, [299] both being members of the Lodge of Lights and the Field Naturalist Society. Roger Charlton-Parr, member of the local banking family that had been behind the building of the Warrington civic Parr Hall, became a Freemason in 1896,[300] the Parr Hall becoming a social focus and entertainment centre for the town. The Parr, Lyon & Co. bank was used by the Stubs and Greenall families,[301] the bank

---

[295] See *Warrington Musical Society Documents: including the secretaries' books, accounts, and list of members and subscribers 1833-1995*, Warrington Library, reference MS2847.

[296] *List of Members of the Lodge of Lights no.148, Warrington, 1765-1981*, Warrington Masonic Hall. Not listed.

[297] John Macnab, *History of The Merchants Lodge, No. 241, Liverpool, 1780-2004*, Second Edition, (Liverpool, 2004), p.145.

[298] *List of Members of the Lodge of Lights no.148, Warrington, 28th of July, 1862*, Warrington Masonic Hall. Not listed.

[299] Ibid., *28th of November, 1870.* There are a number of Masonic graves situated in the Churchyard of St. Paul's belonging to members of the Lodge of Lights.

[300] Ibid. Roger Charlton Parr joined the Lodge of Lights on 24th of February 1896. He was listed as a 'Gentleman' and served in Provincial Grand Lodge and in the Grand Lodge of England, following the footsteps of Sir Gilbert Greenall.

[301] Parr's Bank Ltd was a private bank established in Winwick Street, Warrington, in 1788, originally as Parr & Co., by Joseph Parr (sugar refiner), Thomas Lyon (brewer and sugar refiner), and Walter Kerfoot (attorney); it was also known as Warrington Bank. The bank was styled Parr, Lyon & Greenall from 1825 to 1851 and Parr, Lyon & Co from 1855 to 1865. In 1896 the company's name was abbreviated to Parr's Bank Ltd, amalgamating in 1918 with London County & Westminster Bank Ltd, bankers of London, to form London County Westminster & Parr's Bank Ltd. Royal Bank of Scotland Group Archives, Records of Parr's Bank Ltd, Reference code: GB 1502 PAB/. Also see *National Westminster Bank. '200 Years in Warrington 1788-1988'*, (London: 1988).

also being used by the Provincial Grand Lodge of Cheshire; in a Provincial Grand Lodge meeting in September 1888, it was revealed that Parr's Banking Co. held their securities totalling £1200.[302] The Parr family were also involved in local politics, with Roger's brother, Joseph, became Mayor in 1901.[303] Roger Charlton-Parr and Sir Gilbert Greenall were just two Freemasons who supported the Warrington Continuation School of the People's College in the 1890s, both giving generous donations to cover the expenses rendered.[304]

Local Freemasons and the improvement of local Civic Society

Sir Gilbert Greenall became the 1st Baronet of Walton Hall in 1876, and Greenall went on to finance the building of St. John the Evangelist Church at Walton, Cheshire, which was consecrated in 1885, Greenall also paying for the neighbouring St. John's Sunday school, which was opened for the tenants of his estate. There is no obvious Masonic influence on the architecture, though there is a marble bust of Sir Gilbert Greenall situated inside the church by another Warrington Freemason, the sculptor John Warrington Wood. Sir Gilbert Greenall also contributed to the building of the Penketh Methodist Chapel, and the Greenall family had erected Christ Church in Latchford, which was consecrated in 1861 in memory of the Rev. Thomas Greenall.

Laying the cornerstone or keystone of a new church became a local event for local lodges, especially if lodge members had contributed to the building, the ceremony becoming a public display of Freemasonry and charity. A Masonic ceremony is described as taking place on the 22nd of August, 1843, when the Cheshire Provincial Grand Lodge fixed the keystone in the window of the New Church at Over. The mystical ceremony was concluded by adding:

'coins of the present reign, together with descriptions of the day's proceedings, the names of the local authorities ext., deposited in a cavity in the stone.'[305]

Another Warrington church which had local Masonic support was St. Margaret's and All Hallows Church in Orford. A corner stone was laid

---

[302] Armstrong, *A History of Freemasonry in Cheshire*, p.191.
[303] G.A. Carter, *Warrington Hundred*, Warrington, list of Mayors of Warrington, 1847-1947, (Warrington, 1947), pp.65-69.
[304] Stephens, *Adult Education And Society*, p.104.
[305] Armstrong, *A History of Freemasonry in Cheshire*, pp.110-111.

with a Masonic ceremony on the 18th of October, 1907, the stone dedicated to local Freemason William Sharp and laid by the Provincial Grand Master of Lancashire, the Earl of Lathom. The stone displays the dedication written in-between the Masonic symbols of the set-square and the Seal of Solomon. The architect of the church, Arthur Warburton, later became the architect of the Warrington Masonic Hall, its foundation stone being laid by the Provincial Grand Master in 1932. In 1904 the Earl of Lathom was commemorated by the building of a Chapter House in Liverpool Cathedral, the funding supplied by subscribers such as the Warrington based Lodge of Lights.[306] This kind of charitable and philanthropic support by these local Freemasons reveals how wealthy industrialists and local gentry contributed to their locality, improving their communities.

With education being an important theme in Freemasonry, Masonic ceremonies during the building of places of education were also commonplace, such as the laying of the foundation stone of Fulshaw Memorial School in Wimslow in 1890. The foundation stone of the Technical School in Stockport in 1888 was laid with a Masonic ceremony by the Provincial Grand Lodge, the lodge having met at the local Mechanics Institute on the day. The foundation stone of St. Mary Magdalene School in Ashton-in-Mersey was also laid with a Masonic ceremony in 1895. These centres of education were important to local lodges, the Freemasons taking an active interest in supporting the centres, not just with funding but in the actual building.

Freemasonry in Warrington, though lending itself to educational ideals, was also being used by Warrington's elite as a networking society. Indeed, the *Warrington Guardian* newspaper owned by Alexander Mackie, regularly featured positive reports on the many learned societies which involved his Masonic friends, such as in 1867 when it was reported that the Musical Society had *'elementary classes for youths of both sexes'*, the society *'doing good service to the town'*.[307]

Mackie commented that on his arrival in the town, he was quickly introduced to the prominent figures in Warrington.[308] Mackie supported the School of Art, and was a keen lecturer, giving lectures on witchcraft,

---

[306] *Minutes of the Lodge of Lights no.148, Warrington, 1904, Warrington Masonic Hall.* Not Listed.

[307] Stephens, *Adult Education And Society*, p.35.

[308] G. Nulty, *Guardian Country 1853-1978*, (Cheshire County Newspapers Ltd., 1978), p.12, mentioned in a speech given by A. Mackie on April 24th, 1878, to celebrate the 25th anniversary of the Warrington Guardian, the transcribed speech can be seen in the Warrington Library, reference p1895.

his success leading him to publish his *Twelve Sunday Lectures to Working Men*.[309] He was also a founder of the Bluecoat Brotherly Society, which assisted boys after they had left the Bluecoat School, and Mackie, like his friend and fellow Mason Sir Gilbert Greenall, also aspired to be a Conservative MP, but was unsuccessful in this pursuit.[310] He counted among his closest friends the likes of Sir Gilbert Greenall, William Beamont, the Parr family, and Peter Rylands.

Self help charitable work and educational directives were major themes within localised Freemasonry during this period, similar to the time of the Academy in the eighteenth century. Relative absence of the labouring tradesmen as members in the lodge at this time is however, extremely striking, and the lodge seems to include the majority of Warrington's elite. Factory owners, businessmen, solicitors, and local gentlemen, all dominated the Lodge of Lights in the later nineteenth century, but it was the Greenall and Rylands families that not only began to dominate local Freemasonry in Warrington, but local society as well. Sir Gilbert Greenall was involved in the opening of the successful School of Science in 1878, being one of the school's first vice presidents.[311] Other members of the Lodge of Lights that were on the committee of the School of Science included the Masonic historian John Armstrong, local industrialist Thomas Morris who was also a Fellow of the Geological Society, schoolmaster John Bowes and James Patterson.[312] The School of Science may have attracted so many Freemasons because of the ethos of the promotion of natural philosophy that had been held within Freemasonry since the days of the early 'Premier/Modern' Grand Lodge, the School including lessons in geometry and building construction. The School of Art also included geometrical and architectural drawing, two subjects which were strong within Freemasonry.

Sir Gilbert Greenall jnr, who followed his father into Freemasonry, also donated the grand sum of £750 in 1916 towards the purchase by the Warrington Corporation of Orford Hall, the old residence of the Blackburne family. The Hall, which had also been occupied by William Beamont, was to be purchased for the people of Warrington, with the idea of turning the Hall into a museum, art gallery, library, and a school for girls.[313] The collection of funds for the construction of the

---

309 Ibid., p.35.
310 Ibid.
311 Stephens, *Adult Education And Society*, pp.91-2.
312 *Warrington School of Science Minute Book 1878-1884*, Warrington Library, reference MS239.
313 *Warrington Examiner, 2nd of December, 1916.*

Warrington Museum and Library in 1855 had also attracted the prominent involvement of Sir Gilbert Greenall and Peter Rylands, Rylands being a chairman on the committee of the Museum from 1853-4, and Greenall who played a prominent role during the laying of the foundation stone. Another local industrialist and Freemason Joseph Stubs, was also a chairman on the committee for the Museum in 1851.[314]

A similar process to what was happening in Warrington can be seen in Port Sunlight, with the industrialist Viscount Leverhulme, who was a leading Freemason and local community leader, founding his own lodge, and building an Art Gallery where the lodge met.[315] Leverhulme, who was also a founding member of the University Lodge of Liverpool No. 4274 in 1921, created a hierarchy of lodges within the social structure of Port Sunlight, with separate lodges for management, supervisors and workers. He realised that Freemasonry was an important and beneficial part of the society he had created, forming a bond between the brethren of the lodge and installing strict moralistic and educational principles that would benefit their work and family life.[316] Sir Gilbert Greenall, like Leverhulme, had founded his own lodge in 1869,[317] and a member of the Rylands family also subsequently assisted in founding a lodge.[318] The Lodge of Lights however, remained the central mother lodge of the town, and began to attract mythical status, in a similar way the old Academy had done. The lodge had been founded during the Academy's life time, and the link between Freemasonry and the Academy was celebrated when an Academy Lodge was founded. With the connection to Elias Ashmole and the Academy, Warrington became firmly established as a historical centre for Freemasonry and for independent education.

From the mid-nineteenth century the Warrington based Lodge of Lights recovered from its period of stagnation and became a successful 'Mother Lodge', its membership filled with wealthy industrialists and professionals that went on to found other lodges in the town. The lodge was perfect for networking and establishing business contacts, and this

[314] *Warrington Guuardian, 22nd of September, 1855.*
[315] *Viscount Leverhulme by his son,* (London: Allen & Unwin Ltd., 1928), pp.260-1.
[316] http://www.liverpoolmuseums.org.uk/ladylever/collections/masonicapron.asp [accessed 6th of April, 2009]
[317] Gilbert Greenall Lodge No.1250 was founded in 1869. The lodge still meets at the Warrington Masonic Hall.
[318] Sir William Peter Rylands Bart., was a founder of the Lymm based Domville Lodge No. 4647 in 1924. He was managing director and later the Chairman of Rylands Wire Works, and also had an extremely active public life, working on several committees. See David Harrison, *Domville Lodge No.4647, Lymm, Cheshire, The First 75 Years,* (Lodge Publication, 1999).

can also be mirrored in other lodges in industrial towns like Liverpool, Bolton, Oldham and Stockport. The success of Freemasonry can also be measured in the shift away from pubs and taverns as meeting places for lodges by the later nineteenth century, with Masonic Rooms or Halls being built or converted specifically for the purpose of Masonic meetings, such as in Warrington and Runcorn. However, ideals of charity and education within Freemasonry still retained a certain 'do-it-yourself' attitude to the local community, and the case study of the Warrington Freemasons during the eighteenth and nineteenth centuries reveals this, with local Freemasons forging a cultural identity in the town, creating learned societies, founding civic buildings and constructing centres of education and places of worship for the improvement of the Warrington people. These prominent Freemasons, such as Sir Gilbert Greenall and Peter Rylands, took an active interest in the town's development and in doing so they defined a cultural and civic identity for their community, assisting in providing education and charity to where it was needed.

In the wealthy port of Liverpool, however, Freemasonry had been the preserve of the up-and-coming merchant classes and tradesmen from the eighteenth century onwards, using the Craft as a nexus for business contacts – on both sides of the Atlantic, and the following chapter will analyse their involvement in one trade in particular; the slave trade.

Warrington Masonic Hall, built in a contemporary Art Decorative style. Building work commenced in 1932, and the foundation stone was laid with Masonic honors on the 22nd of September that year by the Provincial Grand Master of the Western Lancashire Division Arthur Foster. The two pillars of Jachin and Boaz preside on either side of the entrance, with globes at the top adorned with Masonic symbolism, such as the crescent moon and stars, overlaid with the 'network'. Freemasonry was no longer hiding in the shadows. (Photograph by David Harrison).

The Warrington Dissenting Academy, showing a modern, though contemporary-looking building extension, with the statue of Oliver Cromwell standing watch outside. The original eighteenth century building, which has been virtually rebuilt, can be seen on the right hand side, the Academy being housed there from 1757-1762. Academy tutors Jacob Bright and John Reinhold Forster were members of the Warrington based Lodge of Lights, and Freemason Jean Paul Marat is mentioned as having taught there. The Academy building was later used as the location of various local learned societies. (Photograph by David Harrison).

Hawarden Masonic Hall in North Wales, built in 1913. The photo reveals the date stone of the beautiful sandstone building set beneath the Masonic symbol of the set-square and compass, with the letter 'G' set in the centre. (Photograph by David Harrison).

The Masonic gravestone of Joshua Wood dated to 1844, situated in the Churchyard of St. Thomas the Martyr in Up Holland near Wigan, Lancashire. Joshua was a weaver and a member of the Wigan based Lodge of Antiquity No.178. The gravestone is quite weathered, and the crudely carved Masonic symbols of the set-square and compass and the plumb line are displayed at either side of what appears to be an 'All-Seeing Eye', giving a somewhat rustic appeal. (Photograph by David Harrison).

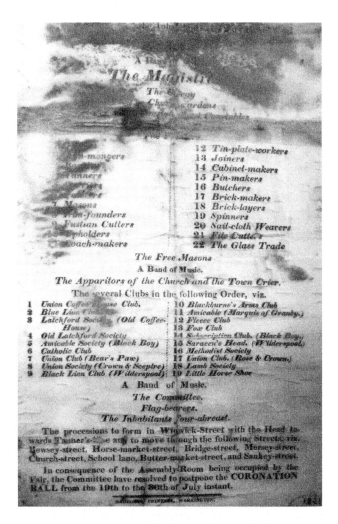

An advertisement for the procession through Warrington of various clubs and societies, led by the 'Free Masons', to celebrate the Coronation of George IV on the 19th of July 1821. This procession was also described in the minutes of the Warrington based Lodge of Lights. (Photograph by David Harrison).

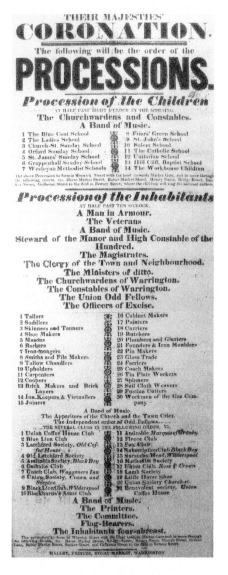

Another similar advertisement for the procession through Warrington ten years later to celebrate the Coronation of William IV. It reveals many of the same clubs and societies taking part, but notably absent are the Freemasons. In their place, the Oddfellows are shown taking a leading role in the procession. It was during this time that the local Lodge of Lights was suffering from very low attendance. (Photograph by David Harrison).

The Masonic gravestone of John Field dated to 1814, located in the ancient churchyard of St. Mary's in Walton-on-the-hill, Liverpool. It reveals an array of distinct Masonic symbolism such as the central set-square and compass, with rays of enlightenment radiating downwards. To the left is the crossed quills, the symbol for the secretary of the lodge, and to the right is the crossed keys, the symbol for the treasurer of the lodge; Field perhaps serving as both at some point. Below, more symbols reveal other elements to the Masonic story of John Field; the Masonic handshake is shown; a symbol which indicates friendship, the plumb rule to the left, the symbol for his lodge is shown with the lion on the crown, and the rule is shown on the right hand side. Field was a member of the Liverpool based Ancients Lodge No. 25c on the 18th of January 1806, a lodge which still exists as the St. George's Lodge of Harmony No. 32, and which stayed loyal during the Liverpool Masonic Rebellion. (Photograph by David Harrison).

A photograph of the Egyptian Suite in Hope Street Masonic Hall, Liverpool. The Egyptian Suite is a Chapter room for the Royal Arch ritual, and though the Egyptian style was only created in modern times, the actual Chapter rooms were part of the Hall refurbishments which date back to the 1920s. (Photograph by David Harrison).

The 'All-Seeing Eye' displayed in a pyramid of gold, emitting rays of enlightenment – a Masonic symbol which is a main feature on the decorated plaster-of-Paris ceiling of the Billiard Room – later the library - of Haigh Hall. The Hall was the residence of prominent Freemason Lord Lindsay, who was a founder of the self-titled Lindsay Lodge in 1870. The Hall witnessed a meeting of Masons in 1910. (Photograph by David Harrison).

The foundation stone of St. Margaret's and All Hallows Church, Orford, Warrington, laid with Masonic honours on the 18th of October, 1907. The stone was dedicated to local Freemason William Sharp and laid by the Provincial Grand Master of the Western Lancashire Division, the Earl of Lathom. It displays the dedication written in the lettering style of the Arts and Crafts Movement, and set in-between the lettering are the Masonic symbols of the set-square and the Seal of Solomon. The architect of the church, Arthur Warburton, later became the architect of the Warrington Masonic Hall, its foundation stone being laid by the Provincial Grand Master in 1932.

Chapter 5

Liverpool, Freemasonry, the Slave Trade and Trans-Atlantic Networking[319]

'before the Slavery Question was pressed among them all parties had merged into Masons and Anti-Masons.'
Richard Carlile discussing Freemasonry in the USA[320]

'Internal slavery, therefore, takes place wherever a whole community is governed by a part, and this perhaps, is the most concise and comprehensive account that can be given of it. The part that governs may be either a single man, as in absolute monarchies; or, a body of grandees, as in aristocracies. In both these cases the powers of government are commonly held for life without delegation, and descend from father to son; and the people governed are in the same situation with cattle upon an estate'.
Freemason Dr. Richard Price, 1777[321]

'That some desperate wretches should be willing to steal and enslave men by violence and murder for gain, is rather lamentable than strange. But that many civilized, nay, Christianized people should approve, and be concerned in the savage practise, is surprising'.
Thomas Paine, 1775[322]

In Liverpool, Freemasonry was extremely popular during the closing decades of the eighteenth century, with around ten lodges emerging in the port, both 'Antient' and 'Modern', supplying an international nexus of networking opportunities for young local merchants and businessmen in the thriving port. The membership of the lodges reflected the social and

---

[319] The author has previously written on this particular subject in David Harrison, 'A Most Miserable Trade', *Freemasonry Today*, Issue 39, Winter 2006, pp.36-38, and David Harrison, 'The American Revolution', *Freemasonry Today*, Number 10, Spring 2010, (London: Grand Lodge Publications), pp.43-45.

[320] Carlile, *Manual of Freemasonry*, p.87.

[321] Richard Price, 'Additional Observations on the Nature and Value of Civil Liberty, and the War with America', (1777), in David Oswald Thomas, (ed.), *Political Writings by Richard Price*, (Cambridge: Cambridge University Press, 1991), p.78.

[322] Thomas Paine, 'African Slavery in America' (1775), in Micheline Ishay, (ed.), *The human rights reader: major political writings, essays, speeches, and documents from the Bible to the present*, (Routledge, 1997), p.130.

economic culture of the port, and as the governance of Liverpool was dominated by local mercantile families, it was not surprising that the young men from these families would want to be involved in a wide-reaching society which extended, not only to other ports and industrial towns in Britain, but also America. Liverpool Freemasonry was to suffer rebellion in the decade after the Union of 1813, but, as we shall see, some of the Freemasons in Liverpool had previously held views in support of the slave trade, support which was tied in to political and economic power in the port.

The slave trade in Liverpool reached its peak during the late eighteenth century, with many Liverpool merchants and businessmen taking part in what was then a legal and legitimate business, making an acceptable profit from slavery, with Liverpool becoming dominant in the trade. Complete surviving lodge membership lists are rare from this period, but there is a surviving list of membership from one particular 'Modern' lodge in Liverpool at this time, aptly named the Merchants Lodge. The list, which contains the names of members and their occupations, dates from 1789, and not surprisingly, considering the name of the lodge, the majority of the Freemasons were merchants. The list is fascinating, not only because it is a rare example of the make-up of a lodge from this period, but because it reveals a number of local Freemasons who were involved in local politics and were directly involved in the slave trade and privateering.[323]

One of the lodge's founders was Thomas Golightly, who was listed in the Company of Merchants trading to Africa for the port of Liverpool. Golightly was mainly a wine merchant, and had powerful political connections in Liverpool, being an associate of erstwhile Mayor of Liverpool and fellow slave trader Peter Baker. Golightly continued to trade in slaves up until its abolition in 1807, and was first elected to the Liverpool Town Council in 1770, serving as Mayor himself in 1772-3 and as a Magistrate in 1779. Roger Leigh, another member of the lodge, was a local Liverpool businessman and politician who owned a number of slave ships, including the *Tuton, Sundet* and the *Pilgrim*.[324]

---

[323] *A List of the Members of Lodge No. 428 (Merchants Lodge), 1789.* Liverpool Masonic Hall, Hope Street, Liverpool. Not Listed. Thanks to Mr. G. A. Gerrard of the Merchants Lodge for his assistance in the research of this chapter. See also John Macnab, *History of The Merchants Lodge, No. 241, Liverpool, 1780-2004*, Second Edition, (Liverpool, 2004).
[324] *Liverpool & Slavery by a Genuine Dicky Sam*, (Newcastle on Tyne: F. Graham, 1969 Edition), p.119, pp.122-3 & pp.126-7. See also *List of the Members of Lodge No. 428 (Merchants Lodge), 1789.*

Freemason Thomas Barton was listed as a 'gentleman' in the lodge list, yet he also ventured into the slave trade, owning the slave ships the *Elizabeth* and the *Will*.[325] The *Will* was captained by the infamous eccentric Hugh Crow, and though the ship is listed in 1799 as being owned by Barton, Crow mentions in his memoirs that it was owned by William Aspinall, the brother of Freemason John Aspinall. Captain Hugh Crow gave an insight as to how he felt about the slave trade at the time, witnessing the slaves in the West Indian ports as well dressed and domesticated servants; he commented how lucky they were in comparison to the primitive and dangerous life experienced by the Negroes in Africa.[326]

This view of the slave trade was also held by the Scottish Freemason James Boswell, who commented on slavery in his *Life of Johnson*, saying that:

'To abolish a status, which in all ages God has sanctioned, and man has continued, would not only be robbery to an innumerable class of our fellow-subjects, but it would be extreme cruelty to the African savages, a portion of whom it saves from massacre, or intolerable bondage in their own country, and introduces into a much happier state of life; especially now when their passage to the West Indies and their treatment there is humanely regulated. To abolish that trade would be to shut the gates of mercy on mankind'.[327]

This *'God sanctioned'* view of slavery which Boswell so stoutly held, can also be seen in his poem *No Abolition of Slavery; or the Universal Empire of Love*, where he warns that *'He who to thwart God's system tries, Bids mountains sink, and vallies rise'*,[328] Boswell reminding the abolitionists that if they were to go against God's Will, they risk upsetting nature itself. Boswell also

---

[325] Ibid., pp.120-1 & pp.124-5. See also *List of the Members of Lodge No. 428 (Merchants Lodge), 1789.*

[326] Hugh Crow, *Memoirs of the late Captain Hugh Crow of Liverpool*, (Liverpool: Longman, Rees, Orme, Brown & Green, and G. & J. Robinson, 1830), pp.289-291. See also John Pinfold, *The Memoirs of Captain Hugh Crow: The Life and Times of a Slave Ship Captain*, (Oxford: The Bodleian Library, 2007).

[327] James Boswell, *Boswell's Life of Johnson*, (London: John Murray, 1847), p.563. James Boswell was a member of the Canongate Kilwinning Lodge in Edinburgh, joining on the 14th of August, 1759. He was an extremely active Freemason, serving as Worshipful Mater of the lodge, and was close friends with Sir William Forbes who served as Grand Master of Scotland from 1776-1778, Boswell serving as Deputy Grand Master at the same time. The family of James Boswell had been intricately linked to Scottish Freemasonry for a number of generations, with evidence existing that John Boswell was involved as an early non-operative Freemason, his signature appearing on the minutes of a meeting of The Lodge of Edinburgh in 1600. The father and uncle of James Boswell were also both Freemasons.

[328] James Boswell, *No Abolition of Slavery; or the Universal Empire of Love*, (London: Printed for R. Faulder, in New Bond Street, 1791), p.17.

insulted the leading abolitionist Wilberforce, writing *'Go, W_____, be gone, for shame, Thou Dwarf, with a big-sounding name.'* [329] He then uses the poem to fully justify his view, describing the slaves as well treated:

The cheerful gang! — the negroes see
Perform the task of industry:
Ev'n at their labour hear them sing,
While time flies quick on downy wing;
Finish'd the bus'ness of the day,
No human beings are more gay:
Of food, clothes, cleanly lodging sure,
Each has his property secure;
Their wives and children protected,
In sickness they are not neglected;
And when old age brings a release,
Their grateful days they end in peace. [330]

It was this view that helped to sanction the trade in the eyes of the Liverpool merchants and politicians. Thomas Barton's brother, William, though not a Freemason, had been a Mayor of Liverpool, and was also involved in shipping, keeping slaves on his West Indian plantation. Another Freemason on the list, William Dennison, was actively engaged in privateering, having a share in the *Enterprise*, the ship actively marauding French vessels.

Thomas Barton had also ventured into privateering, owning the *Harriet*, which took the French brig *L'Agreable*, the ship and its cargo being sold through the office of local broker William Ewart, another member of the Merchants Lodge. Ewart was an associate of John Gladstone, the father of the future Liberal Prime Minister William Ewart Gladstone, being named after his fathers' eminent colleague. John Gladstone also kept slaves on his plantations in the West Indies, and supported the rights of fellow West Indian slave owners during his brief but turbulent political career. Another son of John Gladstone, Robertson, became a Freemason in Liverpool in 1833, [331] the year of the

---

[329] Ibid., p.8.
[330] Ibid., p.21.
[331] Robertson Gladstone joined the St. Georges' Lodge of Harmony No. 32 on the 28th of October, 1833, see the membership list of *St. George's Lodge of Harmony No. 32, 1786-1836, C.D. Rom: 139 GRA/ANT/UNI, The Library and Museum of Freemasonry, UGLE, Great Queen Street, London.* Robertson Gladstone was a local politician and was also present at Provincial Grand Lodge meetings.

Slavery Abolition Act, when John was recorded as having around 1000 slaves on his plantations.[332] Despite John Gladstone's business interests in slavery, his friend and associate, the Freemason George Canning had been against slavery, stating in 1795 that:

'I shall content myself, with giving my vote, without any arguments, for the immediate and unqualified abolition'.[333]

The Freemason and politician Edmund Burke had also supported the abolition of the slave trade, and like Wilberforce, was also targeted in Boswell's anti-abolitionist poem.[334]

The conflict of interests within the slavery debate, even between friends, presented a moral issue against one of business. A similar contrast can be seen in the Merchants Lodge, with Richard Downward, a Liverpool merchant, supporting the abolitionist William Roscoe. Other abolitionists included the industrialist Josiah Wedgwood whose son Josiah Wedgwood II was a Freemason and also an abolitionist.

Freemasons were equally divided on the issue, with perhaps the most famous Freemason in the fledgling United States Benjamin Franklin supporting abolition, being president of the Pennsylvanian Society for the Abolition of Slavery. Thomas Paine, a friend of Franklin's and author of *The Origins of Free-Masonry*, was a founding member of the first Anti-Slavery Society in America. In his essay *African Slavery in America* Paine strongly attacks England's role in the trade:

'By such wicked and inhuman ways the English are said to enslave toward one hundred thousand yearly; of which thirty thousand are supposed to die by barbarous treatment in the first year'.

Paine's anger was intense, especially how the slave trade was given support by the Bible:

---

[332] H. Thomas, *The Slave Trade*, (New York: Simon & Schuster Inc., 1997), p.733.

[333] P. Jupp, (ed.), *The Letter-Journal of George Canning, 1793-1795*, Royal Historical Society, Camden Fourth Series, Volume 41, (London, 1991), p.202. According to Thomas Fenn, *The Prince of Wales's Lodge No. 259: list of members from the time of its constitution*, (London: Jarrold & Sons Ltd., Revised ed. 1938), p.33, Canning joined the Prince of Wales Lodge No.259 from the Somerset House Lodge on 13th April 1810, though in A.W. Oxford, *No. 4 an introduction to the History of the Royal Somerset House and Inverness Lodge*, (London: Bernard Quaritch Ltd., 1928), p.189 it is stated that Canning was initiated and passed in No. 4 Lodge on 30th April 1810, although he was proposed on 12th February 1810.

[334] Boswell, *No Abolition of Slavery; or the Universal Empire of Love*, p.12.

'Most shocking of all is alleging the sacred Scriptures to favor this wicked practice. [335]

Paine's strong worded anti-slavery stance was not alone, and ten years after his *African Slavery in America* appeared, the Freemason Richard Price published his views of slavery and the role that the fledgling United States played in it:

'The Negro trade cannot be censured in language too severe. It is a traffic which, as it has been hitherto carried on, is shocking to humanity, cruel, wicked, and diabolical. I am happy to find that the united states are entering into measures for discountenancing it and for abolishing the odious slavery which it has introduced. Till they have done this, it will not appear they deserve the liberty for which they have been contending. [336]

The slave trade was dependent on business contacts between merchants in British ports such as Liverpool and plantations in the West Indies and in America, the *'Managers'* as Paine called them, being able to network with fellow merchants, creating a Trans-Atlantic nexus of commerce, a nexus that Freemasonry was part of.

Freemasonry, Networking and Trans-Atlantic Trade

The slave trade, like the cotton and tobacco trades, was made possible due to business relationships on either side of the Atlantic. Freemasonry was established in America as early as the 1720s, and by the early 1760s there were two lodges established on the Mosquito Shore in the West Indies – founded by Thomas Marriot Perkins, a merchant who was appointed Provincial Grand Master there in 1761. [337] Freemasonry certainly played an important role in the networking of merchants in the Trans-Atlantic trade, with lodges being set up in the major ports.

Included amongst the Liverpool businessmen in the Merchants Lodge list is a merchant named Melling Wolley, whose residence is given as New

---

[335] Thomas Paine, 'African Slavery in America' (1775), in Micheline Ishay, (ed.), *The human rights reader: major political writings, essays, speeches, and documents from the Bible to the present*, (Routledge, 1997), p.131.

[336] Richard Price, 'Observations on the Importance of the American Revolution and The Means of making it a Benefit to the World', (1785), in David Oswald Thomas, (ed.), *Political Writings by Richard Price*, (Cambridge: Cambridge University Press, 1991), p.150.

[337] See 'From London to the Mosquito Shore – A Unique Jewel From Masonry's West Indian Past', *Freemasonry Today*, Number 10, Spring 2010, (London: Grand Lodge Publications), p.67.

Orleans, and John Samuel Thompson, a merchant from Santa Cruz.[338] Other Liverpool lodges also list a number of merchants and mariners visiting from New York, Boston and Bermuda during this period, testifying to the intricate Masonic links between Trans-Atlantic ports and the networking that could be offered. Indeed, there are obvious parallels between the Liverpool based Merchants Lodge and the Lodge St. Andrews No. 81 in Boston, both having a high percentage of young, well connected and powerful merchants as members, intent on gaining a hold on local politics.[339]

The Lodge St. Andrews, which met at the famous Green Dragon Tavern in Boston, has attracted many legends regarding the Boston Tea Party, which took place on the 16th of December 1773 and was the pivotal event which kick-started the American Revolution. The lodge, long connected to the planning of the Tea Party (which resulted in men dressed as Indians boarding a British vessel and throwing the over taxed tea overboard) included amongst its members the likes of John Hancock, a Boston merchant and future governor of Massachusetts, Dr Joseph Warren, a physician and soldier who fought the British, and Paul Revere, famous in American history for his midnight ride from Boston to Lexington to warn Hancock that *'the British were coming'*. These were all local leaders of the community who played a central role in the Revolution, Hancock being the first to sign the Declaration of Independence on the 4th of July, 1776.[340]

Another American lodge which has attracted study in recent years due to its membership of merchants and powerful local elite was the Virginia based Fredericksburg Lodge No. 4.[341] The lodge included members from numerous countries during the later eighteenth century, including Scottish merchants from Glasgow, which like Liverpool was a thriving industrial port. Scottish Freemasons in the locality included Robert Bogle who represented his father's Glasgow firm in Port Royal, Virginia, and the American Revolutionary naval hero John Paul Jones. Indeed, Masonic

---

[338] *A List of the Members of Lodge No. 428 (Merchants Lodge), 1789, Liverpool Masonic Hall, Hope Street, Liverpool.* Not Listed. A list of the founders of the lodge is also available. Also see R. Craig, & R. Jarvis, *Liverpool Registry of Merchant Ships*, Vol. 15, (Manchester: Chatham Society, 1967).

[339] See S.C. Bullock, *Revolutionary Brotherhood*, (USA: University of North Carolina Press, 1996), pp.91-8.

[340] The record of members of the Lodge of St. Andrews, No. 81, (Boston, Massachusetts, USA), May, 1769. Many thanks to Robert L. D. Cooper, the Curator of the Grand Lodge of Scotland Museum and Library for supplying a copy of the document.

[341] The history of the Fredericksburg Lodge No. 4 can be found at http://masoniclodge4.org/ [accessed 11th of January, 2010]

Scottish roots certainly ran deep in Virginia, with the Port Royal Lodge, which was founded in 1754, applying to 'Mother' Kilwinning Lodge in Scotland for a charter. The request for the charter was eventually passed onto the Grand Lodge of Scotland who honoured the request in 1755. Other prominent Freemasons associated with Fredericksburg were George Washington and James Monroe, both serving as early presidents of the fledging United States and both slave owners, a fact that Boswell's friend and associate Dr. Samuel Johnson referred to in his *Taxation No Tyranny*, when he said:

'If slavery be thus fatally contagious, how is it that we hear the loudest yelps for liberty among the drivers of negroes?'[342]

Freemasonry became vital for the social networking of young merchants and settlers, the Craft allowing them to make new contacts in the area and to form a brotherly bond with like-minded men. Other Scottish members of the Fredericksburg Lodge included Walter Stewart, Andrew Beaty and James Hunter. Hunter was a Scottish émigré who became an extremely successful merchant, his brother Adam negotiating trade contracts with their Scottish relatives while James took care of the business in Virginia, buying goods for sale in Britain. Many of these Scottish-Virginian merchants traded in a variety of commodities, but tobacco became synonymous with many merchant families of this period, such as the Bogle family. Freemasonry was obviously a vital tool in establishing mercantile contacts, and lodges appear habitually in ports where Trans-Atlantic trade was evident, such as in the prosperous port of Whitehaven in Cumberland, were a lodge was active as early as 1740. Whitehaven also imported tobacco from Virginia and exported coal and iron, and there were also mariners from Whitehaven who appeared in Liverpool lodges.[343]

The American Revolution however threatened to destroy this Trans-Atlantic Masonic harmony. The Masonic historian Steven Bullock has discussed how loyalties were divided in America between the Antients, who, he states, were on the whole supporters of the Revolution, and the

---

[342] Dr. Samuel Johnson, 'Taxation No Tyranny' in F.P. Walesby, (ed.), *The Works of Samuel Johnson*, (Oxford: Talboys and Wheeler, 1825), p.262

[343] *Harmonic Lodge No. 216, 1796-1836, C.D. Rom: 139 GRA/ANT/UNI, The Library and Museum of Freemasonry, UGLE, Great Queen Street, London.* See also the history of the Cumberland and Westmorland Province, http://www.cumbwestmasons.co.uk/main/history.shtml [accessed 3rd of May, 2009]

Moderns who appeared to be Loyalists. The St. Andrew's Lodge was under the sway of the Grand Lodge of Scotland, which, unlike the English 'Modern' Grand Lodge, recognized the 'Antients'. The lodge, despite having some prominent revolutionary-minded members, still had brethren fighting for the British, such as the aforementioned Dr. John Jeffries. Compared to the 'Antients', the 'Moderns' did suffer during the war, though this may be explained due to the easiness of 'Antient' lodges to establish travelling Warrants, whereas the 'Moderns' had to suspend meetings during the conflict. Many lodges, such as the Port Royal Lodge, did remain active, its members playing an active role in the formation of the Grand Lodge of Virginia.

After Independence was gained, the Masonic problem arose of also being independent or remaining loyal to the respective Grand Lodge, as the 'Antient', 'Modern', and Scottish Grand Lodges were all British. In this respect, American Freemasonry witnessed a further political dilemma, and though the idea of a national American Grand Lodge was put forward, the future lay in State organized Grand Lodges. Visiting Freemasons could still attend lodges on either side of the Atlantic, the Liverpool lodges, be it 'Antient' or 'Modern', being filled with visiting merchants and sailors from all over America soon after hostilities were ended.

The lodge lists from Liverpool during this time reveals an array of visiting American merchants and sailors, testifying to the continued relationship between the brethren from either side of the Atlantic, such as Master Mariner John Thomas who joined the Ancient Union Lodge in 1851, and Alexander Alcock Nevins who joined in 1852, Nevins being a merchant from New Orleans. There were also a number of brethren from the West Indies, such as Freemason John St. Hill, a merchant from Trinidad who joined the Liverpool based Harmonic Lodge No. 216 in 1815, and a gentleman from Barbados who joined the St. George's Lodge in 1819.[344] A Mariner from Barbados also joined the Sea Captain's Lodge, which perhaps had the largest number of brethren visiting from the United States, such as Mariner John Brown from North Carolina in 1793, and many more from Boston, New York and Philadelphia.[345] The importance of Masonic networks amongst seafaring brethren can also be

---

[344] *A List of the Members of the Ancient Union Lodge No. 203, 1792-1887, Harmonic Lodge No. 216, 1796-1836, & St. George's Lodge of Harmony No. 32, 1786-1836, C.D. Rom: 139 GRA/ANT/UNI, The Library and Museum of Freemasonry, UGLE, Great Queen Street, London.*
[345] *A List of the Members of the Sea Captain's Lodge No. 140, 1768-1836, CD Rom: 139 GRA/ANT/UNI, The Library and Museum of Freemasonry, UGLE, Great Queen Street, London.*

seen in other more inland Lancashire lodges, such as the Bury based Prince Edwin's Lodge No. 128, where ships engineer Hargreaves Hope – who joined the lodge in 1837 – worked on ships crossing the Atlantic, travelling to South America.[346]

Even after the American Civil War, relationships continued, businessmen using Freemasonry to interact on a social level and to maintain contacts, especially in the cotton trade. An example of this is in the Leigh based Marquis of Lorne Lodge No. 1354, were a number of American brethren sought to become joining members. The lodge had included a number of local cotton manufacturers, and in 1871, just after the lodge had been founded, cotton manufacturer Thomas Joseph Lancashire proposed two Masons who were not only members of American lodges but were also cotton manufacturers in Lancashire.[347] In 1876 another Freemason from Memphis, Tennessee wished to join the lodge, and in 1884 a visiting brother from Illinois was refused admission as he was unable to show his Grand Lodge Certificate.[348]

The American Revolution certainly affected American Freemasonry, dividing loyalties, not only politically but in the altering of the structure and organization of the American Craft. Despite the upheavals, Freemasonry undoubtedly assisted in healing the divisions, especially locally, the evidence for which can be clearly seen in the lists of visiting Masons attending lodges from both sides of the Atlantic so soon after the war. Liverpool lodges from the 1780s onwards were filled with visiting American merchants and sailors, and similarly Boston and Virginian lodge lists reveal British merchants and sailors from Glasgow, Liverpool and other British ports. In this way, Freemasonry positively supported Trans-Atlantic trade links, with merchants, seamen and settlers finding familiar and recognizable surroundings in a lodge while being thousands of miles from home. Freemasonry helped heal the political divisions in the post-Independence period, supplying a social system which created a 'special relationship' between merchants and businesses across the Atlantic, repairing attitudes and rebuilding an Atlantic bridge due to the networking offered within Freemasonry. The cotton and tobacco trades assisted in making the port of Liverpool successful, but slavery was also a

---

[346] *Family Papers of Hargreaves Hope, compiled by John Hope.* Private collection. Not listed. Prince Edwin's Lodge No. 128 was warranted under the 'Antient's' in 1803. Hargreaves Hope entered the lodge on the 30th of January, 1837 and was a Freemason until his death in 1885 at the age of 75. Death registered in June 1885, Hargreaves Hope, Bury. Ref: 8c. 331.
[347] P.G. Monk and F. Bent, *A History of the Marquis of Lorne Lodge No. 1354*, (Leigh: P.T.H. Brooks Ltd., 1971), p.9.
[348] Ibid., p.12.

major legitimate trade, and business relationships with the fledgling USA remained vitally important.

The Abolition of Slavery

Despite the large number of merchants in the Merchants Lodge, there where overall only a small number of members directly involved in the slave trade, the merchants being involved in a variety of other trades, and evidence from other lodges in Liverpool only reveals a similar small number of merchants who had direct involvement. The short lived Liverpool based Calladonian Lodge had among its incomplete membership list the conspicuous name of John Aspinall, who appears to have joined in 1786. John was related to James and William Aspinall (both appear to be non-masons), all involved in local shipping and co-owning a number of slave ships. Two lodges in Liverpool during this period do hint at an involvement in local shipping; the Mariners Lodge and the Sea Captains Lodge, though the records are incomplete and at times patchy. Local Freemason and Liverpool merchant, James Chalmers, listed as the co-owner of the slave ship *Union* in 1799, was both a founder member of the Antient Union Lodge in 1792 and the Harmonic Lodge in 1796, and had also been a member of St. George's Lodge of Harmony.[349] These were all 'Antient' lodges in Liverpool, and Chalmers became dominant in all of them.

One prominent member of the Antient Union Lodge who vehemently supported the Liverpool slave trade was General Isaac Gascoyne MP. Gascoyne, a dedicated Tory, joined the lodge on the 16th of June, 1796, and fought hard against abolitionists such as Roscoe, causing Lord Howick to comment that:

> 'he (Gascoyne) considered the slave trade so great a blessing, that if it were not in existence at present he should propose to establish it.[350]

Gascoyne and Howick had confronted each other on the 23rd of February, 1807 in the crucial debate on the slave trade, discussing the

---

[349] *A List of the Members of the Ancient Union Lodge No. 203, 1792-1825, Harmonic Lodge No. 216, 1796-1836, & St. George's Lodge of Harmony No. 32, 1786-1836, C.D. Rom: 139 GRA/ANT/UNI, The Library and Museum of Freemasonry, UGLE, Great Queen Street, London.* See also *the Copy of the Original Warrant & List of Membership for the Ancient Union Lodge No. 203, Garston Masonic Hall, Ireland Road, Garston, Liverpool.* Not listed.

[350] F. E. Sanderson, 'The Liverpool Abolitionist', in Roger Anstey & P.E.H. Hair, (ed.), *Liverpool, the African Slave Trade and Abolition*, HSLC, Occasional Series, Vol.II, (1976), p.222.

economic effects of the abolition of the slave trade to Liverpool. Howick estimated that only £5000 in dock duties would be lost, whereas Gascoyne put forward that 40,000 tons of shipping would be lost and £2 million of investments would be destroyed.[351] Gascoyne added that after the abolition:

> *'great distress, public and private, will follow…and that a number of our most loyal, industrious and useful subjects will emigrate to America'.*[352]

Despite Gascoyne's best efforts, the Slave Trade Act was finally passed on the 25th March, 1807, abolishing the trade, forcing the Liverpool merchants to diversify their trading activities. Isaac's brother, Bamber Gascoyne, had served as an MP before him, and had also gave support for the Liverpool slave trade, the Gascoyne name immortalised in a local poem as a result:

> *'Be true to the man who stood true to his trust,*
> *Remember our sad situation we must;*
> *When our African business was near at an end,*
> *Remember, my lads, 'twas Gascoyne was our friend.*[353]

Isaac Gascoyne's overall political career was viewed later as lacklustre, Gascoyne being described by J.A. Picton in his *Memorials of Liverpool* as *'a man of no special ability'*. Picton did however write of Gascoyne's heroics at detaining the man who had shot and murdered Prime Minister Spencer Perceval in the House of Commons in 1812.[354]

Gascoyne was the Liverpool Corporation's successful nominee for MP since 1796, and had the full support from the merchant class of the port. Songs were composed in honour of the Gascoyne family because of their unwavering support for the slave trade. In contrast, on returning from the parliamentary debate on the trade, the abolitionist William Roscoe was attacked by a mob of out of work seamen during a procession through Castle Street in Liverpool. Roscoe was also an MP for Liverpool, but as a Whig and an abolitionist, he was far from the ethos of

---

[351] Ibid., p.224.
[352] H. Thomas, *The Slave Trade*, p.553.
[353] Gomer Williams, *History of the Privateers and Slave Trade of Liverpool*, (Liverpool: Edward Howell, 1906), p.613.
[354] J. A. Picton, *Memorials of Liverpool*, Vol. I, (London: Longmans, 1875), p.242 & p.297.

Gascoyne and the merchants of Liverpool, Roscoe's political career being far shorter than Gascoyne's.

As a war hero, Gascoyne held instant popular appeal in a port filled with sailors, dock workers and a mainly Tory merchant class. The writer W. Moss, writing in his *Liverpool Guide*, the same year Gascoyne was to enter into Parliament and into Freemasonry, put forward the value of the slave trade to Liverpool:

'It appears that, from the year 1783, to 1793, the value of Slaves imported into the West Indies in Liverpool vessels, amounts to 15,186,850l. Sterl. – 2,278,072l. being deducted from the above for commissions and all contingences in the West Indies, the nett proceeds will be 12,908,823l. Sterl.'

Moss then commented on the moral dilemma of slavery:

'As a simple moral question, considered in the abstract, it can meet with no countenance. In a political point of view, every thing favours it.[355]

It appeared that the wealth which the slave trade supplied to Liverpool contemptuously outweighed the moralistic aspects.

Gascoyne had entered the army as an Officer in 1779, and had gradually risen through the ranks. He was wounded at the Battle of Lincelles in 1793, and though he continued to hold various posts well into the early years of the nineteenth century, Gascoyne was free to follow his brother, the slave trader Bamber Gascoyne, into politics.

In 1796, Gascoyne was elected MP for Liverpool, and in the same year he entered into the local Liverpool Antient Union Lodge, joining the ranks of local merchants and businessmen, including one of the Lodge's founders James Chalmers, who owned an interest in a Liverpool slave ship. Gascoyne's political career strongly reflected the interests of his Tory supporters in Liverpool, and along with his strong opposition to the abolition of the slave trade, he also opposed the Reform Act of 1832, as well as opposing the abolition of bull baiting and Catholic emancipation.

His links to Freemasonry in Liverpool reflected the networking that went on in the port, the Antient Union Lodge being awash with Liverpool merchants and ship owners, the lodge offering a social nexus

---

[355] W. Moss, *The Liverpool Guide*, (Printed for and sold by Crane and Jones, Castle Street, sold by Vernor and Hood, London, 1796), pp.99-100.

for them to maintain relationships and business contacts. Gascoyne served as an MP until 1831, his heroic reputation being defined in the public eye as playing a part in detaining the assassin of the Prime Minister Spencer Perceval. Even though the slave trade was finally abolished in 1807, slaves could still be kept throughout the British Empire, with plantation owners such as John Gladstone keeping up to 1000 slaves in the West Indies. One such Freemason who kept a large number of slaves on his Jamaican sugar plantation was Colonel Thomas Wildman, the Provincial Grand Master of Nottinghamshire who had purchased Lord Byron's ancestral home Newstead Abbey in 1818. The revenue from the plantation certainly assisted in Wildman's repairs and rebuilding work to the Abbey, the Grand Master of the United Grand Lodge of England the Duke of Sussex staying there regularly. The loss of his slaves after the Slavery Abolition Act of 1833 caused Wildman considerable financial losses.

A Freemason who was completely against the use of slavery within the colonies of the British Empire was Sir Thomas Stamford Raffles,[356] who outlawed slavery in Bencoolen - a British garrison located in south west Sumatra - where he served as Lieutenant Governor from 1818, Raffles going on to prohibit slavery in Singapore. Raffles was an employee of the East India Company, and his support for the complete abolition of slavery was displayed in his *Statement of Services* in 1824, in which he described how he played a role in its eventual abolition in Bencoolen:

'Of African slaves the property of Government, there were (men, women, and children) upwards of two hundred, most of them born at Bencoolen, being the children of slaves originally purchased by the East-India Company. They had hitherto been considered as indispensable for the duties of the place, and it had been asserted that they were happier than free men.

I could not be expected to concur in either of these views. They were employed in loading and unloading the Company's ships, and other hard work, for which free labourers ought to have been engaged. No care having been taken of their morals, many of them were dissolute and depraved, the women living in promiscuous intercourse

---

356 Sir Thomas Stamford Raffles was initiated into Freemasonry in July 1812, in the *Lodge Virtutis et Artis Amici*, in Buitenzorg, Java, a lodge under the jurisdiction of the Grand Orient of the Netherlands. He was afterwards raised in the *Lodge De Vriendschap* in Surabaya, Java, in July 1813, serving as Worshipful Master that same year. His close friend and business associate Thomas McQuoid was also a Freemason and a founder of the *Lodge Neptune* which was based in Penang. McQuoid was 'Perfected' with Raffles in *Rose Croix Chapter La Vertueuse* in Batavia in 1816. Thanks to Diane Clements at the United Grand Lodge of England Library and Archive for supplying the records on his Masonic membership.

with the public convicts, for the purpose of keeping up the "breed", and the children left to a state of nature, vice, and wretchedness.

The practice of slavery being very general on the coast, it was my intention to have adopted by degrees all measures which might tend to its entire abolition. I caused the whole of the Company's slaves to be brought before the first public assembly of the chiefs, and after explaining to them the principles and views of the British Government with regard to the abolition generally, I gave to each of the slaves a certificate of freedom: a measure which made a considerable impression, and promised to be followed by the most favourable results.

I had subsequently the satisfaction of passing a Regulation, with the entire concurrence of the Native Chiefs, by which slavery was eventually abolished...[357]

Raffles was extremely pro-active in passing this '*Regulation*', his passion for the complete abolition of slavery within the British colonies being evident in his efforts in Bencoolen and in his later work in defining the constitution of Singapore.

Raffles held a modern vision for the governance of Bencoolen; and he had sent fellow Freemason and politician George Canning a memorandum which set out his aims – especially mentioning the idea of establishing a station at the eastern exit of the straits of Malacca before the Dutch did. The Dutch were always a problem to the British in Southeast Asia, and Singapore, which became the hub for the British Empire in Southeast Asia, was to be free of Dutch influence.

Canning was also against slavery, and was at the time serving as the President of the Board of Control, an office that was responsible for overseeing the East India Company, and thus he was very much interested in British influence in South East Asia. Despite the efforts of Raffles, the Slavery Abolition Act of 1833 had certain notable exceptions, one of which was the territories in the possession of the East India Company. Raffles returned to England in 1824 where he was to die two years later. Because of his anti-slavery stance, he was refused burial inside his local parish church, St. Mary's in Hendon, by the vicar, whose family had made its money in the slave trade.

English Freemasons had been as divided on the issue of slavery as much as the population of England had been, though English Freemasonry had played a role in breaking down barriers of race, with the establishment of the first black Masonic lodge in Boston, America, which

---

[357] Sir Thomas Stamford Raffles, *Statement of the Services of Sir Stamford Raffles*, (London: Cox and Baylie, Great Queen Street, 1824), pp.35-36.

was actually granted a charter by the 'Modern/Premier' Grand Lodge of England in 1784, as American lodges did not permit black membership. Its leader was a black American named Prince Hall, and Prince Hall Masonry has since spread to Canada, the Caribbean and Liberia. English Freemasonry could also boast another connection to the anti-slavery movement, with the Freemasons Tavern in London being famously used as the location for the world's first Anti-Slavery convention on 12th of June, 1840. Despite the abolition of the trade in 1807 and the Slavery Abolition Act of 1833, the Anti-Slavery Society, founded in 1839, continued their work to outlaw slavery in other countries.

The networking aspect of Freemasonry within the busy port of Liverpool would have been important during this period, with many of the members being young businessmen in their twenties and thirties. Freemasonry offered a social nexus for the young merchants within Liverpool, and slavery was mercilessly seen as merely another business enterprise. Slavery during the later eighteenth century thus became a moral dilemma for Freemasons like the abolitionist Richard Downward, yet at the same time, the trade was defended as a profitable business by other Freemasons like Isaac Gascoyne, both ideals inevitably clashing with Abolition in 1807. In Liverpool, Freemasonry was one of the many ways in which merchants and tradesmen could socialise, and through the Craft they could bond together and forge stronger relationships. It was this closeness which would assist in the spread of discontent for some Liverpool lodges in the decade following the abolition of slavery, revolting against the United Grand Lodge and causing the Liverpool Masonic Rebellion.

The Continuation of Trans-Atlantic Networking and Liverpool's support for the Confederacy during the American Civil War

Freemasonry undoubtedly continued to assist in the networking that was crucial to the Trans-Atlantic trade as the nineteenth century progressed, especially between Liverpool and the ports of America. Crucial to the cotton industry of the north-west of England was the trade with the Southern cotton producing States, and with the outbreak of the American Civil War in 1861, the cotton trade experienced a period of uncertainty and instability. The outbreak of the American Civil War followed the secession from the Union by the Southern cotton producing States that depended on slavery. The growing anti-slavery position of the Northern States had made conflict with the South more apparent, the newly elected

President Abraham Lincoln having firmly declared himself against the expansion of slavery, a view that was compounded in a speech he gave in New Haven, Connecticut in March 1860:

'One of the reasons why I am opposed to Slavery is just here...I want every man to have the chance - and I believe a black man is entitled to it – in which he can better his condition – when he may look forward and hope to be a hired labourer this year and the next, work for himself afterward, and finally to hire men to work for him! That is the true system.[358]

With the foundation of the Confederate States of America in February 1861, hostilities followed, and in 1863, the Emancipation Proclamation issued by Lincoln resulted in slaves being freed in Confederate States occupied by the Union.

The maintaining of networking and business contacts were essential to the cotton merchants and brokers of Liverpool, and during the war, despite the neutrality of Britain, some Liverpool merchants were willing to buy cotton that could be smuggled past the Union naval blockade that had been established during the early stages of the conflict. An example of the intricate networking that developed during the Civil War in Liverpool can be seen with the activities of a Confederate naval officer and 'secret serviceman' who operated in the port called James Dunwoody Bulloch, a Confederate 'banker' named Charles Kuhn Prioleau, the Liverpool based shipping firm of Fraser and Trenholm and John Lairds shipbuilding company.

James Dunwoody Bulloch was no stranger to Freemasonry, his family home, Bulloch Hall, was built by his father Major James Stephen Bulloch, a plantation owner, a cotton producer and a Freemason. The Hall, near Roswell, in the Southern State of Georgia, was built in the Neo-Classical Greek revival style in 1840, and displayed Masonic symbolism prominently on each side of the Hall and over the main entrance. The plantation kept a number of slaves, and after being ransacked by Union troops during the war, a legend developed that it had been the prominent Masonic symbolism that ultimately saved the Hall from being

[358] Abraham Lincoln, 'From a Speech at New Haven, Connecticut, March 6th, 1860', in Mario M. Cuomo and Harold Holzer, (ed.), *Lincoln on Democracy; His own words, with essays by America's foremost Civil War historians*, (New York: Fordham University Press, 2004), p.176-177.

destroyed.[359]   Indeed, the legend of Bulloch Hall being saved due to its Masonic links is akin to Albert Pike's home being saved from destruction by a Union commander who was also a high ranking Freemason; Thomas H. Benton, a Union General who had been Grand Master in Iowa from 1860-1862, placed Federal troops around Pike's home at Little Rock, Arkansas, when the city was invaded.[360]

After establishing his base in Liverpool and cultivating his contacts, Bulloch began arranging in secret for the construction of commerce and blockade raiders by the Birkenhead shipbuilders John Laird's, such as the CSS Alabama and CSS Florida. Bulloch also purchased ships, such as the CSS Shenandoah, the purpose of which was as a commerce raider, particularly focussing on Whaling ships – a source of revenue for the Union.   The Alabama became extremely successful; from the ship's launch in July 1862 to her sinking by the USS Kearsarge in June 1864, the Alabama claimed over 60 prizes, her Captain Raphael Semmes also residing in Liverpool for a time. Along with his younger brother Irvine Bulloch, who had been the youngest officer on the Alabama, James remained in Liverpool after the Civil War, both maintaining a relationship with their nephew and future President of the USA Theodore Roosevelt, who was also a Freemason.

The society of Liverpool proved its support for the Confederacy when, in October 1864, the great Southern Bazaar was held at St. Georges' Hall to raise money for the Confederate wounded, and as a result around £20,000 was raised. The woman behind the bazaar was none other than Mary Elizabeth Prioleau, the wife of Confederate 'banker' Charles Kuhn Prioleau, who originated from Charleston, South Carolina, and was a manager and partner of Fraser and Trenholm. The offices of Bulloch and Fraser and Trenholm were located close to each other at Rumford Place, near to the Liverpool Docks.   Prioleau was supplying funds for the shipbuilding at Lairds, and after the war was over, Fraser and Trenholm became bankrupt and he left Liverpool to settle in London.[361]

---

[359] Bulloch Hall is in possession of a 'letter of protection' signed by a Federal General, which ensured the Hall was spared destruction by Union troops. See John Hussey, *Cruisers, Cotton and Confederates*, (Merseyside: Countyvise, 2008), p.91.

[360] See Michael Halleran, *The Better Angels of Our Nature: Freemasonry in the American Civil War*, (Alabama: The University of Alabama Press, 2010).

[361] See the Fraser and Trenholm Archive, The Liverpool Maritime Museum. The archive includes original letters from Prioleau to key figures in the Confederacy, discussing loans and blockade running vessels.

The foundation stone for the Neo-Classical St. Georges' Hall had been laid in 1838 with a Masonic ceremony, led by the Deputy Provincial Grand Master of West Lancashire, with a number of local lodges attending, such as the Lodge of Harmony.[362] Many of the local Liverpool lodges also raised money for the *'distressed operatives'* of the cotton mills throughout Lancashire and Cheshire during the American Civil War period, with lodges such as Lodge of Harmony[363] and the Merchants Lodge, which contributed twenty guineas in 1862, taking the lead.[364] There are no records yet discovered of the Bulloch's and Prioleau being Freemasons in Liverpool, but they certainly mixed in the same social circles, the men enjoying access to Liverpool high society, and Prioleau knew the value of symbolism, decorating his house at 19 Abercromby Square in Liverpool with an elaborate mixture of classical and Confederate symbolism, some of which, such as the fresco on the entrance porch ceiling which displays the palmetto tree, being the State symbol for South Carolina, would be instantly recognisable to Confederate supporters.

The Lancashire Cotton Famine was as much a result of gross overproduction in the years prior to the American Civil War as it was the supply of raw cotton being cut off due to the Union blockade. The cotton workers of mill towns such as Manchester became unemployed as a result, and a rioting took place in Stalybridge in 1863, spreading to Ashton, Hyde and Dukinfield. Despite this hardship, cotton workers had met at the Free Trade Hall in Manchester and had given support to Lincoln and the Union in the fight against slavery. Many of the unemployed cotton workers in Wigan during the Civil War period were found work by the Lindsay family, assisting in landscaping the plantations of Haigh Hall, James Ludovic Lindsay becoming a prominent Freemason in Wigan. However, support was divided in certain Lancashire cotton producing towns, and some mills actually hoisted the Confederate flag on the day the Prince of Wales married Princess Alexandra in 1863.

William Ewart Gladstone, despite his liberalism, had shocked his fellow politicians on his views on the American Civil War and the issue of slavery. Gladstone, whose elder brother Robertson was a high ranking Freemason and politician in Liverpool, and whose father had kept slaves

---

[362] Anon. *The History of The Lodge of Harmony No. 220*, (Liverpool, 1948), p.9.
[363] Ibid., p.13.
[364] John Macnab, *History of The Merchants Lodge, No. 241, Liverpool, 1780-2004*, Second Edition, (Liverpool, 2004), p.57.

on his West Indies plantation, gave a speech in Newcastle in October 1862, where he had effectively recognised the Confederacy:

We may have our own opinions about slavery; we may be for or against the South; but there is no doubt that Jefferson Davies and other leaders of the South have made an army; they are making, it appears, a navy; and they have made, what is more than either, they have made a nation... [365]

Gladstone's reference to the Confederacy *'making a navy'* was certainly uncanny regarding that his home town of Liverpool was central to the ship building activities of Confederate agent James Dunwoody Bulloch at this time. Gladstone's Newcastle speech certainly stirred feelings across the British political spectrum, leading the Liberal spokesman John Bright to comment *'he has no word of sympathy for the four million bondsmen of the South'*.[366] Though he was against slavery, Gladstone ultimately disapproved of the Civil War to bring about its end.[367]

Confederates, Slavery and Freemasonry

The issue of slavery and the political divide it caused found Freemasons on both sides of the American Civil War. Albert Pike, a Freemason who had joined the Southern Jurisdiction of the Scottish Rite in the USA, was an advocate of slavery and a Confederate Officer during the Civil War, who, having built up relationships with various Native American tribes while working as a lawyer, was given a command in the Indian Territory and trained Confederate regiments of Indian Cavalry. Pike fell foul of his superiors and faced an accusation that some of his troops had scalped Union soldiers, so, facing arrest, Pike resigned from the Confederate Army. After the war, Pike continued his Masonic career, re-shaping the Scottish Rite (he had been elected Grand Commander for the Southern Jurisdiction in 1859), and writing the detailed work *Morals and Dogma*. Pike and his work was held in high regard by many Masons in Britain, such as Dr. William Wynn Westcott who founded the Hermetic Order of the Golden Dawn in 1888.

---

[365] Peter J. Parish, 'Gladstone and America' in Peter J. Jagger (ed.,), *Gladstone*, (Hambledon Continuum, 1998), pp.85-105, on p.97.
[366] Ibid., p.99. See also Philip Magnus, *Gladstone A Biography*, (New York, E.P Dutton & Co., 1954), p.154.
[367] Peter J. Parish, 'Gladstone and America' in Peter J. Jagger (ed.,), *Gladstone*, (Hambledon Continuum, 1998), pp.85-105, on p.99

Freemasonry in the Confederate States was undoubtedly affected by the Civil War, with many lodges suffering due to the conflict. One such lodge was the Atlanta Lodge No. 59, which had a number of its brethren actively take part in the conflict, such as General George 'Tige' Anderson who fought in a number of campaigns, including Gettysburg in July 1863. Other brethren who served in the Confederate army included Dr. W.E. Parkhurst who served as Lieutenant in the Fifth (5th) Georgia Cavalry, and Dr. Daniel Cornelius O'Keefe, who was born in Limerick, Ireland, and served as Surgeon with the rank of Major. After the war he campaigned to established public schools in Atlanta. The lodge certainly suffered during the war and from 1861 to the end of the conflict in 1865, Methodist Minister Lewis Lawshe served as Worshipful Master, holding the lodge together. Lawshe also entered the ranks of the Confederate Army as Chaplain.

The war torn Confederate States underwent an economic and social upheaval which obviously affected the membership of Freemasonry in the area. As with the members of the Atlanta Lodge, many Confederate Freemasons were involved in the war, and Freemasonry in the old Confederate States suffered stagnation in the following years. After the war, the lodges in the Northern states however, reveal a different story, and whereas the Confederate lodges were static for many years, the lodges in the Northern States appear to have flourished and enjoyed a period of prosperity - the golden age of fraternalism not applying in the Confederate States.[368]

Many prominent officers in the Union army were also practising Freemasons. One such officer and Freemason who fought the Confederates was the Muscogee Creek Indian Chief Opothleyahola, who, in leading Creeks and Seminole Indians who were loyal to the Union from his plantation in Oklahoma to seek promised refuge in Kansas, fought a number of battles against pursuing Confederates. Suffering great losses through battle, disease and hardship, the remaining followers finally made it to a refuge camp in Kansas, were Opothleyahola died from illness in 1863. Opothleyahola had kept slaves on his plantation, but during the outbreak of the Civil War, he refused pressure to join the

---

[368] John Belton and David Harrison, 'Two Centuries of Masonic Membership Exposed and some light on Post Civil War Fraternalism', a paper presented at the ICHF, Edinburgh, 26th of May, 2007.

Confederacy, his plantation becoming a gathering place for runaway slaves, free blacks and Indian tribes in the early stages of the war.[369]

Perhaps one of the most moving examples of Masonic brotherhood during the Civil War was written by American Masonic historian Joseph Fort Newton, who related the story of how his father; a Freemason and soldier in the Union army, had been taken prisoner, and while at a prisoner of war camp, he became seriously ill. He made himself known as a Mason to a Confederate officer in the camp, and the officer subsequently took him to his home and nursed him back to health. At the end of the war, the same Confederate officer gave Joseph Fort Newton's father money and a pistol for his journey home.[370] Another incident that revealed how Freemasonry bridged the bitter political divide created by the Civil War was during the battle of Gettysburg in 1863, when the Confederate officer and Freemason Lewis Addison Armistead, who was mortally wounded in the field of battle, gave the Masonic sign for distress. He was attended to by fellow Freemason Henry H. Bingham, who recognised the sign. Bingham however, was a Union officer, but the brotherhood of Freemasonry transcended above the political differences and personal beliefs. Armistead gave Bingham his personal effects to pass onto his old friend and fellow Mason Winfield Scott Hancock, who was also a Union officer.[371]

Freemasons had certainly played a part in slavery and the slave trade, and Freemasons had also played a part in bringing an end to it. Freemasonry allowed intimate business relationships to develop and to become established, so mariners and merchants from the United States could be welcomed by other Freemasons who were merchants from Liverpool, maintaining friendships and business links at various ports, cultivating trades such as slavery. Certainly when a mariner stepped off his ship in the old Liverpool docks, he could make his way to a lodge meeting and be among friends, finding a meal and lodgings during his stay. He could then perhaps discuss business, make connections, and

---

[369] See Angie Debo, *The Road to Disappearance, A History of the Creek Indians*, (Oklahoma: The University of Oklahoma Press, 1941). For examples of Native American tribes keeping slaves see Patrick Neal Minges, *Slavery in the Cherokee Nation*, (London: Routledge, 2003).

[370] See Allen E. Roberts, *House Undivided: The Story of Freemasonry and the Civil War*, (Missouri, USA: Missouri Lodge of Research, 1961). Also see Joseph Fort Newton, *The Builders*, (London: Unwin Brothers Limited, 1924).

[371] Brigadier General Lewis Addison Armistead, originally from North Carolina, was a member of Alexandria-Washington Masonic Lodge No. 22, and before the Civil War he had served with his friend and fellow Mason Major General Winfield Scott Hancock, who was a member of Charity Lodge No. 190. Captain Henry H. Bingham, serving under Hancock at Gettysburg, was a member of Chartiers Lodge No. 297. See Halleran, *The Better Angels of Our Nature*.

perhaps extend an invite to his lodge in America or the West Indies. Of the many trades that took place in Liverpool, the slave trade was one that contributed immensely to the development of the port, and certainly increased the wealth of the merchants there.

Chapter 6

The Liverpool Masonic Rebellion and the Grand Lodge of Wigan[372]

'we deny the power of any authority to compel us to adopt a System, which has hitherto been unknown, or not practised by the ancient Masons of this Kingdom.'
Copy of the Address sent to H.R.H Prince Augustus Frederick, Duke of Sussex, read out by Michael Alexander Gage, September, 1819[373]

'My son forgot not my Law, but let thine heart keep my Commandments and remove not the Ancient Landmark which thy Father's have set.'
Michael Alexander Gage, Deputy Grand Master, *The Magna Charta of Masonic Freedom*, 22nd of December, 1823[374]

'you who have been the Main Instrument in Asserting and vindicating our rights in both private and public and to whom the tyrants in the Masonic world would have always looked upon with dread.'
Grand Secretary Robert Bolton writing to Michael Alexander Gage on his resignation, 14th of June 1842[375]

On the 22nd of December 1823, a group of Masonic rebels met at the Shakespeare Tavern in Williamson Square in Liverpool to re-establish the 'Antient' Grand Lodge, a Grand Lodge that had officially merged with

---

[372] The author has previously written on this particular subject in various articles and papers, see David Harrison, 'The Masonic Rebellion in Liverpool and the Wigan Grand Lodge', *Freemasonry Today*, Issue 30, Autumn 2004. This article also appeared in *Symbols and Mysteries, Freemasonry Today: The Best of 10 Years* (Lewis Masonic, 2007). The original paper was presented at the Urban History Seminar, University of Liverpool, on the 17th of March, 2004. See also David Harrison, 'James Broadhurst and the Liverpool Masonic Rebellion', in *MQ*, Grand Lodge Publications, Issue 13, April, 2005, and David Harrison, 'The Grand Lodge of Wigan: Its Rise and Fall', in *MQ*, Grand Lodge Publications, Issue 16, January, 2006. The topic was also presented as a paper by the author to the Historic Society of Lancashire and Cheshire on the 24th of March, 2010.
[373] E.B. Beesley, *The History of the Wigan Grand Lodge*, (Leeds: Manchester Association for Masonic Research, 1920), p.5 and p.130.
[374] Ibid., p.36.
[375] Ibid., p.86.

the 'Moderns' ten years previously. The group of Freemasons, led by local tailor Michael Alexander Gage, were rebelling against the central control of London and what they saw as the *'tyranny'* of the Duke of Sussex, who had neglected their grievances concerning the ritualistic and administrative practices which had been imposed on them. The rebellion in Liverpool was the culmination of discontent within the large Lancashire Province, which seemed to have been simmering since the Union of the Antients and the Moderns in 1813. The Lodge of Friendship No. 277 in Oldham had witnessed disruption in 1817, the bickering between the brethren splitting the lodge in two, the rift only being healed the following year after the direct intervention of the Provincial Grand Master, Francis Dukinfield Astley.[376]

Other areas also experienced disruption during the early part of the nineteenth century, such as in Gloucestershire, which suffered due to the personal dispute between the infamous William Pitt Fitzhardinge and the United Grand Lodge. Fitzhardinge, otherwise known as 'Bad Billy', was the illegitimate son of the fifth Earl of Berkeley and a close friend of George IV, who was also a Freemason. Fitzhardinge had a reputation of being a bully, and was a rampant womaniser with a fierce vindictive nature. He was a member of the Berkeley based Royal Lodge of Faith and Friendship No. 270, and forced the lodge to petition him for the position of Provincial Grand Master for Gloucestershire in 1835, a demand which resulted in a stand-off with the United Grand Lodge. They refused to accept Fitzhardinge as only the Grand Master himself had the right in choosing the Provincial Grand Masters. Because of this stand-off, the Province of Gloucestershire had no official serving Provincial Grand Master from 1835-1856, and thus had no regular Provincial Grand Lodge, the Province suffering as a result, with Freemasonry in the area declining severely. The Royal Lodge of Faith and Friendship has no records of meeting from 1851-1857, the brethren only officially meeting again the year after Fitzhardinge's death.[377]

Disruptions in Liverpool had previously taken place in 1806, when the Grand Secretary of the Antients Grand Lodge was forced to write a letter to Lodge No. 53b which met at the Cheshire Coffee House at Old Dock Gate, after receiving a complaint - apparently from other Liverpool Antient lodges - that the lodge was open at unreasonable hours and that several members of the lodge were confined for breaking into a

---

[376] See *Minutes of the Lodge of Friendship, No.277, Masonic Hall, Oldham, 26th of February, 1817 – 20th of May, 1818.* Not listed.
[377] See C.M. Malpus, *A History of the Royal Lodge of Faith and Friendship, No. 270,* (Berkeley, 2002).

warehouse and stealing. The Grand Secretary requested that the lodge should suspend all Masonic business until they were cleared of the charges brought against them, but despite this request, the lodge continued to meet. The Mayor of Liverpool became involved when he received a letter from the other Antient lodges of the port, and the Committee of the Masters of the Antient lodges in Liverpool started an official investigation which concluded that Lodge No. 53b had been involved in *'unmasonic behaviour'* resulting in their Warrant being withdrawn by the Antient Grand Lodge in 1807. The following year however, despite all the trouble, a number of the brethren of the erased lodge were desperately seeking a new Warrant to form a new lodge.[378]

The Liverpool rebellion of 1823 certainly reflected the spirit of internal bickering and *'unmasonic behaviour'* that had resulted in the closure of Lodge No. 53b. The rebellion was also tainted with an element of isolationism and networking 'cliques' within the lodges; some of the outlying industrial towns such as Wigan, Warrington and Ashton-in-Makerfield, had strong business links to Liverpool, mainly in relation to the cotton and coal trade, and these towns became the location for lodges which came under the sway of the rebels. Many of the Liverpool lodges, like other lodges based in the neighbouring industrial towns, were also suffering from low membership, and in the acrid climate where the threat of closure and the loss of traditional rights caused increasing dissatisfaction amongst the Masons, revolt spread quickly, gaining momentum and stamina.

Many of the Liverpool Masonic rebels, who were mainly a collective of Liverpool and Wigan based tradesmen and merchants, eventually returned to the United Grand Lodge renouncing their initial grievances and apologising. But a hardcore remained, and under the leadership of the tempestuous Michael Alexander Gage, the rebels created the groundbreaking *Magna Charta of Masonic Freedom* and formed the *Grand Lodge of Free and Accepted Masons of England According to the Old Constitutions*, which was later to become the *Grand Lodge held at Wigan*.[379] *The Magna*

[378] *Letters concerning the Lodge at the Cheshire Coffee House, Old Dock Gate, No. 53b [erased], Liverpool Annual Returns, AR/906, 1797-1809, Library and Museum of Freemasonry, UGLE, Great Queen Street, London.*

[379] The *Grand Lodge of Free and Accepted Masons of England According to the Old Constitutions*, first met officially in Liverpool in the July of 1823, which resulted in the declaration of the 'Magna Charta of Masonic Freedom' which was read out in the aforementioned meeting in the Shakespeare Tavern the following December. The 'Magna Charta of Masonic Freedom' was a document which put forward the theme of a new dawn in Masonry; free from what seen as the *'despotic power'* of the United Grand Lodge. The Grand Lodge first met in Wigan on the 1st of March, 1824, and with no

Charta of Masonic Freedom was a bold Masonic statement for the time, the majority of which was probably written by Gage himself. It reflected the rebels' grievances and outlined their hope for an independent future, but it also reflected Gage's egotistical personality, and set him up as a 'founding father' of the re-launch of 'Antient' Freemasonry. Ironically, many of the Liverpool based Masonic rebels were originally from outside Liverpool, such as Gage, who was born in Norfolk, John Robert Goepel, a Jeweller who originated from London, and James Broadhurst, a watchmaker from Great Sankey near Warrington.

James Broadhurst: naval hero, watchmaker and Masonic Rebel

A study of some of the men involved in the rebellion presents a fascinating insight into their character and the nature of the rebellion. James Broadhurst was baptised on the 25th of August, 1771, at St. Mary's Church, Great Sankey. He was the son of a watchmaker, and James followed in his father's footsteps, eventually moving to Liverpool, where he set himself up as a watchmaker and married Christian Litherland at St. Nicholas' Church in Liverpool in 1794. Christian was the sister of Liverpool watchmaker Peter Litherland, who had also originated from Warrington, and was famous for inventing the patent lever watch. Litherland had relocated to Liverpool in 1790, and James developed a close relationship with the fellow watchmaking family. With the outbreak of the French wars, Liverpool was rife with press gangs, and Broadhurst was forcibly *'inrolled'* into the Navy in 1795. He served as an able seaman on the *Namur*, taking part in the decisive Battle of Cape St. Vincent on the 14th of February 1797, which was an outstanding victory for the British, revealing the brilliance of Nelson.

In the December of 1800, Broadhurst was transferred to the *San Josef*, one of the two captured Spanish ships from the battle, which displayed Nelson's flag for a time in early 1801. It would be another two years before Broadhurst was released from service, and he returned to Liverpool and to watchmaking. He was later to receive the Naval General Service medal in 1847, the medal only being presented to the veterans still surviving at the time.[380] In 1817, like many veterans of the Napoleonic Wars, he entered into Freemasonry, joining the Merchants

---

mention of the Grand Lodge meeting in Liverpool again after 1825, it became known as The Wigan Grand Lodge.

[380] See 1841 Census for Liverpool, Lancashire. Liverpool Library. Ref: HO107/561/15, where Broadhurst is still working as a 'Watchmaker' aged 69.

Lodge, (listed as No. 442 on his certificate), and in 1820 he joined the Ancient Union Lodge (listed as No. 348 on the records), where he was to serve as Worshipful Master. Both of these lodges included members that became actively involved in the rebellion,[381] and Broadhurst, having served on the *San Josef* when Nelson had hoisted his flag on the ship, would have been seen as a naval hero, giving him a respect which would have made him an obvious leading figure in the rebellion.[382]

Broadhurst took an active part in the Provincial Grand Lodge meetings, and was quick to join his fellow Masonic tradesmen in the rebellion, sharing the same grievances, freely giving his signature to the document which outlined these issues. The discontent had developed a year after Broadhurst had become a Freemason, and quickly gathered pace, the Lancashire Province suffering in part due to the neglect of its Provincial Grand Master, Francis Dukinfield Astley, who never took action in Liverpool or Wigan to diffuse the situation. Perhaps, like his fellow tradesmen, after surviving through the Napoleonic Wars and hardships of the early decades of the nineteenth century, Broadhurst sought equality and freedom of speech, which was perhaps the initial attraction to a society which he felt held those qualities.

At a Provincial Grand Lodge meeting held at Ye Spread eagle Inn, Hanging Ditch, Manchester, in the October of 1818, a motion was passed which declared that any lodge whose membership is reduced to less than seven, should not be considered as a regular lodge and the Warrant be declared void. This motion, which was seen as a move to correct a defect in the *New Constitution-Book*, was actually made by Michael Alexander Gage with the overwhelming support of his fellow brethren. This motion was then duly passed on to the Board of General Purposes, but instead of it being presented by them to the United Grand Lodge, the motion was

---

[381] *Family papers of James Broadhurst.* Private collection. Not listed. See also *Minutes of the Ancient Union Lodge no. 203, 1795-1835, Garston Masonic Hall, Liverpool.* Not Listed. The lodge numbers have changed several times; see Appendix II.

[382] Nelson hoisted his flag on the *San Josef* in January, 1801, after arriving at Plymouth, but transferred his flag to the *St. George* less than a month later. The respect for able seamen who had served under Nelson is displayed in early nineteenth century literature, such as in *Redburn* by Herman Melville. *Redburn* was based on Melville's own visit to Liverpool in 1839, and in the book, on arriving in Liverpool docks, a description of the *'Dock-Wall Beggars'* is given. The sailors walking past the beggars ignored them, except for one; *'an old man-of-war's man, who had lost his leg at the battle of Trafalgar'*, his wooden leg being made from the oak timbers of the *Victory*. This beggar was respected by the sailors and *'plenty of pennies were tost into his poor-box'* by them. See Herman Melville, *Redburn*, (Middlesex: Penguin, 1987), p.261. A reference to the status of being a naval hero is also made in Charles Dickens's *David Copperfield*, by Mr. Micawber, a character who is down on his luck but who is also honest. Micawber describes himself as *'a gallant and eminent naval Hero'*, see Charles Dickens, *David Copperfield*, (New York: Sheldon and Company, 1863), p.138.

not reported and the Board remained silent on the issue. Certain Liverpool lodges, such as the Ancient Union Lodge No. 348, an old 'Antient' lodge, only had ten members at the time and the lodge had held an emergency meeting prior to the Provincial Grand Lodge meeting, sending a brother to attend, keeping an eye on the proceedings.[383]

As previously discussed in chapter 2, many lodges at this time, especially in the industrial areas of Lancashire, had suffered a decline in the wake of the Unlawful Societies Act of 1799. Freemasonry had suffered stagnation in the province of Lancashire, and only a few new lodges had been founded in the area during the early decades of the nineteenth century.[384] The majority of the Liverpool lodges, some suffering more than others from low attendance, bonded together; the low attendance leading some Freemasons to join other lodges, such as when Broadhurst and some other brethren from the Merchants Lodge - who were to play an important role in the rebellion - joined the Ancient Union Lodge, a move, which ensured not only the survival of the struggling lodge but would have created greater bonding between the brethren.[385]

In September 1819, it was proposed by Gage that a letter should be drafted,[386] addressed to the Grand Master himself – the Duke of Sussex, which would thus outline the grievances of Gage and his supporters; focussing on the fact that the motion passed during the meeting the previous year had not been presented by the Board of General Purposes to the United Grand Lodge. In the letter to the Duke, the rebels also referred to an incident in Bath, were Petitions for Royal Arch Chapters were dismissed by the Grand Chapter because it was:

'not desirable to make the Number of Chapters in any place equal to the Number of Lodges'.[387]

---

[383] Beesley, *Wigan Grand Lodge*, pp.2-4.

[384] A somewhat rare example of a surviving lodge that emerged during this stagnant period was the Blackburn based Lodge of Perseverance No. 345, constituted in 1815, a lodge that certainly lived up to its name.

[385] See *A List of the Members of the Ancient Union Lodge No. 203, 1792-1887, Harmonic Lodge No. 216, 1796-1836, & St. George's Lodge of Harmony No. 32, 1786-1836, C.D. Rom: 139 GRA/ANT/UNI, The Library and Museum of Freemasonry*, UGLE, Great Queen Street, London.

[386] Beesley, *Wigan Grand Lodge*, pp.4-5.

[387] A Copy of the Address to His Royal Highness Prince Augustus Frederick, The Duke of Sussex, Grand Master of the United Grand Lodge of Ancient Free and Accepted Masons of England, in Beesley, *Wigan Grand Lodge*, p.132.

The rebels seized upon this example, and, being of 'Antient' persuasion, they indicated that they saw the Royal Arch as part of Craft Masonry, and the rejection of the Petitions was an abuse of power. The Duke of Sussex however, did not reply to the letter. Indeed, the Masonic historian Beesley puts forward that the letter may have been destroyed as it was addressed directly to the Duke of Sussex and not addressed through the normal administrative channels of the United Grand Lodge.[388] The fact there was no reply only intensified the anger of the rebels and culminated in a decisive meeting in the Castle Inn, North Liverpool on the 26th of November of 1821 which would launch the revival of the 'Antients'.

The Duke seemed to have been quite dismissive of any disagreeable elements within Freemasonry and had little sympathy for rebels within the society. Such was the case with the outspoken Freemason Dr. George Oliver, whose removal from his Provincial office was engineered by the Duke after Oliver incurred his dislike.[389] The letter had been extremely direct and revealed the anger felt by the rebels, complaining how certain 'Modern' practices were being enforced and how new rules concerning the Royal Arch conflicted with the *'Ancient Landmarks'*. Gage and his fellow rebels had given the Duke plenty of time to reply, but with no response, it could be said the Duke had played into their hands.

This period was certainly a sensitive one, and certain local lodges had their own, slightly different – almost eccentric practices. Hampered by the neglect of the Provincial Grand Master within the rebellious areas of Liverpool and Wigan and with a growing feeling that their rights in the society were being eroded by the tampering of London based officials, the Liverpool rebels grew extremely sensitive to the transition of the Union regarding the 'Antient' and 'Modern' practices. Trouble had been simmering slowly during 1819, with disruptions in Liverpool with the Merchants Lodge, the Sea Captains Lodge and the Lodge of Harmony, and with Lodge No. 394 in Chorley, near Wigan. It had been thought that the trouble had been settled by a visit from the Provincial Grand Secretary in the May of that year, but it was just a sign of more serious trouble to come.

The decisive meeting at the Castle Inn, North Liverpool, in the November of 1821, set the final scene for rebellion. A document was drafted with 34 signatures, including Gage and Broadhurst, outlining the

---

[388] Beesley, *Wigan Grand Lodge*, p.5.
[389] R.S.E. Sandbach, *Priest and Freemason: The Life of George Oliver*, (Northamptonshire: The Aquarian Press, 1988), p.99.

dissatisfaction felt by the rebels. The other lodges included in the rebellion were Lodge No. 74 and Sincerity Lodge No. 486 (both based in Wigan), as well as a number of brethren from the Liverpool based Mariners Lodge No. 466, the Ancient Union Lodge, the Sea Captains Lodge and the Merchants Lodge.

Broadhurst was the Worshipful Master of the Ancient Union Lodge in 1821, and along with a number of brethren including William Walker and Thomas Berry, he represented their lodge in the rebellion, adding their signatures to the Castle Inn document. Broadhurst, apart from being the senior member of his lodge, became vital in gaining support for the rebellion from the Ancient Union Lodge, and would have been secure in gaining an important role in the rebel Grand Lodge. Representatives from Broadhurst's original lodge; the Merchants Lodge, included liquor merchant John Eltonhead – who later was connected to the Castle Inn as landlord,[390] tailor Daniel Mackay, tanner John Manifold and excise man Samuel Money Blogg.

Michael Alexander Gage: tailor and Masonic Rebel

The 34 brethren who signed the document were subsequently suspended by the United Grand Lodge, and Gage's lodge, Lodge No.31, was erased, an action that mirrored the erasing of Lodge No.53b in 1807. This action created further isolation for the suspended rebels as they were not allowed to visit any other lodges, ultimately providing greater bonding between them and giving them further cause to complain about the *'tyranny'* of the United Grand Lodge. The dissent spread rapidly through Liverpool as certain lodges began to support their fellow brethren. The Liverpool based Sea Captain's Lodge No. 140 threatened to separate itself entirely from the United Grand Lodge if Lodge No. 31 was not re-instated, and by the middle of 1822, an increased number of 65 brethren from Liverpool and Wigan were recorded as being suspended.

Gage's Lodge No. 31 had been the 'senior' lodge amongst the 'Antient' lodges in Liverpool, having the oldest Warrant, and therefore having the position to settle the disputes that occurred within other

---

[390] Liverpool Mercury Friday 16th of May 1823, Issue 624, in which is stated that *'A well accustomed Inn, known by the name of the Castle Inn North, situated on the West side of Scotland Road, now in the occupation of Mr John Eltonhead, with good stabling for 7-8 horses and rooms over.'* Also in the Liverpool Mercury 4th of November, 1825, issue 754, which recorded the death of Mary Kirby age 67, widow of Thomas Kirby and mother of John Eltonhead, Castle Inn North, on the 29th of October 1825. *Family papers of John Eltonhead.* Private collection. Not listed.

'Antient' lodges within the town. The lodge had been called Lodge No. 20 before the Union, but had been subsequently re-numbered, and, in doing so, had lost some of its local prestige. This re-numbering was obviously a sore point for the lodge as they reverted back to No 20 on the creation of the rebel Grand Lodge in 1823. The Warrant for Lodge No. 20 had been purchased by a number of brethren from the Ancient Union Lodge shortly after it was founded in 1792, and, with the original Warrant dating from 1753, Lodge No. 20 became the oldest 'Antient' lodge operating in Liverpool, out-dating and thus displacing the local St. George's Lodge, which, despite being founded in 1786, had a Warrant which dated from 1755.[391] St. George's Lodge became extremely aggressive in its attitude to the rebels, particular against the conduct of Gage and Lodge No. 31, and when looking at the membership makeup of the St. George's Lodge, a greater number of local gentlemen are evident, whereas in Lodge No. 31, the membership makeup had a greater number of tradesmen, such as Gage who was a tailor. There was a clear issue of class within the dispute, and this may explain the anger felt by Gage - a man with aspirations.

On the 2nd of December, 1822, a meeting was held at the Lodge of Harmony, No. 385, at the Magpie and Stump in Key Street, Liverpool. The Lodge of Harmony, like the Ancient Union Lodge, had belonged to the 'Antient' Grand Lodge before the Union in 1813. This heated meeting had visitors from The Merchant, Mariners, and Ancient Union Lodges, all local Liverpool lodges which had certain members involved in the rebellion. The meeting revealed a lodge in crisis as the Worshipful Master and Wardens were appointed during an emergency meeting, and not elected or installed as they usually were. The result of this particular gathering was the wish by all the members present to write a letter to the United Grand Lodge declaring the present state of the Lodge of Harmony. It seems that the lodge decided against the rebellion and kept their distance, deciding to give their support to the United Grand Lodge of England. Despite this show of loyalty, the Worshipful Master at the time of the meeting was suspended in 1824 for twelve months, and another brother for seven years, for what is described as *'unmasonic conduct'*.

---

[391] St. George's Lodge of Harmony No. 32 had been No. 25c, changing to No. 38 in 1814. It was renumbered again to No. 35 in 1832, and changed to its present number in 1863. See Lane's Masonic Records 1717-1894 online: http://freemasonry.dept.shef.ac.uk/lane/ [accessed 25th of January, 2010]

On the 5th of March, 1823, the United Grand Lodge finally expelled 26 brethren, stating that the rebels had:

> *'been found guilty of various Acts of insubordination against the Authority of the Grand Lodge, and having been summoned to show cause why they should not therefore be expelled from the Craft; have not sent any sufficient apology for their late misconduct'.*

Their rebellious activities were described as an *'insult'* by the United Grand Lodge and the brethren, having *'violated the laws of the Craft'*, were ostracized.[392] Gage and his followers were now free to proceed with their master-plan – to resurrect the 'Antient' Grand Lodge. The plan was certainly to go national and to spread the influence of the rebel Grand Lodge, and it was declared that the causes which led to the re-establishment of the 'Antient' Grand Lodge were to be advertised in four of the London Papers, a public declaration which would be guaranteed to reach the eyes of the leaders of the United Grand Lodge.

Gage took on the role of Deputy Grand Master, while George Woodcock Esq. was duly elected as the Grand Master of the Rebel Grand Lodge. Woodcock was a prominent member of the Barnsley based Friendly Lodge No. 557 and fully supported the *'Antient landmarks of Freemasonry'*. He was in correspondence with Gage and Lodge No. 31 in Liverpool from early 1823, Woodcock seeking to write an eight part resolution which outlined the *'sorrow and regret at these severe measures which the G. Lodge has thought it proper to exercise towards Twenty-six respectable members of the Society'*.[393] Woodcock struck up a long-distance friendship with Gage, with the new Grand Master seeking advice from him on numerous occasions in regard to the administration of the Rebel Grand Lodge. The correspondence continued between them until Gage distanced himself from Freemasonry; in a letter to Woodcock dated June 1828, Gage declined meeting Woodcock and the brethren of the Barnsley lodge in Manchester, and also declined an invitation by Woodcock to spend Christmas at Barnsley. Gage also outlined in the letter how he had been putting Masonry before business for too long, and that he must now start devoting himself to the inhabitants of Liverpool and concentrate on his *'plan of Liverpool'*.[394]

---

[392] Beesley, *Wigan Grand Lodge*, pp.16-19.
[393] Will Read, 'The Spurious Lodge and Chapter at Barnsley', in *AQC*, Vol. 90, (1978), pp.1-36, on p.10.
[394] Ibid., p.26 and p.31.

The new Grand Master was listed as a Gentleman in the minutes of his lodge meetings, but he worked as a bank manager for a fellow member of the lodge; John Staniforth Beckett – a member of a local banking family. Despite this, Woodcock appears to have been in control of the lodge and certainly engineered the lodge joining the rebellion; a decision that split his lodge in two, mirroring the incident which had occurred at the Lodge of Friendship in Oldham. Woodcock certainly shared the same spirit as his fellow rebels in Liverpool and Wigan, though events were to dampen the fire of revolt.

The new Grand Lodge soon ran into trouble; at a meeting of the Grand Lodge held at the Cross Keys in Wigan on the 23rd of June, 1824, the ex-Grand Secretary John Eden was:

> *'for ever expelled…in consequence of his having Embezzled the funds of the Grand Lodge for his contempt of Summonses and other unmasonic conduct.*[395]

Eden had been a member of Gage's lodge, and this would have been a personal blow to the leader and would have created difficulties for the financial status in the early days of the rebel Grand Lodge. Part of the Grand Secretary's job would have been to assist in looking after funds, and Eden had certainly abused the trust that had been placed in him. The returns paid to the Grand Secretary from certain lodges under the sway of the new rebel Grand Lodge, such as the Barnsley lodge, had not been passed on to the Grand Treasurer, Eden fraudulently using the funds. It seems that this incident had certainly shaken the fledgling rebel Grand Lodge, affecting the brethren deeply, some of whom became quickly disenchanted.

During the same year, James Broadhurst turned his back on the rebellion and conformed. Along with a number of other rebels, Broadhurst presented an apology to the United Grand Lodge, which brought them back into the fold. He immediately rejoined the Merchants Lodge, but his payments ceased in 1826, the experience of the rebellion and the subsequent fall out perhaps affecting the camaraderie of the lodge. Out of the original rebels representing the Ancient Union Lodge, only Thomas Berry remained to become an active member of what would become the Grand Lodge of Wigan, Berry having attended the first meeting of the rebel Grand Lodge at the Shakespeare Tavern in 1823 and serving as Secretary in the March meeting of 1825.

---

[395] Beesley, *Wigan Grand Lodge*, pp.46-47.

George Woodcock's Barnsley Lodge became alarmed at the financial irregularities occurring in the administration of the rebel Grand Lodge and formally separated themselves from their Lancashire brethren in 1827, Woodcock going on to resign his office as Grand Master.[396] The Barnsley lodge – being the only Yorkshire lodge in support of the rebellion – thus styled themselves as *'The Yorkshire Lodge of Ancient Masons'*, and Woodcock continued to lead his lodge in isolation until his death in 1842.[397]

If Broadhurst and the rest of the fellow Liverpool brethren that had apologised would have stayed with the rebels, the rebel Grand Lodge may have remained in Liverpool, and not have moved permanently to Wigan. Gage himself seemed to have slowly distanced himself from the rebels, and it was if the Liverpool brethren were becoming disillusioned, the energy of the rebels quickly ebbing away. Broadhurst continued to work in Liverpool as a watchmaker, and died in October 1851, being buried at the Wesleyan Brunswick Chapel in Liverpool.

The Wigan Grand Lodge

The Masonic Rebellion in Liverpool had included from the outset a number of Wigan lodges, and after 1825, no minutes exist of the Grand Lodge meeting in Liverpool, though in Gage's resignation letter written in 1842, he stated that he had:

> *'not had the pleasure of meeting the Grand Lodge, nor in fact any private Lodge during the last fifteen years'.*[398]

The makeup of the Liverpool and Wigan lodges that were involved in the rebellion were similar, with the majority being tradesmen and merchants, all sharing the same grievances, but the shift from Liverpool to Wigan was to become a permanent one. Another leading Liverpool rebel, John Eltonhead, returned to the United Grand Lodge on the 7th of March 1827,[399] the same year that Gage had stated that he had last attended a lodge. With these two leading rebels gone, it left only a handful of active Liverpool brethren, such as Thomas Page, Thomas

[396] Read, *AQC*, Vol. 90, pp. 16-17.
[397] Ibid., p.23.
[398] An excerpt from Michael Alexander Gage's resignation letter, 10th of June, 1842, in Beesley, *Wigan Grand Lodge*, p.85.
[399] Michael J. Spurr, 'The Liverpool Rebellion', in *AQC*, Vol. 85, (1972), pp.29-60, on p.42.

Berry and John Robert Goepel, mixing with an influx of leading Wigan rebels, such as John Atherton, Ralph Ball and Robert Bolton.

Despite the abolition of slavery in 1807, the port of Liverpool continued to grow as merchants and investors found new trade and new business. William Ewart, the Liverpool broker and a leading member of the Merchants Lodge, became a founder of the Committee to support the proposition of the building of the Liverpool and Manchester railway.[400] On the 15th of September, 1830, the Liverpool and Manchester railway was finally opened by the Freemason the Duke of Wellington, an event attended by an array of local dignitaries, and connected the port, not only to the cotton producing town of Manchester, but the whole of the industrial north-west of England, bringing the area closer together, cutting down the transport time between Liverpool and Manchester to an hour.

The railway also brought social and business networking closer together, and especially aided the cotton, coal and iron making industries in the area.[401] The north-west of England soon became criss-crossed by interlinking railways and within a few years of the opening of the Liverpool to Manchester railway, the cotton and coal producing town of Wigan became connected, this new easy transport bringing the Masonic rebels closer together. Indeed, it was not long after the introduction of the railways that the Masonic rebels moved their centre of operations to Wigan, though a number of Liverpool brethren still attended. The rebellion in Liverpool had struck a blow to Freemasonry in the port, but, like Masonry in its neighbouring industrial towns, by the mid-nineteenth century, the society had started to expand. The newly constructed Provincial Grand Lodge of West Lancashire – formed in 1826 to make the large province of Lancashire more manageable - soon made its presence known within Liverpool, and prominent local figures such as Robertson Gladstone were appearing in the membership list of St. George's Lodge of Harmony – especially as the lodge could now claim to be the oldest surviving lodge in the area.[402]

There is a large gap in the minute book from the last known meeting in Liverpool in 1825, until April the 13th, 1838 when the Grand Lodge

---

[400] John Macnab, *History of The Merchants Lodge, No. 241, Liverpool, 1780-2004*, Second Edition, (Liverpool, 2004), p.34.

[401] 'The Manchester and Liverpool Rail-Road' in the *Monthly Supplement of The Penny Magazine of The Society for the Diffusion of Useful Knowledge, March 31 to April 30, 1833*, pp.1-3.

[402] *List of Members for Lodge No. 35 held at the Adelphi Hotel – Liverpool, December 18th, 1839.* Masonic Hall, Hope Street, Liverpool. Not listed.

suddenly met in Wigan at the Hole I'th' Wall tavern in the Market Place. Gage was not in attendance, but original rebels Thomas Page, from the 'Antient' Liverpool Lodge No. 31, (renumbered to its original pre-Union number of 20 after the rebellion) and Robert Bolton, from the Wigan based Sincerity Lodge No. 492, were present. A new Grand Master William Farrimond Esq. was elected, officially replacing George Woodcock who – according to the surviving minutes - had never actually attended the Grand Lodge meetings, and the rebel Grand Lodge began a new phase as it took on more of a Wigan identity, gradually severing its ties with Liverpool.

After 1838, the meetings for the Grand Lodge took place regularly every quarter in various Wigan taverns, some of which were run by its own Freemasons, such as the Hole I'th' Wall which was run by Brother Thomas Johnson; the Banker's Arms, which was run by Brother Thomas Bolton, and the Angel Inn in nearby Ashton-in-Makerfield, which was run by Brother Timothy Turton. Wigan was well placed in the centre of Lancashire, and at its height in the early 1840s, the Wigan Grand Lodge had lodges in Wigan, Liverpool, Ashton-in-Makerfield, Warrington, and had been in close contact with an 'Antient' lodge in Lynn Regis in Norfolk, which may have had more to do with Gage having originated from there and having continuing links with the town.[403]

By mid 1842, Gage finally resigned from the Wigan Grand Lodge, angry at not being asked to review the re-numbering of lodges and the granting of new Warrants, a decision that had taken place in a meeting held on the 15th of August, 1838. The Wigan based Sincerity Lodge became Lodge No. 1, and the Liverpool Lodge No.20, became Lodge No. 2, a move which may have added to Gage's anger and revealed how Wigan had become more dominant and more pro-active in the administration. This new pro-active stance by the new Wigan based Grand Lodge began to pay off, and it slowly begun to spread its influence, having five lodges under its jurisdiction by the early 1840s, though George Woodcock's Barnsley lodge had declined an offer to join the Wigan Grand Lodge, and a lodge in nearby Warrington, called the Lodge of Knowledge, was relatively short lived. Two more lodges were given Warrants; one based in nearby Ashton-in-Makerfield named Harmony and Perseverance, the other, named the St. Paul's Lodge, which was based in Ashton-under-Lyne. All of these lodges except for the Lodge of Sincerity seemed to have disappeared by the 1860s.

---

[403] 1851 Census for Liverpool, Lancashire. Liverpool Library. Ref: HO153/2183.

Gage had always been given the title of Deputy Grand Master, courteously being given the task of overlooking some of the activities by correspondence. However, he was deeply upset that the 'Magna Charta' had been breached, as it had originally stated that on the creation of the rebel Grand Lodge, all lodge numbers per 1823 had been reverted back to their pre-Union numbers before 1813. On the 10th of June 1842, Gage wrote a lengthy letter of resignation, in which he outlined his feelings at not being asked to review the decision of the new Warrants. He was a proud man, and as he was the person who had instigated the Liverpool Masonic Rebellion, he appeared to have been hurt by the decision. In the letter, he made references to the Magna Charta of Masonic Freedom, reminding the brethren of their origins:

'It was therefore from an ardent desire to hand down to posterity the Ancient Landmarks Customs and Usage of Masonry that we re-established the Ancient Grand Lodge this act however could only justified by a strict Adhereance on our parts to the Ancient Laws Landmarks and Usages of Masonry. [404]

Gage also sternly refused a request to write a pamphlet detailing the causes of the rebellion. Despite Gage's coldness, he was still the spiritual leader of the 'Antients', and in the reply to his resignation, Gage was described by the Grand Master as a man whom:

'the tyrants in the Masonic world would have always looked upon with dread'. [405]

Perhaps Gage's opinion was not sought by the Wigan Grand Lodge in fear of his reaction to the changes. The Magna Charta of Masonic Freedom, originally written under the influence of Gage, was re-written in 1839. This re-organisation, decided by a Grand Lodge now dominated by Wigan brethren, began to forge a new identity. The original rebels, Gage in particular, were still held in high regard, seen as the founding fathers of the resurrected 'Antient' Grand Lodge, and Robert Bolton's reply to Gage's resignation, though tinted with expectation and hinting at Gage's lack of interest, effectively left the door open for his return. Gage however, never came back and never replied to Bolton's letter. Increasing the isolation of the Wigan Grand Lodge, Thomas Page and John Robert Goepel, two of the last remaining original rebels from

---

[404] An excerpt from Michael Alexander Gage's resignation letter, 10th of June, 1842, in Beesley, *Wigan Grand Lodge*, p.84.
[405] Ibid., pp.83-88.

Liverpool, returned to the United Grand Lodge on the 1st of December, 1858.[406] Like Gage, John Robert Goepel had dramatically changed his career, going from a jeweller to a dentist after the Masonic Rebellion, a profession that he engaged in until his death in 1862.[407]

Gage was by this time older and was still based in Liverpool, and though seemingly showing a lack of interest in Masonry, he still held a sense of importance when it came to his position within the Wigan Grand Lodge. His disinterest may have been as a result of his close colleague John Eden's embezzlement of Masonic funds, possibly the re-location of the Grand Lodge to Wigan, or perhaps down to Gage having a family and changing his career from a tailor to a Land Surveyor, Gage going on to publish a map of Liverpool which was based on his surveys of the port in 1836.[408] He was however, to remain a rebel to the end, effectively rebelling against the rebels. Gage was always an obstinate man, passionate, arrogant and confident in the face of opposition, and his fight for the cause of Antient Freemasonry had been extremely fierce and pro-active.

He held the respect of his fellow rebels, and without Gage, there would have been no Wigan Grand Lodge, his leadership influencing its original design. He had aspired to greater things, Gage, a mere tailor having written to the Duke of Sussex complaining about the way certain brethren in Liverpool were being mistreated being an excellent example of an attempt to break down the class and social divisions. Gage died in 1867 aged 79, though as his ex-Masonic rebel had noted, Gage would continue to inspire the Wigan Grand Lodge.[409] The success of the rebellion – albeit on a local basis - is revealed in its organization and the pro-active stance of the Wigan Grand Lodge, its effect on the United Grand Lodge also proving permanent, with the rather large Lancashire

[406] Spurr, 'The Liverpool Rebellion', *AQC*, Vol. 85, p.42.
[407] Goepel's occupation is given as 'Dentist' age 50, and his birthplace as London in the 1851 Census for Liverpool, Lancashire. Liverpool Library, Ref: HO107/2180. However, Goepel was listed as a 'Jeweller', aged 40 in the 1841 Census for Liverpool, Lancashire. Liverpool Library, Ref: HO107/556/28. Deaths registered in June, 1862, John Robert Goepel, Liverpool. Ref: 8b. 113.
[408] 1851 Census for Liverpool, Lancashire. Liverpool Library. Ref: HO153/2183, where Gage's occupation is listed as a 'Civil Engineer', and also in the Church Records for St. Peters, Liverpool; *Baptism of William Henry, son of Michael Alexander Gage, Land Surveyor, & his wife Sarah*, 25th of December, 1833. Liverpool Library. Ref: 283PET2/21. Also see the 1841 Census for Liverpool, Lancashire. Liverpool Library. Ref: HO107/558/3. Gage's occupation is given here as 'Land Surveyor'. A map of Liverpool published in 1836 was based on Gage's expert survey of the port, see Liverpool Map, 1836, M. A. Gage, Maritime Archives and Library, Drawer Z/F3.
[409] Deaths registered in January, February and March, 1867, Michael Alexander Gage, aged 79, West Derby, Liverpool. Ref: 8b. 331.

province being divided in two shortly after the rebellion, creating the more manageable western and eastern divisions.

The end of the 'Antients'

The minute book for the Wigan Grand Lodge ends in 1866, though James Miller, who wrote his memories of the Lodge of Sincerity in the 1950s, stated that the Grand Lodge of Wigan did survive, supervising the last remaining lodge, the Lodge of Sincerity, its last Grand Master being John Mort who served as Grand Master from 1886 until the lodge returned to the United Grand Lodge in 1913. James Miller was a young man when he was initiated into the Lodge of Sincerity in 1908. He followed his father, his grandfather, and great-grandfather, in becoming a Freemason under the Wigan Grand Lodge, and would become instrumental in the survival of its memory. Miller discusses in his memoirs the festival of St. John, which was celebrated by all lodges before the Union, and mentions the practice of the Royal Arch; its apron being worn by the Grand Master, John Mort, at all times. The Knights Templar was also practised, and Miller mentions a sickness and burial society within the lodge, which may be a continuation of the 'funeral fund' which was mentioned in the minutes of the Wigan Grand Lodge in 1839.

John Mort seems to have held the Grand Lodge of Wigan together during its final years, and he appears in the Wigan Grand Lodge minutes for the first time in 1866, when Peter Seddon was Grand Master. Mort, like Miller, passed on his memories of the Wigan Grand Lodge, enabling Eustace Beesley to write his *history* in 1920. According to Miller, Mort was initiated in 1864. He served as Master of the Sincerity Lodge on a number of occasions, and became the last Grand Master in 1886. Miller paints a cosy picture of an isolated lodge filled with friends and family members; Mort's son, also called John, was a member, and Miller's uncle, Richard Warburton, was initiated on the same day as Miller was. Miller recited the merriment of the lodge festive board, where each member of the lodge was allowed one drink from the lodge funds. When the drinks had been consumed, the Worshipful Master would call out *'mortar'*, and a Steward would take the trowel around so each Brother could give his contribution to the next round of drinks. After these funds had been exhausted, a cry for *'more mortar'* would ensure further drinks, accompanied by the fine tenor voice of John Mort jnr, who was also a member of the Wigan Parish Church Choir.

These eccentricities reflect the lodge as an apparent time capsule, surviving in isolation, having an independent and inward looking attitude. The drinking and socialising seemed to have created a deep bond between the brethren, keeping the last remaining lodge alive. The Grand Lodge had met at numerous inns and taverns around Wigan, some meetings taking place in the centre of Wigan, such as the infamous Dog Inn at Wigan Market Place, where the Grand Lodge met on a number of occasions in 1839. Other meetings took place on the periphery of the Wigan area, such as the Angel Inn in Ashton-in-Makerfield. The use of these inns were vital as important meeting places for the Grand Lodge, many of them, like the Angel Inn and the Rope & Anchor Inn in Scholes, were run by fellow brethren, enabling the Grand Lodge to establish regular meetings, ensuring its continuity and allowing it to carry on its own unique culture.

As the Wigan Grand Lodge descended into solitary isolation, 'regular' Freemasonry under the United Grand Lodge of England flourished in Wigan; the Provincial Grand Lodge of West Lancashire met there in October 1886, and in the November of the same year the Wigan Freemasons under the United Grand Lodge celebrated the centenary of the Lodge of Antiquity No. 178. More visits by prominent figures within the United Grand Lodge followed; in October 1889, the Freemasons accompanied the Mayor to church and a sermon was given by the Grand Chaplain of England the Rev. T. Barton Spencer. Perhaps these very public displays by the ever more powerful and confident United Grand Lodge sent a message to the dwindling Wigan Grand Lodge.

Indeed, 'regular' Freemasonry in Wigan, like in other industrial towns at the time, attracted the local aristocracy. One such local aristocrat was James Ludovic Lindsay FRS, who resided at Haigh Hall, an elegant neo-classical manor house on the outskirts of Wigan.[410] Lindsay was to become the 26th Earl of Crawford and 9th Earl of Balcarres, and he founded the Lindsay Lodge No. 1335 in 1870, Lord Lindsay serving as Conservative MP for Wigan from 1874-1880. Lindsay became as much a central figure for Freemasonry in Wigan as Sir Gilbert Greenall was in Warrington, and like Greenall, Lindsay became involved in the development of local education and charity; his family had been

---

[410] James Ludovic Lindsay was first initiated into the Isaac Newton University Lodge No. 859 in Cambridge in February 1866. He subsequently joined a number of other lodges including the Prince of Wales Lodge No. 259 in 1868 and the Lodge of Edinburgh No. 1 in 1870. Lord Lindsay – as he was styled from his grandfather's death in 1869 until he succeeded to his later titles on his father's death in 1880 – also served as Deputy Provincial Grand Master for West Lancashire.

concerned in the opening of the local Mining and Mechanical School, and Lord Lindsay had been involved in the building of local school houses.[411] Lindsay became a celebrated astronomer, and, together with his father, they had built up one of the most impressive libraries in Britain; the *'Bibliotheca Lindesiana'*. Lindsay also constructed a private observatory in Dunecht, Aberdeenshire, his interest in astronomy leading him to mount expeditions to Cadiz in 1870 to observe an eclipse of the sun and to Mauritius in 1874 to observe the transit of Venus. He also made a substantial donation of astronomical instruments and books from the *'Bibliotheca Lindesiana'* on the history of astronomy by the likes of Johannes Kepler and Isaac Newton so the new Royal Observatory in Edinburgh could be founded, the observatory opening in 1896. In 1910, Haigh Hall played host to a visiting contingent of Manchester Masons, again confirming the power and status of 'regular' Freemasonry against the increasingly secluded Wigan Grand Lodge.

Miller was to witness the end of the Grand Lodge of Wigan, its last surviving lodge being isolated and alone, and as a relic of the 'Antients' of the eighteenth century, it was not recognised by other local Masonic lodges. Despite the ruling passed in the early days of the Grand Lodge that it was forbidden to discuss the United Grand Lodge, Miller mentions that *'heated arguments'* on re-joining had been going on for two or three years leading up to 1913. The matter was brought to a head, as Miller puts it, in 1912, when an un-named newly raised brother received an invitation to visit a Masonic lodge under the United Grand Lodge of England. On presenting himself to the lodge, and showing his certificate, he was refused admission, which led him to write a rather abusive letter, calling the lodge a bogus institution, and stating he was the victim of a fraud. This incident seemed to confirm that the Sincerity Lodge, the last surviving lodge under the Grand Lodge of Wigan, had a bleak future, and if it was to survive, it needed to adapt.

A meeting between both Grand Lodges was sought, and the Sincerity Lodge was visited by Worshipful Brother J. D. Murrey from Provincial Grand Lodge, who was satisfied with what he witnessed of the working of the lodge. Miller recites that developments moved quickly, and the lodge could keep the name 'Sincerity' but would have to be re-numbered.

---

[411] See Cornelius McLeod Percy, *History of the Mining and Technical School, Wigan,* (Wigan, 1900). The Agent of the Earl of Crawford had chaired a Public meeting in 1857 which duly decided that the Wigan Mining and Mechanical School should be established. Many public buildings in the Wigan area bare the distinctive Crawford and Balcarres mark on the date stone, an example of one such building is the School House on Red Rock Lane near Haigh Village which was built in 1871.

Ironically, the issue over the renumbering of lodges after the Union was an issue which had moved Gage to rebel against the United Grand Lodge in the first place. The lodge would lose its original number of 486, it would surrender its old Warrant, and despite being founded in 1786, it would have a new number of 3677 and in the official United Grand Lodge records, the Lodge of Sincerity would have the 26th of September, 1913 as the date of its consecration.

All the brethren of the Wigan Grand Lodge then had to be initiated, passed and raised, in a ceremony which was reminiscent of the pre-Union 're-making' ceremony, when an 'Antient' Mason joined a 'Modern' lodge. Miller seemed to have mixed feelings of his lodge rejoining the United Grand Lodge, and he ended his memoirs with a haunting image:

But one can still wonder if the ghosts of those old brethren of an unrecognised Lodge still linger around Sincerity'.[412]

Miller was speaking with some regret of the surrender of what was effectively the last surviving relic of the 'Antients' and was perhaps referring to the ghost of Michael Alexander Gage, still lingering in the lodge room with his Masonic rebels. It had been 90 years since Gage presided over the first meeting at the Shakespeare Tavern in Liverpool, and in the Masonic Rooms at Wigan, Gage's dream finally ended, as the last surviving lodge under the Grand Lodge of Wigan re-joined the United Grand Lodge of England, bringing the rebellion to an end.

The rebellion represented feelings of dissatisfaction and discrimination amongst some Freemasons, especially within the then large Lancashire province. Feeling that their grievances were being unanswered, they broke away from the United Grand Lodge in London and went their own way. The rebellion can also be seen to reflect a revolt by the merchants and tradesmen of Liverpool against the *'tyranny'* of the Duke of Sussex; Freemasons and tradesmen such as Gage and Broadhurst seeing the leadership of the United Grand Lodge firmly being in the hands of London based aristocracy, a leadership that had neglected the issues raised by the brethren of the leading port in the industrial north-west of England. This is evident, not only in the name and the wording of the 'Magna Charta of Masonic Freedom', but also in the aggressive attitude of the leading rebels, some of whom, such as Gage, clearly had personal

---

[412] *Reminiscences of an Unrecognised Lodge, namely Old Sincerity Lodge No. 486 by James Miller.* Some of Miller's regalia is currently held by the Library of the United Grand Lodge of England. Many thanks to the Rev. Neville Cryer who supplied a copy of the memoirs of James Miller. Not listed.

aspirations. The rebellion was the last stand of the 'Antients', and despite it taking place, the expansion of Freemasonry under the United Grand Lodge of England continued apace during the later half of the nineteenth century.

Chapter 7

The Royal Arch and the Pathway to the Search for Lost Knowledge

'It is regrettable that Masonic research during recent years has failed to throw light upon the origin and early history of the ROYAL ARCH'
Arthur Edward Waite, 1921[413]

'…go and prepare for the foundation of the Second Temple. But let me lay this injunction upon you – that should you meet with anything belonging to the First Temple, you will communicate no part thereof to any one, until you have faithfully made your report to the Sanhedrim here sitting in chapter.'
Richard Carlile, 1825[414]

'In 1740 he (Ramsay) came over to England, and remained in this country for more than a year; after which he returned to France, where the rage for innovation had now fairly commenced. It was during this period, I am persuaded, that the English Royal Arch was fabricated; for very soon afterwards, the ancients publicly announced that 'Ancient Masonry consisted of four degrees' while modern Masonry had only three, the fourth signifying the Royal Arch'.
Dr. George Oliver, The American Freemason, 1859[415]

The 'Moderns' and the 'Antients' had finally come together in Union in 1813, the rift between the two Grand Lodges being healed. One of the main problems had been the Royal Arch ritual, seen by the 'Antients' as a fourth degree, but practiced by the 'Moderns' as the completion of the third degree. The bitterness and feuding had escalated until both sides finally came together, and after the Union, it was settled that the Royal Arch was the completion of the third degree, though was practiced in separate 'Chapters', the Chapter room set out differently than the Craft lodge room. Despite this, the Royal Arch was still referred to as a fourth

---

[413] Arthur Edward Waite, *New Encyclopaedia of Freemasonry Vol. II*, (New York: Wings Books, 1996), p.376.
[414] Richard Carlile, *Manual of Freemasonry*, (Croydon: New Temple Press, 1912), p.121.
[415] George Oliver, 'Origin of the Royal Arch Degree', in *The American Freemason Magazine*, (New York, 1859), p.216.

degree by some stubborn lodges until around 1850 and the rebel Grand Lodge of Wigan still practised the Royal Arch as a separate degree. In fact during the Liverpool Masonic Rebellion, the Royal Arch became a point of debate.

In my book *The Genesis of Freemasonry* I put forward how Dr. John Theophilus Desaguliers had reconstructed the Masonic ritual in the 1720s, creating the three degree structure set within Solomon's Temple, describing its initial construction by chief architect Hiram Abiff, disclosing his murder and the attempt at raising him from the dead to regain his lost knowledge. The Royal Arch ritual continues this theme, with the rebuilding of Solomon's Temple under Zerubbabel and the search for lost knowledge within the Temple ruins, the ritual revealing a number of lost artefacts set within the keystones of three arches in the Temple. These artefacts were lost in the destruction of the original Temple, but with their discovery, the Temple could be reconstructed, the divine measurements of God being found to recreate the most sacred holy place on Earth.

The Royal Arch ritual has obscure origins, and the first tantalising mentions of the ritual reveal hints that it was put together after the three Masonic degrees were formed, continuing the mystical dramatisation of the building and rebuilding of Solomon's Temple. Elements of the ritual have all the hallmarks of being put together by Desaguliers himself, the ritual continuing the education of the Master Mason, and revealing the Biblical story of Solomon's Temple with its embedded themes of the search for hidden knowledge. It does make sense that this could be a fourth degree, and it could be easy to speculate that there could have been ideas for other degree rituals to follow it; perhaps continuing the story of the Temple, presenting the construction of Herod's Temple and completing the cycle. Perhaps because it was left unfinished may be the reason why, after the death of Desaguliers, the Royal Arch was seen as an awkward 'add on' to the third degree, it should have been the fourth degree, but without other rituals to complete the story, it caused debate and confusion, especially with the 'Moderns'.

The ritual reveals similar language to the third degree, with poetical elements and references to Newtonian language, the *'science of sciences'* taking the Master Mason to a higher level of secret knowledge. Indeed, Carlile writing in his *Manual of Freemasonry* in the 1820s calls the Royal Arch a degree in its own right, and the story does stand alone rather than acting as a mere add-on to the third degree. In this sense, the Royal Arch seems to be the next chapter in the unfolding story of the Temple, taking the search for hidden knowledge and the understanding of the divine measurement of God to another educational level. As the rebuilding of the Temple is announced, *'three sojourners from Babylon'* arrive to offer their services in the rebuilding. They explain that they suffer the wrath of God because their ancestors *'deviated from the true Masonic principles'* and *'ran into every kind of wickedness'*. These three men are thus travelling on a path of enlightenment, and have been sent by God to complete a task which will not only redeem them, but will educate them. They *'deem the lowest situation in the Lord's house an honour'* and beg for employment as labourers. During the construction work to rebuild the Temple, a discovery is made and the workers report back:

'being at our work early this morning, our companion broke up the ground with his pickaxe; and we judging from the sound thereof that it was hollow, called upon our companion with his shovel to clear away the loose earth, and discovered the perfect crown of an arch. With my crow-bar I removed the key-stone.' [416]

The Royal Arch ritual describes an ancient archaeological excavation, and the workers from Babylon are deemed trustworthy as they report back to *'the Most Excellent Principal'* with their discoveries. Like the third degree, a moralistic and educational drama is being enacted, and though not exactly of Shakespearian quality, the ritual is vibrant, embracing themes of how the weakness and wickedness of man can lead to the loss of God's sacred word; the divine measurement of the Temple itself. Through trust, unity, and industry, the workers first retrieve a lost scroll from an excavated arch, a scroll which is the long-lost book of the holy law. The workers return to the excavation, and find a second *'crown of an arch'*, though after removing the key-stone, they find nothing. However, judging from the hollow sound beneath, the workers continue to search, and find a key-stone of a third arch, and on removing it:

'the sun, having now gained its meridian height, darted its rays to the centre. It shone resplendent on a white marble pedestal, whereon was a plate of gold. On this plate was engraved a triple triangle, and within the triangles some characters which are beyond our comprehension'. [417]

---

[416] Carlile, p.121. Carlile produced an in-depth presentation of the rituals with a commentary, sometimes critical, but he was renowned for his accuracy. Indeed, his ritual expose was used, albeit unofficially, for decades by Freemasons who wished to revise the ritual for practice in the lodge.
[417] Ibid., p.122.

The word 'meridian' was also used in the third degree ritual, again suggesting Desaguliers had an influence, who in 1724, wrote his *Dissertation Concerning the Figure of the Earth*, a work based on Newtonian principles, in which he discussed the *'proper method for drawing (the) Meridian'*, and *'observations of the rising and setting sun'*, putting forward the importance of the meridian in creating more accurate maps.[418] The Royal Arch, like that of the third degree, certainly celebrates the Newtonian obsession for the search for lost knowledge, and when the workers report back with their glittering find, they are informed as to the importance of the gold plate, which displays *'the Grand Omnific word'*. *The three mysterious words'* displayed *'in a triangular form, is the long-lost sacred word of the Master Mason'*, and the secret signs of the Royal Arch are thus revealed to the workers. Redemption and trust is earned, and the mysteries are revealed, God's sacred word has been rediscovered and the Temple can be rebuilt.[419]

The essence of the Royal Arch ritual is undoubtedly a continuation of the Temple story, in effect a sequel to the third degree, continuing the themes of lost knowledge being found by the worthy, and that the lost divine word will be revealed to those who seek it for selfless reasons. A strong moralistic overtone is portrayed as the ritual is dramatically set amongst the Temple ruins, and the Mason is reminded of the destruction of the most sacred place on Earth, which has been destroyed by man's selfish greed and lust for war. As in the third degree were Hiram Abiff is murdered by selfish Masons who lust after the secret for themselves, man's weaknesses have led to the destruction of the Temple, which can only be rebuilt by finding the true path to enlightenment, the men involved in the reconstruction rediscovering the true way to God. The rebuilding of the Temple in the Royal Arch ritual reflects the interest within the 'Premier/Modern' Grand Lodge of the rebuilding of St. Paul's Cathedral by the Freemason Sir Christopher Wren after its destruction, the parallel being evident when recognising St. Paul's as the new Temple built in London.[420]

The Royal Arch ritual is a powerful reminder of man's folly, and it would be natural for the cycle to continue, with another degree perhaps revealing the story of the building of Herod's Temple, again reflecting the

[418] J.T. Desaguliers, *A Dissertation Concerning the Figure of the Earth*, The Royal Society Library, London, (1724), Reference: RBC.12.494. See also David Harrison, *The Genesis of Freemasonry*, (Hersham: Lewis Masonic, 2009), pp.122-123.
[419] Carlile, p.123.
[420] See Harrison, *The Genesis of Freemasonry*, p.96.

theme of the search for lost knowledge and its rediscovery, leading to a rebuilding of the Temple and a reminder of the importance of following a moralistic and righteous path. The person who wrote the Royal Arch ritual was astutely aware of Biblical knowledge, the rebuilding taking place after Nebuchadnezzar of Babylon's destruction of Jerusalem and the Temple, and the ritual is filled with Biblical characters such as the Principal Zerubbabel and Nebuzaradan, who is described as the chief of Nebuchadnezzar's officers.

Herod the Great rebuilt the Temple again, and this version of the Temple was finally destroyed by the Romans. The ritual also contains poetical elements and rhythmic style which reflects the presentation of the third degree ritual. When reminded that Desaguliers was a practicing Reverend and a poet, as well as being the driving force behind Freemasonry in the 1720s and 1730s, he once again becomes the obvious contender for the authorship of the Royal Arch, or at least producing the ideas behind its conception. Desaguliers would have been familiar with the moralistic themes of searching for lost knowledge, especially concerning Solomon's Temple, as his mentor Isaac Newton worked obsessively on searching for the divine measurements of the Temple for many years.

Masonic historian Dr. George Oliver, writing in the 1850s, had suggested that the Royal Arch was purely an 'Antient' Grand Lodge invention, inspired by Jacobite Freemason's in France and brought over to England by Chevalier Ramsay. Oliver rather confusingly put forward that the Modern's had not properly practiced the Royal Arch until the 1770s:

The introduction of the Royal Arch degree into the modern system could not be earlier than the dedication of Freemasons Hall in 1776. [421]

Oliver was a prolific Masonic writer in the nineteenth century, though he was never far from criticism, his views bringing him into conflict with the Grand Master of the United Grand Lodge of England the Duke of Sussex. Oliver's confusing views on the origin of the Royal Arch have been well and truly criticised over the years, an example being the Masonic historian Leon Hyneman who politely sums up Oliver's misinterpretations:

---

[421] Oliver, 'Origin of the Royal Arch Degree', *The American Freemason Magazine*, p.219.

'Dr. Oliver, in his "Account of the Schism" in England, and his elaborate letters on the "Origins of the English Royal Arch" with seemingly the best intentions to be unbiased in writing to his friend and reverend brother, Dr. Crucifix, yet he wrote as if trammelled and confined in his range of thought to views in accord with all his other Masonic writings.[422]

There had been a Grand Chapter of England formed in London under the authority of Lord Blaney in 1766, Blaney having previously served as Grand Master of the 'Moderns'. From this governing body, many Royal Arch Chapters soon emerged all over England, Wales, and even several in Scotland.[423] Thus the 'Moderns' were as keen as practising the Royal Arch as their Antient counterparts.

Oliver's proposed Jacobite culprit for the creation of the Royal Arch degree was an associate of Desaguliers' named Chevalier Ramsay. Andrew Michael Ramsay had been granted the rather exalted title of Chevalier of the neo-Chivalric Order of St. Lazarus by the Duke of Orleans while in France. Ramsay was a Scottish Jacobite who had gone to France, tutoring the sons of aristocrats, and when in London in 1730, he entered Desaguliers' prestigious Horn Tavern Lodge. In his 'Oration' to the Paris Grand Lodge in 1737, Ramsay presented that Freemasonry was originally linked with the Crusaders and the Chivalric Orders, and after being preserved in the British Isles, it was thus passing to France. There is no historical evidence for what Ramsay put forward in his address in 1737 regarding a link to the Crusaders or Chivalric Orders, but it does reveal that he desired a noble and Chivalric origin for Freemasonry. Ramsay was an idealist, and the Oration was a presentation of his ideal of Freemasonry; that its principles and values should reflect the romantic Chivalrous attitudes of the medieval Knights. Though Ramsay did not set out plans for new Masonic Orders in his Oration, he certainly inspired them, with his ideals of virtuous principles that were reflected in his romantic views of medieval Crusader Chivalry, and as aristocrats became increasingly interested in Freemasonry, exotic degrees and rituals with romantic Chivalric themes would certainly appeal.[424]

---

[422] Leon Hyneman, *Freemasonry in England from 1567 to 1813*, (Montana: Kessinger Publishing, 2003), p.14. See also R.S.E. Sandbach, *Priest and Freemason: The Life of George Oliver*, (Northamptonshire: The Aquarian Press, 1988), p.99. For Dr. Crucefix see R.S.E. Sandbach, 'Robert Thomas Crucefix, 1788-1850', in *AQC*, Vol. 102, (1990), pp.134-163.

[423] Robert Currie, *Early Royal Arch Chapters in the South of Scotland*, http://www.lodgehope337.org.uk/lectures/rcurrie%20L1.PDF [accessed 15th of March, 2009]

[424] See L.A. Seemungal, 'The Rise of Additional Degrees' in *AQC*, Vol. 84, (1971), pp.307-312.

Oliver's views that the Royal Arch was an Antient Jacobite creation had some support at the time, and in a feature entitled *The Antiquity of The Royal Arch* in the *Freemasons Magazine and Masonic Mirror* dated January 1868, his theory was discussed again:

'it is clear that Dermott and his associates extended the second part of the third degree, until they made it a fourth degree, and gave it the name of the Royal Arch. The fact is also clear to me, and to my mind quite conclusive that the English Royal Arch – as a degree or in name – did not exist before 1740.'[425]

Lawrence Dermott had been the spiritual leader of the 'Antients', founding the successful 'Antient' Grand Lodge in 1751, though there had been earlier references to the Royal Arch by the 'Premier' or 'Modern' Grand Lodge which had been founded in 1717. Desaguliers' associate James Anderson, when writing the first edition of the *Constitutions* in 1723, writes about the *'Arch'*, saying it was the cement of brotherhood preserved *'so that the whole Body resembles a well-built Arch'*.[426] In this respect, the *'Arch'* symbolized strength, not just within architecture but within the society of Freemasonry.

The writer of the above feature in the *Freemasons Magazine and Masonic Mirror* was sternly taking the official line that the Royal Arch was the *'completion'* of the third degree, being its *'second part'*, referring to Dr. Oliver's *Origin of the Royal Arch Order of Masonry*, a new edition of which had been published the previous year. The writer, who praised Oliver as *'the greatest modern light of Freemasonry'* also discussed Oliver's theory on the mysterious *'Rite Ancien de Bouillon'* manuscript,[427] of which, he stated, had displayed the first *'faint glimmerings'* of the Royal Arch Ritual, *'styled by its fabricators as the fourth degree'* being *'designed by the brethren who seceded from the Constitutional Grand Lodge* (the 'Moderns') *in 1739'.*[428] Oliver had discussed this secession of the 'Antients' in 1739 in his work *A Dictionary of Symbolic Masonry*, this date fitting his theory of the 'Antients' creating the Royal Arch soon after:

---

[425] 'The Antiquity of The Royal Arch' in the *Freemasons Magazine and Masonic Mirror*, January 1868.

[426] James Anderson, *The Constitutions of The Free-Masons*, (London: Senex, 1723), p.48.

[427] The 'Rite Ancien de Bouillon' has mysterious origins, but Oliver put forward that it had links to Ramsay, possibly from him being on good terms with a noble family who pretended descent from the Crusader Godfrey de Bouillon. See George Oliver, *The Origin of the Royal Arch Order of Masonry*, (London: Bro. Richard Spencer, 1867), p.31.

[428] 'The Antiquity of The Royal Arch' in the *Freemasons Magazine and Masonic Mirror*, January 1868.

'In the year 1739 a few brethren, having violated the laws of Masonry, were expelled from the Grand Lodge…they appropriated to themselves the exclusive and honourable title of Ancient Masons'.[429]

Although the Antient Grand Lodge was officially founded in 1751 by Lawrence Dermott, there had been an incident of *'irregular Making of Masons'* by certain brethren reported in the minutes of the 'Premier/Modern' Grand Lodge in 1739,[430] and the Grand Lodge faced increasing ridicule and criticism throughout the early 1740s with 'Mock Masonry'.[431] Oliver omitted the official 'Antient' Grand Lodge foundation date of 1751 from his discussion on the Antients, again presenting a confusing picture. The ritual displayed in the *'Rite Ancien de Bouillon'*, which Oliver dismissed as *'unsatisfactory jumble'*, has also been described as a 'deviant ritual', and though dated to 1740, it largely presented a different version of the Hiram legend which makes up the third degree ritual. However, what the *'Rite Ancien de Bouillon'* also reveals is the way writers were experimenting with the Hiramic legend at this early stage, introducing different versions of the legend, and emphasising the search for the divine lost word.[432]

The mysterious *'Rite Ancien de Bouillon'* puts forward a very early mention of the golden plate which appears in the Royal Arch ritual as displaying the lost word, and, like the Royal Arch ritual, it also mentions Newtonian terminology with the word 'meridian':

'…when we retired from labour to refreshment, at High Meridian…'[433]

Oliver recited the origin of the gold plate as put forward by the *'Rite Ancien de Bouillon'* in his *Origin of the Royal Arch Order of Masonry*:

'We permitted our lamented Brother, after casting the two Pillars of the Porch, to engrave the mysterious Word upon a plate of gold within the cabalistic figure of our signet, and to wear it as a mark of our royal favour and good will'.[434]

---

[429] George Oliver, *A Dictionary of Symbolic Masonry including The Royal Arch Degree*, (London: Richard Spencer, 1853), p.21.

[430] James Anderson, *The Constitutions of The Antient and Honourable Fraternity of Free and Accepted Masons*, (London: J. Scott, 1756), pp.228-229.

[431] Harrison, *The Genesis of Freemasonry*, pp.180-181.

[432] See Joannes A.M. Snoek, *The Evolution of the Hiramic Legend in England and France*, (2003), http://www.scottishrite.org/what/educ/heredom/articles/vol11-snoek.pdf [accessed 8th of June, 2009]

[433] Oliver, *The Origin of the Royal Arch Order of Masonry*, p.91.

A ceremony of finding the golden 'medal' on the corpse of Hiram then took place, with the description of the 'medal' revealing a *'double triangle enclosed within a circle, and the Tetragrammation in the centre. The medal was then placed upon the Holy Bible'.*[435] Oliver discusses how the mysterious word would have been forever lost if not recovered, as *'if it had fallen into improper hands, they might have prized it for its metallic value'* and not *'its symbolic worth'.*[436]

A similar manuscript displaying the confessions of Freemason John Coustos, made before the Portuguese Inquisition on the 21st of May, 1743, also puts forward an early reference to the gold plate of the Royal Arch, when Coustos, who had been a member of a London lodge, stated that:

'when the destruction of the famous Temple of Solomon took place there was found below the First Stone a tablet of bronze upon which was engraved the following word, JEHOVAH, which means GOD'.[437]

John Coustos had been made a Freemason in London, but after moving to Lisbon, Portugal, were he had founded a lodge; he had been arrested and tortured by the Inquisition. Coustos survived the numerous tortures, and in 1744, he was finally released, going on to write an account of his sufferings.[438]

What is certain is that the Royal Arch story – the re-discovery of the lost word of God hidden amongst the ruins of the first Temple – was known by the early 1740s. Desaguliers died in 1744, and it is around this time that more evidence of the Royal Arch in practice appears; the earliest record of the Royal Arch in a possible ceremonial context comes from Youghal in Ireland, during a public procession on St. John's Day, in the Winter of 1743, when a local newspaper account describes that the Master was preceded by *'the Royal Arch carried by two excellent masons'*,[439] and

---

[434] Ibid., p.92-93.
[435] Ibid., p.93.
[436] Ibid.
[437] See Joannes A.M. Snoek, *The Evolution of the Hiramic Legend in England and France*, (2003), p.31, http://www.scottishrite.org/what/educ/heredom/articles/vol11-snoek.pdf [accessed 8th of June, 2009]. See also John Coustos: Confession of 21 March 1743, in S. Vatcher, 'John Coustos and the Portuguese Inquisition', *AQC*, Vol. 81, (1968), pp.50-51.
[438] John Coustos had been initiated into Freemasonry in London in 1730, and was a member of Lodge No. 75, held at the Rainbow Coffee House, London. Also see John Coustos, *The Sufferings of John Coustos for Free-Masonry And For His Refusing to Turn Roman Catholic in the Inquisition at Lisbon*, (London: W. Strahan, 1746).
[439] Waite, *New Encyclopaedia of Freemasonry*, Vol. II, p.376.

in 1744, a certain Dr. Fifield Dassigny, spoke to an assembly of Masons at York, who had gathered under the title of *'Royal Arch Masons'*.[440]

Oliver had dismissed the importance of *'Rite Ancien de Bouillon'* and confusingly used it as 'evidence' for the Royal Arch as being an 'Antient' concoction, suggesting it was an early attempt at creating a degree. But the manuscript does verify the development of the popular Hiram story of the re-discovery of hidden knowledge in the ruins of the Temple, a story that Desaguliers could have easily influenced, a story that remained unfinished and left open for adaptation. Oliver created a confusing picture of events, linking the Royal Arch to the Jacobites, and with the Royal Arch being used as a fourth degree by the 'Antients', he thus produced a Jacobite agenda.

Further degrees and the continuation of the journey

During the period that Oliver was writing about his dubious theory of the origins of the Royal Arch, other Masonic 'degrees' were becoming highly fashionable. The Grand Lodge of Master Mark Masons was founded in 1856; the medieval masons marks becoming a popular fascination with Freemasons of the prosperous middle classes,[441] who were developing an interest in medieval churches and cathedrals, many of which were being renovated or rebuilt in extravagant High-Victorian Gothic style.[442] The foundation of the Mark Grand Lodge has been linked to the increasingly prosperous middle class Freemasons separating themselves socially from the older ruling aristocrats who were held responsible for the disastrous running of the Crimean War.[443] It also reveals the desire to form new organising bodies for further attainable Masonic 'degrees', Oliver

---

[440] Gould, *History of Freemasonry*, pp.407-8.

[441] See Jennifer S. Alexander, 'The Introduction and Use of Masons' Marks in Romanesque Buildings in England', in *Medieval Archaeology*, 51, (2007), pp.63-81. http://www2.warwick.ac.uk/fac/arts/arthistory/research/staffinterests/ja/med51-alexander.pdf [accessed 25th of July, 2009]

[442] An excellent example of this Masonic interest in Victorian renovation of churches and Cathedrals was the restoration of Worcester Cathedral, for which Worstershire Masons donated a large sum in 1874. In this year, the local Worcester Freemasons were involved in a procession from the Guildhall to the Cathedral for a service, and the Worstershire Province then paid for a commemorative window to be installed in the North Transept of the Cathedral. A large three pane stained glass Masonic window to commemorate a certain Brother Joseph Bennett had also been installed in the Cathedral in 1867. See 'Freemasonry's 270 years of Lodges in Worcestershire' in *Worcester News*, Saturday, 15th of June, 2002, http://archive.worcesternews.co.uk/2002/6/15/264560.html [accessed 1st of May, 2009]

[443] Andrew Prescott, *Well Marked? Approaches to the History of Mark Masonry*, http://www.freemasons-freemasonry.com/prescott01.html [accessed 15th of March, 2009]

referring to the fact that during *'the building of Solomon's Temple, every Fellowcraft undoubtedly had his own mark, and was therefore a Mark Mason'.*[444] This was yet another mysterious Masonic degree which could reveal further secrets, though as with the Royal Arch, the Mark degree had originally emerged in the eighteenth century.

As the Victorian era progressed, interest in Freemasonry grew, Masonry becoming a conventional culture. The desire for networking combined with the yearning to discover deeper secrets within Masonry resulted in the success of further rituals and degrees such as the Royal Arch and the Master Mark Mason. With thriving trans-Atlantic ports such as Liverpool, where trade with the USA led to established business contacts, Masonic ideas were also being traded, and a glance at the lodges from Liverpool at this time reveals many visiting brethren from ports in the USA, notably New York. There are a number of Masonic graves in cemeteries in Liverpool that display tales of American brethren who had died at sea and received a Masonic burial in Liverpool. Indeed, there was such a close relationship with Liverpool Masonry that a report on a Masonic Ball held in the Town Hall in Liverpool *'in aid of the funds of the West Lancashire Masonic Educational Institution'* attended by the local Masonic dignitary including the Earl of Zetland and Earl de Grey and Ripon, was featured in the Boston based *Freemasons' Monthly Magazine* in 1864.[445] Further Masonic degrees and rituals soon took hold in the USA, and Oliver's Masonic writings became extremely popular over there.

The desire for further degrees and Masonic mysteries in the USA led to the success of the 'Ancient and Accepted Rite' commonly referred to the 'Scottish Rite', which was nurtured from an obscure Masonic practice in the early 1800s to a Rite of foremost importance by the attorney, Confederate officer and Freemason Albert Pike. The Scottish Rite enables the Mason to complete 33 degrees, each ritual revealing deeper mysteries to the Freemason as he continues his journey to gain the ultimate 33rd degree. Pike received the 4th to the 32nd degree in South Carolina in 1853 from the Masonic writer Dr. Albert G. Mackey, eventually receiving the 33rd degree and becoming the Grand Commander for the Southern Jurisdiction in the USA. The Scottish Rite has its beginnings in the later eighteenth century and like the 'Antients', it has

---

[444] George Oliver, *The Historical Landmarks and other Evidences of Freemasonry: Explained in a Series of Practical Lectures*, (New York: Masonic Publishing and Manufacturing Co., 1867), p.308.
[445] Charles W. Moore, Grand Secretary of The Grand Lodge of Massachusetts, 'Masonic Ball at Liverpool', in *Freemasons' Monthly Magazine*, Vol. XXIII, (Boston: printed by Hugh H. Tuttle, 1864), March 1, 1864, No. 5, p.158.

been linked to Jacobite origins by certain writers. It was Pike however, who reworked and revised the rituals, and by 1872 he published the gargantuan work *Morals and Dogma of the Ancient and Accepted Scottish Rite of Freemasonry*. The Scottish Rite also captured the keen interest of Dr. George Oliver and Dr. Robert Thomas Crucefix in England, and together they helped to form the Supreme Council 33° in 1845 which was warranted by the Northern Jurisdiction in the USA.[446]

Pike's work cleverly promoted the Scottish Rite, and though quite a heavy read, it puts forward a tantalising glimpse of the inner most mysteries of this version of Freemasonry. It discusses Pike's theories on the degrees, giving 'lectures' on each, drawing knowledge from the Old Testament, the Kabala, and Pythagorean principles, and presents Pike's in-depth intellect on the secrets and symbolism of Freemasonry, the search for the lost word of God, and the hidden mysteries of Nature and Science, which according to Pike *'was taught to Moses and Pythagoras'*.[447] The work became widely published and was accessible to all kinds of Freemasons, and though quite in-depth in discussing the lost word of God, he expertly guides the reader through the lectures of 32 degrees (the 33rd being the ultimate degree and is only revealed at the end of the physical Masonic journey).

One particular degree, the 13th, is called *The Royal Arch of Solomon* within the Southern Jurisdiction, and Pike puts forward how *'every Masonic Lodge is a temple of religion'*. He discussed how the Holy of Holies is a cube *'by which the ancients presented Nature'*, describing the Temple as having a *'starred'* ceiling and that *'every Masonic Lodge represents the Universe'*.[448] In its presentation of the Temple and the search for lost knowledge – the word of God itself - amongst hidden artefacts, this particular degree bears a slight resemblance to the Royal Arch ritual of the United Grand Lodge of England. The 18th degree is called the Rose Croix, its name echoing a romantic connection to the Rosicrucians, the degree becoming of particular interest to Oliver and Crucefix, with Oliver discussing how the Rose Croix was believed to have been practiced by King Arthur and his Knights of the Round Table.[449] The Scottish Rite is proof of how Masons desired deeper knowledge about Freemasonry, and yearned for

---

[446] See Sandbach, *The Life of George Oliver*, p.108-109. For Dr. Crucefix see Sandbach, 'Robert Thomas Crucefix, 1788-1850', in *AQC*, Vol. 102, (1990), pp.134-163.
[447] Albert Pike, *Morals and Dogma of the Ancient and Accepted Scottish Rite of Freemasonry*, (NuVision Publications LLC, 2007), p.186.
[448] Ibid., pp.187-191.
[449] Oliver, *The Origin of the Royal Arch Order of Masonry*, p.4.

more rituals. In this sense the Scottish Rite, and indeed other rituals in Britain, provided a pathway for promotion within the structure of Freemasonry, the society containing intricate organizations of higher Orders, creating routes of progression.

The York Rite was also an American Masonic organization, but unlike the Scottish Rite, was an assemblage of Masonic 'grades' including the Royal Arch, giving the Mason access to a progression of higher degrees such as the Mark Master degree and the Chivalric Orders of the Knights Templar. The name was inspired by the legend of Edwin who organized the first Grand Lodge of Masons ay York in 926 AD. The Ancient York Rite was discussed in detail in *Duncan's Masonic Ritual and Monitor* which was published in the USA in 1866, Duncan stating the purpose of the work being so the Mason could *'progress from grade to grade'.*[450] The Royal Arch is alluded to in the York Rite as the seventh degree, but the version of the Royal Arch presented by Duncan is very similar to the earlier version presented by Carlile in his *Manual of Freemasonry.*

The Royal Arch was also practised by the rebel Wigan Grand Lodge throughout its existence, the Masonic historian Eustace Beesley putting forward that it was used as a *'degree'.*[451] With the Wigan Grand Lodge being the last practitioners of the 'Antients' in England, they considered the Royal Arch as a distinctive fourth degree, separate from the third Master's degree. Wigan Grand Lodge member James Miller described the installation of Worshipful Master in a lodge, and how *'no brother was advanced to the Royal Arch unless he had passed the chair but the ceremony was performed in the lodge'*. Miller also mentioned the *'Ceremony of Installation'* was *'also for the purpose of admission to the Royal Arch'*, the ceremony itself being described as a *'simple'* one. Besides the 'degree' of the Royal Arch, the Wigan Grand Lodge also practised the *'Sublime Degree of Knights Templars.'*[452]

The Knights Templar as a Masonic Order can be traced back to the mid-late eighteenth century,[453] and is described as a *'Masonic Order of Chivalry'* by Carlile in his *Manual of Freemasonry*, the ritual discussing the resurrection of Christ and taking place within a *'well guarded grand Christian encampment'*. The candidate has a number of questions put to them, and is asked about *'The Sign and Word of a Royal Arch Mason'* and if they have

---

[450] Malcolm C. Duncan, *Duncan's Masonic Ritual and Monitor*, (Forgotten Books, 2008), p.1.
[451] E.B. Beesley, *The History of the Wigan Grand Lodge*, (Leeds: Manchester Association for Masonic Research, 1920), pp.76-77.
[452] Ibid., pp.102-3.
[453] Seemungal, 'The Rise of Additional Degrees' in *AQC*, Vol. 84, pp.310-311.

worked on the second Temple. The Christian encampment is, like the Temple, a sacred space, and the candidate is asked if they have received a Christian Baptism and are willing to protect the Christian Faith. The candidate is described as *'a poor weary pilgrim'* and offers to devote his life to Christ and the service of the poor and sick, and thus becomes a Knight Templar.[454] The *'pretended'* link between Freemasonry and the medieval Order of the Knights Templar was discussed as early as 1864 in the Boston *Freemasons' Monthly*, the confusion in regards to the history of the Masonic Order was already beginning to blur.[455]

The search for lost knowledge within Freemasonry during the nineteenth century continued, with the industrialists and professionals yearning for a deeper insight into the secrets of Freemasonry and the hidden mysteries of Nature and Science. As in the eighteenth century, knowledge of science was still sought after, and Freemasonry offered an intellectual pathway to the understanding of natural philosophy. Further degrees could assist with this journey, and the Royal Arch was the beginning of a new voyage of discovery for the Master Mason, the Craft offering a road to the discovery of lost knowledge, with further rituals such as the Master Mark degree and the Knights Templar revealing new mysteries. As the American Masonic writer Albert G. Mackey once put it, Royal Arch Masonry was *'that division of Speculative Freemasonry which is engaged in the investigation of the mysteries connected with the Royal Arch, no matter under what name or what Rite.'*[456]

Freemasonry became fashionable again for the industrialists and professionals after the mid-nineteenth century, the up-and-coming middle classes becoming involved in a wider social scene which involved joining a network of other clubs and societies. The next chapter will analyse this social scene of the nineteenth century gentleman, focussing on how Freemasonry and gentlemen's clubs were both used for networking, making connections and social climbing. The symbiotic relationship between Freemasonry and gentlemen's clubs will be explored, and certain Freemasons who were also members of these clubs will be discussed, their affiliation to both creating a cross-over culture of social and business networking opportunities.

---

[454] Carlile, pp.137-146.

[455] Charles W. Moore, Grand Secretary of The Grand Lodge of Massachusetts, 'Order of Knights Templars: Its Pretended Continuation and Connection with Freemasonry', in *Freemasons' Monthly Magazine*, Vol. XXIII, (Boston: printed by Hugh H. Tuttle, 1864), December 1, 1863, No. 2, p.41.

[456] Albert G. Mackey, *Encyclopedia of Freemasonry Vol. II*, (Chicago: The Masonic History Company, 2003), p.884.

The Masonic gravestone of Benjamin Blundell, who died on the 6th of July, 1881, aged 57. The gravestone is located at St. Peter's Church in Newton-le-Willows, Lancashire. Blundell was a Freemason who was a grocer residing on the High Street of the small town. The gravestone reveals an elaborate set square and compass with the letter 'G' in its centre, which was the regular symbol used on the gravestones of deceased Masons during this period. (Photograph by David Harrison).

A Masonic gravestone at St. James' Cemetery, Liverpool revealing the mystical 'All-Seeing Eye' above the set-square and compass. The gravestone tells the story of Captain Charles H Webb of the Barque St. Lawrence from New York, USA, who was buried in Liverpool by local Freemasons in 1856. Being a Freemason ensured that, no matter where you were in the World, you could always rely on your brethren to help you if needed, especially supplying funds for burial, which, in the nineteenth century, was socially important, a 'good send off' being much preferred to the social stigma of a paupers burial. Captain Webb had committed suicide by poisoning himself with *two wine glassfuls of laudanum*. The gravestone also gives evidence for the Masonic relationship between New York and Liverpool.

Another Masonic gravestone from St. James' Cemetery in Liverpool, dating from 1848, erected in the memory of Captain David Davies of the Brig Naiad from Milford in South Wales. The Masonic symbols of the set-square, plumb line, and crossed keys appear at the top, the iconography being different to the other Masonic graves in the cemetery.

A Masonic monument from St. James' Cemetery in Liverpool, revealing the story of Captain Elisha Lindsay Halsey, from Charlestown, South Carolina, USA, who died on his ship 'Thomas Bennett' while on the Bay of Biscay off the coast of Spain in 1844. Captain Halsey had been stabbed to death on his ship during a dispute with the ship's cook, after the Captain had produced a pistol with the intent of killing the cook. The ship arrived in Liverpool, and the remains of the Captain, a Freemason, was buried, and this very elaborate monument erected *'by American ship masters and a few friends in Liverpool'* indicating it was a local lodge which assisted in the arrangements and the funeral. The American flag appears on one side of the monument while the Masonic symbols of the set-square and compass and the 'All-Seeing Eye' set within two inverted triangles dominate another side. Again this monument testifies to the Trans-Atlantic relationship of Freemasonry at this time. The cook was tried for the Captain's murder and a verdict of 'justifiable homicide' was reached by the Jury.

The Masonic monument of Capt. Elisha Lindsay Halsey in detail, revealing the 'All-Seeing Eye' set within two inverted triangles and the set-square and compass.

A magnificent marble Masonic monument from St. James' Cemetery dated to 1901, erected by members of the Liverpool based Royal Victoria Lodge in memory of their Worshipful Master Alexander J. Mackey. The Royal Victoria Lodge was a daughter lodge of The Merchants Lodge, and was founded in 1864, during a period of growth for Freemasonry.

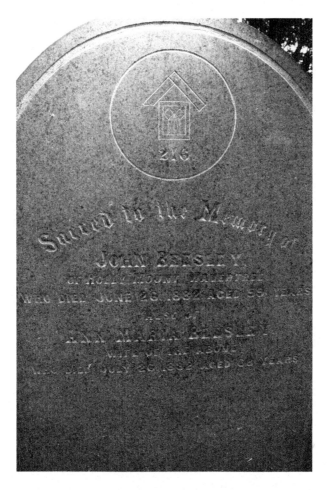

A beautiful marble Masonic gravestone located at Holy Trinity Church, Wavertree in Liverpool, in memory of John Beesley, a pawnbroker who resided at Holly Mount in Wavertree. Dated to 1882, the striking Masonic symbol of the set-square above Euclid's 47th problem is one which represents the Worshipful Master of a lodge. Also displayed is the lodge number 216. Like grocer Benjamin Blundell, Beesley is typical of the 'High Street' business men that became Freemasons in the Victorian period. The play Hobson's Choice which was set in Salford, portrays another 'High Street' business man - a Cobbler - as a Freemason, revealing how these local business men were commonly linked to the Craft during the period.

The Masonic gravestone of Thomas Brookes of Birmingham, dated to 1876, and situated in the Churchyard of St. Mael & St. Sulien in Corwen, Wales. The set-square and compass is revealed set within a shield. The gravestone again supplies evidence of a Freemason who traveled and was laid to rest with the help of a local lodge.

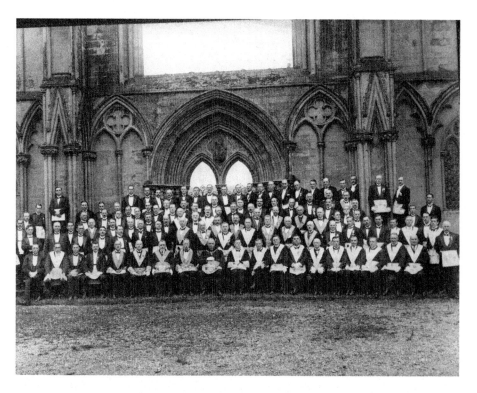

A photograph of a meeting for an installation ceremony in 1923 of the Byron Lodge No. 4014 at Newstead Abbey – the old seat of the Byron family. Some of the Freemasons are still wearing Evening Dress, despite a policy – started during the Great War, which promoted the wearing of Morning Dress. The 'Wicked' Lord Byron had been Grand Master during 1747-51, and the poet Lord Byron had mentioned Freemasonry in his poetry. Byron sybsequently sold Newstead Abbey to his school friend Col. Thomas Wildman, who became Provincial Grand Master of Nottinghamshire. Many thanks to John Allcock for supplying the photograph.

RACOBITE WALKS BROAD O TH LANE 1917

A photograph dating from 1917 showing the Independent Order of Rechabites marching through the village of Shevington in Lancashire, wearing sashes – their regalia and oath taking, like that of other 'Friendly Societies' which emerged in the nineteenth century, being similar to Freemasonry. Many thanks to the Shevington Conservative Club for supplying the photograph and to the Reprographics Department at Liverpool Hope University for the digital reproduction.

The foundation stone of St. Mary's Catholic Church, Standishgate, Wigan, laid on St. Patrick's Day, 1818. In his memoirs of the last days of the Wigan Grand Lodge, James Miller mentions that the lever and heavy maul used to lay the stone was presented to the Lodge of Sincerity in 1826 by the Master, John Bimson. (Photograph by David Harrison)

Above the busy shops of Mostyn Street in Llandudno lies the Masonic Hall - a beautiful late Victorian building with Cathedral-like Gothic windows, displaying three pentacles. The Masonic Hall almost lies hidden from view above the shops, and it is only when recognising the symbolism that you would realise it was there.

The sign of the Druid Inn, Gorsedd in North-east Wales. This is one of three public houses named The Druid Inn, all in close proximity to each other, all dating from the later nineteenth century. The sign shows the typically romantic scene of robed Druids practising a ceremony in a stone circle. Just over the road from the pub is a standing stone called the Druid Stone. Romantic interest in the Druids developed during the nineteenth century, and links are evident with Freemasonry, especially in the symbolism and in the rituals. Interest in the Druids was also evident outside Wales, an example being The Druid Inn at Birchover in Derbyshire, which is situated near to the mysterious Rowter Rocks were, according to local tradition, the ancient Druids practised rituals.

Chapter 8

Freemasonry in Fashion: Gentlemen's Clubs, Occultists, and the Search for Elitism and Hidden Knowledge

'The members elect by ballot. When 12 and under 18 members ballot, one black ball, if repeated, shall exclude; if 18 and upwards ballot, two black balls exclude, and the ballot cannot be repeated. The presence of 12 members is necessary for a ballot.'
Charles Dickens (Jr.), discussing the London based Travelers Club in
Dickens's Dictionary of London, 1879[457]

'Once a priest, always a priest; once a mason, always a mason; but once a journalist, always and forever a journalist.'
Freemason Rudyard Kipling, *A Matter of Fact, Many Inventions*, 1893[458]

'That no dice and no game of hazard be allowed in the rooms of the Club, nor any higher stake than guinea points, and that no cards be introduced before dinner.'
Peter Cunningham, *Hand-Book of London*, 1850[459]

'...I will send you a cheque to-morrow. What is your club?
I have no club. That is to say, not just at present.'
Freemason Oscar Wilde, *Lord Arthur Savile's Crime*, 1891[460]

As Freemasonry became an increasingly desirable social activity for the industrialists and professionals in the mid nineteenth century, other gentlemen's clubs and learned societies became part of their social culture; the dining, gambling and reading rooms of the clubs and societies became places were the young up-and-coming gentlemen could learn and then flaunt their newly acquired social skills. As with many gentlemen's clubs in England, there are those who are in, and those who are not, and for most ambitious young gentlemen who were in pursuit of networking and securing a career, it was almost certainly better to be in. The many gentlemen's clubs situated in London represented this attitude, as many

---

[457] See Charles Dickens Jr, *Dictionary Of London: An Unconventional Handbook*, (London: Charles Dickens and Evans, 1879).
[458] Rudyard Kipling, *Many Inventions*, (Kessinger Publishing Reprint, 2005), p163.
[459] Peter Cunningham, *Hand-Book of London, past and present*, (London: J. Murray, 1850), p.511.
[460] Oscar Wilde, *The Complete Works*, (London: Magpie, 1993), p.174.

clubs were founded in the eighteenth and nineteenth centuries for various types of gentlemen; be it for aristocratic Whig or Tory gentlemen, for travelling gentlemen, for authors and poets, or for Army and Navy Officers. Most clubs had their exclusive premises situated within private buildings of high neo-classical architectural splendour, and, like Freemasonry, had strict club rules, stringent dress codes, were strictly for men only, they had high subscription fees and balloted for new members. Many of these fashionable clubs were centred on the prestigious and elegant area of St James' Square and Pall Mall.

Aristocratic Whig and Tory clubs had flourished in the eighteenth century, such as White's (the oldest surviving club established in 1693), situated on St James', which was Tory, and Brooks's, founded in 1764, which was Whig, and was situated just down the road from White's in St. James' Street. Brooks's was just opposite from Boodle's which was another prestigious aristocratic Tory club that had been established in 1762. Notable Freemasons who were members of Boodle's included the Duke of Wellington and historian Edward Gibbon.[461] The Whig club Brooks's was an extremely exclusive club which attracted many leading politicians, and also included many aristocratic and Royal Masonic members, such as the Prince of Wales (later George IV), and his brothers Prince Frederick, the Duke of York, who was for a time the Grand Master of the 'Antients', and Prince William, Duke of Clarence (later William IV).

Other members of Brooks's that were linked to Freemasonry were Tory Minister Charles Watkin Williams Wynn (the elder), who's family had a lodge which had operated from their family home at Wynnstay in North Wales. Charles retained his administration under Freemason George Canning, and though a Tory, he also held the position of Secretary of War for a time under the Whig Lord Grey, who was one of the principal designers of the Reform Act of 1832. Other Masonic members included the Whig politician Edmund Burke, and historian Edward Gibbon, who, though having been linked to the Whigs, was also a member of the Tory Boodle's club. Gibbon was a member of many London clubs, such as Samuel Johnson's Literary Club, and moved with ease through London society, being comfortable in both Tory or Whig club alike. Burke was also a member of Johnson's Literary Club, along with Freemasons James Boswell and Joseph Banks. Brooks's was famous

---

[461] F. H. W. Sheppard (General Editor), 'St. James's Street, East Side', in *Survey of London: volumes 29 and 30: St James Westminster, Part 1* (1960), pp.433-458. http://www.british-history.ac.uk/report.aspx?compid=40621 [accessed 16th of April, 2009]

for its gaming room, and a member could gamble throughout the day and night with the company of his like-minded friends, the club being a gentlemen's 'refuge', not only from their Creditors, but also from their wives and the many mistresses they may have.

Other exclusive clubs began to appear in London, such as The Travellers Club which was founded in 1819, specifically for gentlemen that had travelled at least five hundred miles in a direct line from London. The current building which houses The Travellers Club on Pall Mall was built in 1832 by the architect Sir Charles Barry, and was based on Raphael's Palazzo Pandolfini in Florence, Barry having recently returned from the Grand Tour. The club library is extensive and decorated with a cast of the Bassae Frieze, which were originally reliefs from the Temple of Apollo, discovered by architect and founder member Charles Robert Cockerell, who had assisted Freemason Robert Smirke in rebuilding the Covent Garden Theatre. Freemasons the Duke of Wellington and George Canning were both members, and the club's membership later became linked to Foreign Office officials.[462]

Canning was also a member of other clubs, dining frequently at White's, of which he commented in his journal on visiting in February 1795:

'In the evening we went to White's, which was more brilliant tonight than I have ever yet seen it. The faro table was open for the first time that I remember since I have been in the habit of going there.[463]

He also frequented the Crown and Anchor Law Club of which he mentioned the introduction of a fine for absent members:

'they have just passed a law, inflicting upon every member, who is in town, and who fails attending for a whole week, a fine of 5 shillings. So I went and dined at my own expence out of pure economy to save the fine.[464]

For a young up-and-coming MP like Canning, being a member of influential clubs such as White's would certainly help him in forming networking relationships in London, and his references to them in his

[462] See the official website for the Travellers Club http://www.thetravellersclub.org.uk [accessed 16th of April, 2009]

[463] P. Jupp, (ed.), *The Letter-Journal of George Canning, 1793-1795*, Royal Historical Society, Camden Fourth Series, Volume 41, (London, 1991), p.214 and p.281.

[464] Ibid., p.120.

journal provide an insight into how popular and essential they were. When Canning became a Freemason in 1810, he joined two of the most prestigious lodges in London; Lodge No. 4 which was one of the four original lodges that had formed the 'Premier/Modern' Grand Lodge of 1717, and the Prince of Wales Lodge No. 259, the membership of which included the Prince of Wales himself.

The Duke of Wellington was also a patron of the Army and Navy Club, which was originally founded as a Commissioned Officers Army Club in 1837. However, when Wellington was initially asked to be a patron, he refused unless membership became open to commissioned officers from the Royal Marines and Royal Navy. This was agreed upon and the club duly opened in St James' Square. A new club building was opened on Pall Mall and the corner of George Street in 1851, and was especially designed by C.O Parnell and Alfred Smith and influenced by the Palazzo Corner della ca' Grande in Venice. The foundation stone was laid on the 6th of May 1848 by the chairman of the committee of management Lieutenant Colonel H. Daniell, though without the lavishness and ritual of a Masonic foundation stone laying ceremony. Wellington was President of the club from 1838-1841. Prince Adolphus, the Duke of Cambridge was President from 1845-1850, though unlike his six brothers, he didn't become a member of the Craft.[465]

It would have been prestigious for any club to obtain the membership of Wellington after his success at Waterloo. He was epitome of the English war hero, and though his Masonic career was brief and had taken place in his younger years, he would have recognised the value of becoming a member of an influential London gentlemen's club, and would have been familiar with the traditions, etiquette and conventions of the clubs. Wellington was however suspicious of the radical clubs, and in later life he somewhat distanced himself from Freemasonry, and had never again attended a lodge after 1795. Wellington also sponsored William Crockford in founding Cockfords, the famous gaming club in 1828, of which the gambler, Waterloo veteran and society gentleman Captain R.H. Gronow once said:

'...*the most agreeable conversation, the most interesting anecdotes, interspersed with grave political discussions and acute logical reasoning on every conceivable subject, proceeded from the soldiers, scholars, statesmen, poets, and men of pleasure, who, when*

---

[465] See the official website for the Army and Navy Club http://www.armynavyclub.co.uk/the-club/index.php [accessed 16th of April, 2009]

the "house was up" and balls and parties at an end, delighted to finish their evening with a little supper and a good deal of hazard at old Crockey's. [466]

Crockfords certainly seemed to be a very agreeable club, attracting society gentlemen like Gronow, who, writing in 1864, noted an already stark difference in the social make-up from his time:

'The tone of the club was excellent. A most gentlemanlike feeling prevailed, and none of the rudeness, familiarity, and ill-breeding which disgrace some of the minor clubs of the present day'. [467]

Indeed, Gronow noted how the class of the clubs had changed since the early nineteenth century:

'in 1814 – The members of the clubs in London, many years since, were persons, almost without exception, belonging exclusively to the aristocratic world. "My tradesmen," as King Allen used to call the bankers and the merchants, had not then invaded White's, Boodle's, Brookes', or Wattiers'. White's was decidedly the most difficult of entry; its list of members comprised nearly all the noble names of Great Britain. [468]

These 'tradesmen' as they were referred to by Gronow and his aristocratic associates, would become the burgeoning middle class, intent on gaining access to gentlemen's clubs and Freemasonry in the later half of the nineteenth century, infiltrating them with the desire to mix with the aristocracy, network and ultimately improve their social status. As a member of the elite aristocratic gentlemen of society who dominated the clubs in the early nineteenth century such as Count D'orsey and Beau Brummell, Gronow was obviously angered by this infiltration by the up-and-coming middle-classes.

The 'mystery' and 'aesthetic' of the London gentlemen clubs included the essential excusive dining room, library, coffee, morning or smoking rooms, and the games room, all to aid the creative and stimulating conversation of like-minded gentlemen. Though there were instances of disagreements and progressive thought which led to the formation of new

---

[466] Captain R.H. Gronow, *Celebrities of London and Paris*, (London: Smith, Elder & Co., 1865), p.104-105.
[467] Ibid., p.105.
[468] Captain R.H. Gronow, *Reminiscences of Captain Gronow*, (London: Smith, Elder & Co., 1862), p.76.

clubs, such as the Reform Club, which was founded in 1836 by the new Liberal supporters of the Reform Act of 1832, formed as a result of the older Whig Brooks's Club being unwilling to admit a large number of new members. The building, like the nearby Travellers Club, was designed by Sir Charles Barry in 1841 and was influenced by the Farnese Palace in Rome. Masonic members included Winston Churchill and Sir Arthur Conan Doyle, and Liberal Prime Minister William Ewart Gladstone, who, though not a Freemason came from a family with Masonic associations.[469] The Reform Club was one of the first clubs to offer bedrooms to its members, a feature that became essential to most of the London gentlemen's clubs for out of town members.[470]

The Athenaeum Club was another highly influential club with an equally highly influential membership list, which, throughout the nineteenth and early twentieth century, has had many Freemasons as members such as the Duke of Wellington, Rudyard Kipling, Sir Walter Scott, Sir Arthur Conan Doyle and Winston Churchill. It was founded in 1824 for gentlemen involved in scientific, literary, artistic pursuits and those involved in public service, and as a result, included what appeared to be the intelligentsia of the London social scene. The club building was designed in a neo-classical style with friezes copied from the Parthenon, and like the other Pall Mall clubs, reflected the aesthetic of a London gentlemen's club. Other notable members during the nineteenth century were Charles Dickens and Charles Darwin.[471]

Freemasonry, Occultists, and the Victorian Search for Hidden Knowledge

The networking that took place in the London gentlemen's clubs attracted the vivid imagination of Victorian writers, some who had even experienced the mysterious activities that occurred behind the closed

---

[469] William Ewart Gladstone's elder brother Robertson Gladstone was an influential Freemason in his family home of Liverpool, being a member of the Ancient Union Lodge No. 203. The Prime Minister was named after William Ewart, a close friend and associate of his father John Gladstone, Ewart being a member of the Merchant Lodge No. 428 in Liverpool.

[470] See the official website for the Reform Club http://www.reformclub.com [accessed 16th of April, 2009]. See also F. H. W. Sheppard (General Editor), 'Pall Mall, South Side, Existing Buildings: The Reform Club', *Survey of London: volumes 29 and 30: St James Westminster, Part 1* (1960), pp.408-415, http://www.british-history.ac.uk/report.aspx?compid=40611 [accessed 16th of April, 2009]

[471] Archives in London, The Athenaeum, Reference code: GB 1969, http://www.aim25.ac.uk/cgi-bin/search2?coll_id=7253&inst_id=87 [accessed 16th of April, 2009]. See also the official website for The Athenaeum Club, http://www.athenaeumclub.co.uk/ [accessed 16th of April]

doors. Writer and Freemason Sir Arthur Conan Doyle[472] made a literary reference to a London gentlemen's club in his 1893 Sherlock Holmes short story *The Adventure of the Greek Interpreter*, were Sherlock Holmes visits his brother Mycroft at the mysterious 'Diogenes Club' which he describes as:

'the queerest club in London' being for gentlemen *'who have no wish for the company of their fellows. Yet they are not averse to comfortable chairs and the latest periodicals.'*

The bizarre rules of the club are described:

'No member is permitted to take the least notice of any other one. Save in the Strangers' Room, no talking is, under any circumstances, permitted, and three offences, if brought to the notice of the committee, render the talker liable to expulsion. My brother (Mycroft) was one of the founders, and I have myself found it a very soothing atmosphere.'

The location of the club in the story was given as being on Pall Mall, a short distance from the Carlton Club, Conan Doyle presenting its interior as having a games room and *'a large and luxurious'* reading room. The 'Diogenes Club' was fictional, but with Mycroft's secretive career in the government, the club was presented as having possible deeper mysterious political agendas.[473] Unlike the 'Diogenes Club', the Carlton Club was very real, and was yet another Tory club, which was formed in the wake of the Reform Act of 1832. William Ewart Gladstone had joined as a young aspiring politician but resigned as his political persuasions became more liberal.[474] Conan Doyle was obviously being inspired by the secrecy and mysterious nature of such Gentlemen's Clubs, so it is not surprising that he also occasionally referred to Freemasonry in his Sherlock Holmes stories, such as in *The Red-Headed League*, when Holmes – who was obviously very familiar with Masonic symbolism - recognised that a gentleman was a Freemason, the particular gentleman being surprised that Holmes knew of his membership:

---

[472] Sir Arthur Conan Doyle was initiated into the Pheonix Lodge, No. 257, at Southsea, Hampshire, on the 26th of January, 1887.

[473] Sir Arthur Conan Doyle, *The Adventure of the Greek Interpreter*, in *The Adventures of Sherlock Holmes*, (Herefordshire: Wordsworth Editions Limited, 1992), pp.399-401.

[474] Philip Magnus, *Gladstone A Biography*, (New York, E.P Dutton & Co., 1954), p.146.

'I won't insult your intelligence by telling you how I read that, especially as, rather against the strict rules of your order, you use an arc and compass breastpin.'[475]

Sir Arthur Conan Doyle, along with fellow Freemasons Rudyard Kipling, Henry Rider Haggard and Jerome K. Jerome, wrote letters of goodwill when the Authors' Lodge No. 3456 was consecrated in November 1910, the lodge having a direct connection to the London based Authors' Club, which had been founded in 1891. The lodge was constituted by the Masonic members of the Authors' Club, one of the founders being Masonic historian A.F. Calvert, who had famously discovered an early Masonic *Catechism* dating from the early eighteenth century, which he eventually sold to Masonic historian Douglas Knoop.[476] The consecration of the Authors' Lodge reveals the intricate relationships between certain gentlemen's clubs and Freemasonry; the founding of the lodge being seen as not only a way of promoting the Authors' Club amongst Freemasons, but also providing a means of promoting Freemasonry within the club, attracting literary men into the Craft *'could not fail to add lustre to the Order.'*[477] Other Freemasons involved in the Authors' Club included Oscar Wilde and Winston Churchill.

Kipling and Rider Haggard were very close friends, both conveying Freemasonry in their writings. Indeed, Masonic themes can be seen in Rider Haggard's late Victorian works *King Solomon's Mines* and the wonderfully exotic novel *She*, a story which deals with death and re-birth. Both of these works present the idea of the heroic explorer searching lost civilisations for hidden knowledge and, along with Kipling's *The Man Who Would Be King*, testify not only to the popularity of Freemasonry at the time, but also the acceptance of the Craft in Victorian society, which, within these literary contexts also conveyed an element of mystery and the occult. Rider Haggard was also a close friend of Egyptologist and occultist Ernest A. Wallis Budge, both of them, along with Kipling, being celebrated members of the literary Savile Club. Conan Doyle, like fellow Freemason and writer Arthur Edward Waite, took a keen and almost obsessive interest in the occult, both men becoming deeply involved with psychic research. Waite also co-created the influential Rider-Waite-Smith

---

[475] See Sir Arthur Conan Doyle, *The Adventure of the Red-headed League*, in *The Adventures of Sherlock Holmes*, (Herefordshire: Wordsworth Editions Limited, 1992), p.133. Conan Doyle also referred to Freemasonry in other Sherlock Holmes stories, such as *The Adventure of the Norwood Builder* and *The Adventure of the Retired Colourman*, as well as mentioning Freemasonry in his other works.
[476] *Authors' Lodge Transactions iii*, (London, 1919), p.408.
[477] *History of the Authors' Lodge No. 3456*, (London, 2000).

Tarot card deck, which, when published in 1909, displayed elements of Masonic symbolism embedded within the mysterious pictures.

Waite had become a member of the Hermetic Order of the Golden Dawn in 1891, an occult society which had been founded three years earlier by Freemasons Dr. William Robert Woodman, Dr. William Wynn Westcott and Samuel Liddell MacGregor Mathers. His search for the deeper secrets of initiation led him to join Freemasonry in 1901, Waite becoming a rather prolific Masonic writer and historian, who seemed to be in constant search for the more magical origins of the Craft, writing *A New Encyclopaedia of Freemasonry* which, when published in 1921, part projected Waite's more mystical Masonic fancies.[478] Of his initiation, Waite commented:

'For myself it was a curious experience in more ways than one, and perhaps especially because it was so patent throughout that I could have told the Worshipful Master all that he was communicating to me. My Initiation was nothing therefore but a means to an end: I awaited the Grades beyond'.[479]

Indeed, Waite was anxious to explore the more mysterious and exotic further degrees which Freemasonry opened up to him, and by 1903 he had achieved acceptance into various other Masonic 'Rites' and Orders; having entered into the Rosicrucian Society of England, the Holy Royal Arch and the Knights Templar, even traveling to Scotland to receive the 'Early Grand Rite' and then on to Geneva to receive the 'Rectified Rite'. Waite was exploring all the further degrees, quenching his thirst for deeper knowledge, seeing Freemasonry as a pathway of mystical enlightenment, and in this respect, to Waite, Masonry was almost similar to the Hermatic Order of the Golden Dawn; a society which would endow him with the hidden secrets of Nature and Science. He saw the symbolism of Freemasonry has having the same original source as other esoteric pursuits, such as alchemy, Kabbalism and Rosicrucianism; all providing a pathway to enlightenment through the search for hidden knowledge. Waite referred to his experience by saying that:

---

[478] Arthur Edward Waite was initiated into the London based St. Marylebone Lodge No. 1305, on the 19th of September, 1901. See also Arthur Edward Waite, *A New Encyclopaedia of Freemasonry*, Vol. I & II, (New York: Wings Books Edition, 1996) and R.A. Gilbert, 'The Masonic Career of A.E. Waite', in *AQC*, Vol. 99, (1986).

[479] See Gilbert, 'The Masonic Career of A.E. Waite', in *AQC*, Vol. 99, (1986). Also see Arthur Edward Waite, *Shadows of Life and Thought. A Retrospective Review in the Form of Memoirs* (London: Selwyn and Blount, 1938), p.162.

'there is a Masonry which is behind Masonry and is not commonly communicated in lodges, though at the right time it is made known to the right person'.[480]

He believed he was special enough to be accepted into the 'Masonry which is behind Masonry' – those more mysterious rituals which would only be revealed to the chosen few. He was also interested in gaining enough secret knowledge and experience to create his own rituals, Waite having plans at one stage to establish the more obscure 'Rites' in England. The Hermetic Order of the Golden Dawn certainly offered a more 'magical' experience, practising ceremonial magic and using many Masonic symbols within the ritual. The Order became extremely popular and attracted writers and poets such as Waite, W.B. Yeats and Arthur Machen, though unlike many of the clubs and societies of the era, the mysterious and magical Hermetic Order of the Golden Dawn accepted women members.[481]

The founding of the Golden Dawn can be traced back to 1887, when Dr. William Wynn Westcott, a Freemason who was constantly in search for hidden knowledge, and had joined many Orders and Rites such as the Rosicrucian Society of England, obtained a mysterious manuscript in cipher from fellow Freemason the Rev. A.F.A. Woodford. The cipher – on translation - turned out to be a series of rituals, and Westcott asked fellow Freemason and Rosicrucian Samuel Liddell MacGregor Mathers to work on and expand the rituals. Amongst the papers of the cipher manuscript that Westcott had received from Woodford, he had found the name of a certain Fraulien Anna Srengal, a Rosicrucian adept from Germany, and after writing to her, Westcott was 'granted permission' to form an English version of the Golden Dawn.

The occult Order needed three Chief's, so Westcott and Mathers brought on board fellow Freemason Dr. William Robert Woodman, who was at the time the Supreme Magus of the Rosicrucian Society of England, and thus the Hermetic Order of the Golden Dawn was founded. Westcott even invited the elderly Southern Jurisdiction of the Scottish Rite leader Albert Pike to join, but he declined. Nevertheless, the Golden Dawn became exceedingly fashionable, attracting the likes of Waite and Yeats, and by 1896, there were five Temples and over three hundred members, and a Second Order was also thriving. Despite this success, there was disruption as the leaders began to fall out after

---

[480] See Gilbert, 'The Masonic Career of A.E. Waite', in *AQC*, Vol. 99, (1986).
[481] See Mary K. Greer, *Women of the Golden Dawn; Rebels and Priestesses*, (Rochester, Vermont: Park Street Press, 1995).

Woodman's death in 1891; Westcott resigned in 1897 after his work in the magical Order conflicted with his career as Coroner and accusations of forging the papers which had led to the founding of the society by Mathers followed.[482]

The Victorian interest in the occult and the search for lost ancient knowledge was fuelled by many sources, such as developments in archaeology – especially in Egypt - capturing the imaginations of many intellectuals at the time. The founding of the Egypt Exploration Fund in 1882 and an array of widespread publications on Egypt, such as Amelia Edwards' *A Thousand Miles up the Nile* in 1877,[483] all assisted in stirring interest in the lost civilisations of Egypt and of course, the hidden secrets of the ancients. Occultist, Rosicrucian and Freemason Kenneth Mackenzie – most famous for his *Royal Masonic Cyclopaedia* which was published in six parts between 1875-77, had previously edited and translated *Discoveries in Egypt, Ethiopia, and the Peninsula of Sinai* in 1852 - a work written by the German Egyptologist K.R. Lepsius. Mackenzie claimed to have secret knowledge of obscure Orders and rituals, most notably the 'Hermetic Order of Egypt' and the 'Order of Ishmael', the latter of which was ruled by Three Chiefs, which was very reminiscent of the Hermetic Order of the Golden Dawn. Indeed Waite, writing in his *Shadows of Life and Thought*, suggested that Mackenzie may have been behind the Golden Dawn ciphers.[484]

Masonic interest in Egyptian mysteries was nothing new; as early as the eighteenth century, certain Freemasons, such as the infamous occultist and alchemist Count Cagliostro, were claiming to possess the secrets of mysterious Egyptian Rites.[485] In England, the early Masonic interest in Egyptian mysteries can be seen in the naming of the London based Egyptian Lodge No. 27 in 1811, and as the nineteenth century

---

[482] R.A. Gilbert, 'William Wynn Westcott and the Esoteric School of Masonic Research', in *AQC*, Vol. 100, (1987), pp.6-20.

[483] See Amelia Edwards, *A Thousand Miles up the Nile*, (London: George Routledge and Sons, 1891). Amelia Edwards was the co-founder of the Egypt Exploration Fund. For a further insight into the late Victorian obsession of Egyptian archaeology see Ernest A. Wallis Budge, *The Mummy, Funeral Rites & Customs in Ancient Egypt*, (Guernsey: Senate Press, 1995), which was first published in 1893.

[484] Kenneth Mackenzie, *The Royal Masonic Cyclopaedia*, (Worcester: The Aquarian Press, 1987), pp.vi-ix, in which John Hamill and R.A. Gilbert discuss Mackenzie's life and work in their 'Introduction' to the edition. Waite had put forward that Mackenzie may have partly invented the mysterious cipher, and partly been inspired by his translation of '*German Grade experiences*', Hamill and Gilbert also supporting Waite's claims, mentioning that Mackenzie had translated manuscripts on magic and astronomy.

[485] See Philippa Faulks and Robert L.D. Cooper, *The Masonic Magician; The Life and Death of Count Cagliostro and his Egyptian Rite*, (London: Watkins, 2008).

progressed, occultist Freemasons such as Mackenzie and Waite vividly explored ideas of Egyptian mythology, trying to discover the lost knowledge of the ancients.[486]

The Victorian era also witnessed an explosion in gothic poetry and novels – most famously exemplified with the publication of Bram Stoker's *Dracula* in 1897, although this was not the first literary portrayal of the vampire. Dr. William John Polidori, the personal physician to the Romantic poet Lord Byron became a Freemason in 1818,[487] Polidori being credited with the beautiful evocative gothic short story *The Vampyre*, written in 1816 during his stay at the Villa Diodati at Lake Geneva in Switzerland. Polidori had stayed at the Villa with Byron, Percy Bysshe Shelley and Mary Wollstonecraft Godwin Shelley, and during a number of days in which they were kept inside due to bad weather, they recited ghost stories and *The Vampyre* and Mary Shelley's gothic masterpiece *Frankenstein* were written.

Polidori's story was finally published in 1819 and featured the secretive 'Byronic' aristocrat Lord Ruthven as the Vampire and followed his introduction into London Society and his travels to Rome and Greece, the gothic and occultist themes of the story being hauntingly evident.[488] As the nineteenth century progressed, Freemasonry increasingly attracted writers and poets such as Kipling, Conan Doyle and Rider Haggard, the mysterious nature of the Craft and the status it provided as a networking 'club' made it an essential element of their social scene and presented an obvious inspiration for their work. Writers and poets had been linked to Freemasonry since the early part of the eighteenth century, with Jonathan Swift and Alexander Pope being famous literary members who had also found inspiration in the Craft.[489]

Another Freemason and celebrated psychic researcher who, like Mackenzie and Waite, had also become involved in the Rosicrucian Society of England, was Frederick Bligh Bond, an architect and a keen student of the occult. Bligh Bond knew Conan Doyle and they shared similar interests in psychic research, Bligh Bond having used psychic mediums to assist him in his famed excavation of Glastonbury Abbey in Somerset, which, according to Bligh Bond, led to the discovery of the

---

[486] See Mackenzie, *Masonic Cyclopaedia*, pp.185-188, and Waite, *Encyclopaedia of Freemasonry*, pp.218-225.

[487] William John Polidori was a member of the Norwich based Union Lodge No. 52, Initiated on the 31st March 1818, Passed on the 28th April 1818, and was Raised on the 1st June 1818.

[488] See William John Polidori, *The Vampyre*, (London: Sherwood, Neely and Jones, 1819).

[489] See David Harrison, *The Genesis of Freemasonry*, (Hersham: Lewis Masonic, 2009).

Abbey being built with sacred geometry. According to Bligh Bond, his mediums received information from dead monks which assisted him in discovering archaeological remains of the Abbey. This rather unorthodox approach to his archaeological work eventually led him to be dismissed from the site by his employers, the Church of England. Bligh Bond went on to write about the Geometric cubit as a basis for proportion in the plans of medieval buildings and published his account of the Abbey excavation in his celebrated work *The Gate of Remembrance* in 1918.[490]

Conan Doyle had embraced psychic research after the death of his wife and several other close family members, and until his death in 1930, he ardently supported spiritualism and constantly sought proof of life after death, a curiosity which can be paralleled with writer and Freemason Mark Twain's interest in parapsychology in the USA. Conan Doyle's book *The Coming of the Fairies* in 1922 put forward his support for the infamous Cottingley Fairies; where two girls, from Cottingley near Bradford in the north of England, had supposedly taken five pictures of fairies.[491] Decades later, the girls, then elderly women, admitted faking the photographs, but in 1922, Conan Doyle strongly supported their claims. His 1926 work *The History of Spiritualism* also lent his support to séances conducted by various psychics at the time and their supposed spiritual materialisations.[492] One of the spiritualists that Conan Doyle supported was Daniel Douglas Home. Fellow Freemason Lord Lindsay was also a supporter of Home, having witnessed the spiritualist mysteriously levitate out of a third story window only to return through the window of an adjoining room.

Interest in occult philosophy grew during the later Victorian period, not only amongst the literati of the period, best exemplified with Yeats and Conan Doyle, but with the prosperous and educated who wished to explore the mystical esoteric belief systems, and Freemasonry became a fascination to many because of this. An example of this is how Freemasonry stirred an interest in the occultist Aleister Crowley, who, in

---

[490] Frederick Bligh Bond was a member of the Bristol based St. Vincent Lodge No. 1404, being initiated on the 28th of November, 1889. He served as Worshipful Master of the lodge in 1894, although his membership ceased in 1914. He was a member of the Rosicrucian Society and the infamous Ghost Club, a club which also had links to Sir Arthur Conan Doyle and occultist and Egyptologist E. A. Wallis Budge. See Frederick Bligh Bond, *The Gate of Remembrance, The story of the psychological experiment which resulted in the discovery of the Edgar Chapel at Glastonbury*, (Kessinger Publishing Co., 1999). Also see Frederick Bligh Bond, *Central Somerset Gazette Illustrated Guide to Glastonbury*, (Glastonbury: Avalon Press, 1927).
[491] See Arthur Conan Doyle, *The Coming of the Fairies*, (Forgotten Books, 2007).
[492] See Arthur Conan Doyle, *The History of Spiritualism*, (Teddington: Echo Library, 2006).

the closing years of the nineteenth century, became involved in the Golden Dawn, joining in 1898, and from there went on to sample the hidden mysteries of Freemasonry after joining an irregular 'Scottish Rite' lodge in Mexico and the irregular Anglo-Saxon Lodge No. 343 in Paris. Crowley later joined the Ordo Templi Orientis, which like the Golden Dawn, admitted both men and women, having a Masonic influence within the ritual. Crowley's closeness to Mathers added to growing tensions within the Golden Dawn, and it soon splintered into different groups, with Arthur Edward Waite, who was disliked by Crowley, becoming involved in the leadership of one particular faction.[493] Crowley, like Waite, went on to co-design his own Tarot card deck entitled the Thoth deck.

In Wales, pseudo Masonic and occultist interests merged with the search for a cultural identity to form Druid Societies during the nineteenth century. Welsh poet and scholar Iolo Morganwg had founded the *Gorsedd* in the later eighteenth century, performing a mysterious ceremony on Primrose Hill in London in 1792, Morganwg claiming links to the ancient Druids. Morganwg was linked to Freemasonry by later writers, and he was certainly inspired by the radical writings of Thomas Paine.[494] Freemasonry certainly seemed to have inspired elements of the regalia, symbolism and ritual of the new Druids, for example the Welsh *Eisteddfod* which was held in Liverpool in 1884, witnessed the *Gorsedd* wearing ceremonial dress which was reminiscent of Masonic regalia. The celebrated eighteenth century Welsh poet Goronwy Owen was also a Freemason, entering into the Craft when he was a Curate of St. Mary's Church at Walton-on-the-Hill near the port of Liverpool in 1754.[495]

The romantic connections between the ancient Druids and Freemasonry had been written about by eighteenth century writers such as William Stukeley and Thomas Paine,[496] and the importance and the

---

[493] Martin P. Starr, 'Aleister Crowley: Freemason!', in *AQC*, Vol. 108, (1995), pp.150-161.

[494] See Philip Jenkins, *A History of Modern Wales 1536-1990*, (London: Longman, 1992), p.182.

[495] For a biography of Goronwy Owen's career in Walton 1753-1755, see G. Barrow, *Celtic Bards, Chiefs and Kings*, (London: John Murray, 1928), pp.231-295. Owen describes his membership in a letter to Welsh antiquarian William Morris dated 16th of October, 1754, stating that he believed Freemasonry was a branch of the 'Druids of old'. See D. Knoop, *On the Connection Between Operative & Speculative Masonry*, (1935), The Inaugural Address delivered to the Quatuor Coronati Lodge, No. 2076, (London, 8th of November, 1935), pp.38-9. See also J. A. Davies, (ed.), *The Letters of Goronwy Owen (1723-1769)*, (Cardiff: William Lewis Ltd, 1924) and Jenkins, *A History of Modern Wales*, p.73.

[496] See Thomas Paine, *Origin of Free Masonry*, in *The Works of Thomas Paine*, (New York: E. Haskell, 1854) and William Stukeley, *Stonehenge a temple restor'd to the British Druids*, (W. Innys and R. Manby, 1740).

power of ritual, embraced with tradition certainly captured the Welsh imagination, with Druid societies being formed under the auspice of Friendly Societies, leading to the foundation of the United Ancient Order of Druids, which used very similar symbolism to Freemasonry.[497] An example of this is the Druid symbol for Awen /|\ – a Welsh word for inspiration (poetic or musical), a word which describes the inspiration of the bards in Welsh poetic tradition, and is reminiscent of the radiating downward light which emits from the All-Seeing-eye in Freemasonry. Other Druid symbols which have a similarity to Masonic symbolism include the skull and the tree of life.[498] Like Freemasonry, the revived interest in the Druids filtered into the minds of the nineteenth century Welsh people, and many public houses began to be named after them. An example of this popular romantic interest in the Druids can be seen with three existing Druid Inns in North-east Wales; one in the atmospheric setting of Llanferris, one just a few miles away in the village Pontblyddyn, and another situated in the aptly named village of Gorsedd near Holywell, all three dating to the Victorian period.

The Druidical career of Dr. William Price presents an example of a Welsh radical who embraced the romantic ideology of the ancient Druids to put forward his idea of a Welsh identity. Price, like Iolo Morganwg before him, forged a romantic view of the past, for example he traced the roots of Greek civilisation to the Pontypridd area where he was also a Chartist leader and became a supporter of local miners' organisations and co-operative movements. His desire for ritual and what he perceived as the ancient practices of the Druids came to climax when he cremated his dead son 'Jesus Christ' Price in 1884, in doing so Price became a pioneer for cremation in Britain. As a self appointed Arch Druid, Price was seen regularly wearing his self styled ceremonial regalia which included a fox fur headdress and the obligatory Druid robes, his healthy appetite for women resulting in a number of children, even when he was late in life. He was also involved in the Chartist Newport rising of 1839, Price's

---

[497] See Andrew Prescott, "THE VOICE CONVENTIONAL' Druidic Myths and Freemasonry', a paper given to the Kirkcaldy Masonic Research Conference, May 2001, and at the Fourth International Conference of the Canonbury Masonic Research Centre, November 2002, http://www.lodgehope337.org.uk/lectures/prescott%20S01.PDF [accessed 20th of August, 2009] See also Owain Morgan, *Pabell Dofydd Eglurhad ar anianyddiaeth grefyddol yr hen dderwyddon Cymreig*, (Caerdydd: argraffwyd gan Daniel owen d'I ywmni, 1889), in which Morgan puts forward the history of the Druid Order in Wales.

[498] Ibid. Morgan uses the Awen symbol on the cover of his work along with the symbol of the skull set within a megalithic burial chamber.

political radicalism going hand-in-hand with his radical views on Druidical ideology and his ideas on Welsh national identity.

The Cymmrodorion Society, started in 1751, celebrated Welsh culture and literature, with the Freemason Watkin Williams Wynn, the fourth Baronet, being the Chief President dressing ceremoniously as a Druid when attending London masquerades.[499] The Williams Wynn family had been ardent Jacobite supporters in Wales, and had also been involved in the secret Jacobite club 'The Circle of the White Rose'. In 1822, the Cymmrodorion Society began to publish its Transactions, and, along with its North Welsh counterpart The Gwyneddigion, founded in 1770, attracted the interests of radical Welshmen, such as the Painite John Jones, also known as 'Jac Glan-y-Gors.[500]

Gentlemen's Clubs and societies in the Industrial North West of England

For gentlemen residing outside London, there were clubs being founded that were of a similar ilk. An Athenaeum Club was founded in Liverpool in 1797, one of the founding members being the abolitionist William Roscoe, who also founded the Liverpool Lyceum Club. The Lyceum Club's beautiful Temple-like Neo-Classical building was built in Bold Street, Liverpool by Thomas Harrison of Chester in 1800-1802. Both of these clubs, situated quite close to each other, were gentlemen's clubs, attracting the cream of Liverpool society, including many with Masonic connections, such as John Gladstone, a member of the Athenaeum Club, whose close associates George Canning and William Ewart were both prominent Freemasons. Both clubs offered a library and reading room, the Lyceum becoming home to Liverpool's circulating library, which had been founded in 1757, a year before the aforementioned circulating library in Warrington.[501]

The Liverpool Lyceum and Athenaeum inspired Manchester's Portico Library, which was designed in a similar Neo-Classical style by Thomas Harrison, and opened in 1806. The Manchester Portico Library was built by the Manchester based builder and industrialist David Bellhouse, who was also a founder of the Royal Manchester Institution and the Manchester Mechanics Institute. There is no evidence that Bellhouse was

---

[499] See Harrison, *The Genesis of Freemasonry*, p.174.
[500] Jenkins, *A History of Modern Wales*, p.181-184.
[501] The library is mentioned in W. Moss, *The Liverpool Guide*, (Printed for and sold by Crane and Jones, Castle Street, sold by Vernor and Hood, London, 1796), p.96.

a Mason, but he certainly held ideals which were mirrored in the Craft; he was interested in architecture, promoted local education and was a leading philanthropist.

The Manchester Athenaeum followed in 1836, designed by the renowned architect Charles Barry, and like the Portico Library, was built to supply an education, not just for the professional classes but for labouring men and women also, with Charles Dickens even giving a speech in support of the Manchester Athenaeum in 1842. Manchester also had its own Reform Club, which was established in 1867, and from 1871 was located in the prestigious Manchester thoroughfare of King Street, in an extravagantly gothic building designed by the architect Edward Salomons. King Street became the financial centre of Manchester, being the location of many of its banks, building societies and insurance headquarters, and just around the corner in Bridge Street, the Manchester Masonic Hall was built in 1929.

In the eighteenth century, *'English men would set up a club where they could be at ease smoking, talking or indulging themselves in blissful silence'.*[502] An example of this is an early gentleman's dining club founded in Liverpool called the Unanimous Society, formed in 1753 by the Freemason and merchant Thomas Golightly. Another Liverpool based club called The Free and Easy Society whose Treasurer was none other than Masonic Rebel John Eltonhead, seemed to be another dining society which also donated to charity.[503] The Liverpool Athenaeum pre-dated the founding of its London's namesake, but the gentlemen who were members were certainly extracted from a similar stratum of society; professional men of business and men of culture, like-minded gentlemen with a philanthropic ethos who could relax within the aesthetic atmosphere and exchange thoughts and ideas. Later prominent members who also had Masonic links included the 2nd Viscount Leverhulme who was president of the Athenaeum in 1930, his father, the 1st Viscount, being the influential Freemason who created Port Sunlight.

The intricate relationship between Freemasonry and gentlemen's clubs during the latter nineteenth century can be seen in the minutes of The Merchants Lodge in Liverpool, were in March 1882, three candidates

---

[502] Roy Harper, *Enlightenment*, (London, Penguin, 2000), p.440.
[503] Liverpool Mercury 27th of December 1816, issue 289, a meeting of the Anniversary Dinner of the Free and Easy Society was advertised as meeting at the home of James Sweeney of Mersey St. on the 1st of January, 1817, were *'After dinner members will dispose of cash in the Treasurers Funds to Charities they think proper.'* John Eltonhead was listed as the President of the society. The 'Free and Easy Johns' were assembled into Lodges, and can be traced back to the later eighteenth century.

were each managers of three local clubs; the Exchange Club, the Reform Club and the Liverpool Club. Social etiquette was vitally important for the up-and-coming gentlemen of this period, and access to Freemasonry and the many gentlemen's clubs not only became places to display these social skills but allowed networking across the complex and elaborate 'clubbing' nexus. To become influential in the community it was essential that a sociable gentleman could interact in this 'clubbing' social scene, a scene which Freemasonry was part of. Gentlemen who were in search of culture and seeking to climb the social ladder could, as in Freemasonry, find access to a club - if they knew existing members.

The Liverpool Cotton Brokers' Association, founded in 1841, was an essential part of the clubbing nexus in Liverpool, especially in the cotton trade, which was a vital part of the economy, not just for the north-west of England but also for the whole of the country. In 1882 it became known as the Liverpool Cotton Association, and links with local Freemasonry were extremely close, with a lodge being connected to the Association. The President of the Association from 1940-1942, William Sinclair Scott Hannay, had also been Provincial Grand Master for West Lancashire from 1952-1957, with members of the Hannay family having previously served as President of the Association during the later nineteenth and early twentieth centuries. Hanney had joined the prestigious Liverpool based St. George's Lodge of Harmony in 1910, a lodge which also featured a hefty number of cotton brokers. The Liverpool Cotton Association met at the Cotton Exchange, which was built in 1906, the building containing a ballroom which was used by the members for all kinds of social events, including Masonic functions.

Like the previously discussed learned societies and gentlemen's clubs situated in the industrial north-west of England, such as Warrington, Oldham and Liverpool, which attracted the cream of the professional classes, the London gentlemen's clubs did the same, but on a much grander scale, the clubs attracting high ranking aristocrats, leading politicians, natural philosophers, artists and writers. These were the people who were running the country and were involved in government. The old paradigms of Whig and Tory were becoming a memory, and the staunch old political clubs of the earlier eighteenth century, such as the legendary anti-Stewart 'Calves' Head Club', were long gone.[504] Indeed,

---

[504] Leigh Hunt, *The Town*, (Oxford: Oxford University Press, 1907), pp.434-6. The 'Calves' Head Club met at a tavern in Suffolk Street, London during the eighteenth century, and at a meeting on the 30th of January (a date which commemorated the beheading of Charles I), the members apparently threw a calf's head wrapped in a napkin out of the tavern window and drank damnation

the Victorian gentlemen's clubs were far removed from the early eighteenth century Whig and Tory clubs; for example Jonathan Swift's Tory Brothers Club and the Whig Kit-Kat Club, with their sometimes hostile and overtly political divisions and ritualistic persuasions well and truly in the past. Politicians, no matter what their political background, could move through the gentlemen's social scene with ease. These clubs had no ritual, but some did retain traditional elements, be it toasting during the meal or traditional after dinner speeches. Club rules dictated the culture of polite society, something that Freemasonry had promoted in the previous century, the Craft creating a neutral space, uniting Whig and Tory and creating a political bridge.[505]

For a country gentlemen, there was his country lodge, which might have met at his private estate, such as the Masonic lodge of Sir Watkin William Wynn at Wynnstay in North Wales. Lord de Tabley's country estate in Cheshire also witnessed Masonic meetings, and a De Tabley lodge also met in the rural market town of Frodsham in Cheshire.[506] This particular lodge, founded in 1862, had amongst its founder members Lord de Tabley, the Hon. Wilbraham Egerton M.P, and George Cornwall Legh M.P., all leading Cheshire gentry. The Masonic historian John Armstrong commented on the excusive membership of the lodge when writing his *History of Freemasonry in Cheshire* in 1901:

'Probably no Lodge in the Province of Cheshire was ever established under more favourable circumstances…If in 1840 the rich men of the neighbourhood took little notice of Masonry, the same certainly could not be said in 1862.[507]

Other social networking activities for the country gentleman was the hunt, an example of which is the Cheshire Hunt, which in 1839 included

---

to the Stuarts. However, when writing about the club, Hunt put forward that this was untrue, and though mentioning the club had a Protestant political nature, the members never threw a calf's head out of the window at all on this date, but a Catholic led mob had gathered outside the tavern and threatened the members of the club, surrounding the tavern and causing a riot. The riot was eventually dispersed but an enduring myth was made about the club. Hunt also mentions how the Tories stirred up mobs against the Whigs in London when Mug-Houses became centres for political meetings in the early eighteenth century, with political factions forming beer-drinking clubs were political singing and toasting took place, see Hunt, p.410-11.

[505] Lawrence E. Klein, 'Liberty, Manners, and Politeness in Early Eighteenth-Century England', *The Historical Journal*, Vol. 32, No. 3, (September, 1989), pp.583-605, on p.587. Also see Lawrence Klein, 'The Third Earl of Shaftesbury and the Progress of Politeness', *Eighteenth-Century Studies*, Vol. 18, No. 2, (Winter, 1984-1985), pp.186-214.
[506] See Harrison, *The Genesis of Freemasonry*, pp.141-144.
[507] John Armstrong, *A History of Freemasonry in Cheshire*, (London: Kenning, 1901), pp.384-385.

various members of the Cheshire gentry who were also leading Masons such as Lord de Tabley, Tatton Egerton and George Cornwall Legh. In a list of local gentry included in the Cheshire Hunt of 1823, Sir Harry Mainwaring, Bart., of Peover is mentioned, a prominent local Freemason who served as Deputy Provincial Grand Master of Cheshire in 1832,[508] Sir Harry Mainwaring being related to Col. Henry Mainwaring who had been made a Freemason with Elias Ashmole in 1646. The second Lord de Tabley, whose family had also married into the Mainwaring's of Peover,[509] would become Provincial Grand Master of Cheshire in 1865, followed later by Allen De Tatton Egerton in 1887.[510]

Freemasonry became an attractive social networking 'club' for gentlemen, industrialists and professionals, offering an element of exclusiveness that the 'middle classes' yearned for, supplying another elitist society for them to join as it became increasingly fashionable. The promotion of education and service to their community was important in many of the clubs that emerged during the nineteenth and early twentieth centuries, such as the Rotary Club and certain learned societies, reflecting the so called '*voluntary code of behaviuor*', that the middle classes adhered to.[511] Other clubs, such as the gentlemen's clubs of London were clubs of privilege, while other societies, such as the Hermetic Order of the Golden Dawn, explored the more occult interests of the educated who sought deeper hidden knowledge. With Freemasonry however, these prosperous middle classes could access a society which included the aristocracy, elevating their social status as they searched ever fervently for secret lost knowledge, some of them delving ever more experimentally into ritual and symbolism. The gentlemen's clubs in the town and the hunting clubs in the country were social havens for the gentry, but Freemasonry not only offered a ritualistic experience that itself provided an element of mystery and a culture of secret symbolism, it presented a multi layered

---

508 Ibid., p.95. See also *History of the Mainwaring Chapels in the Church of St. Laurence, Over Peover*, (Local Publication, 1972).

509 Peter Leicester of Tabley (1588-1647) married Elizabeth daughter of Sir Randle Mainwaring of Peover in 1611, in *Cheshire Visitations pedigrees*. See also *History of the Mainwaring Chapels in the Church of St. Laurence, Over Peover*, (Local Publication, 1972), p.20, in which a monument dated to 1573 records that Philip Mainwaring of Peover had married Anne, daughter of Sir Raffe Leycester.

510 See Armstrong, *A History of Freemasonry in Cheshire*, pp.186-189.

511 See C.R. Hewitt, *Towards My Neighbour: The Social Influence of the Rotary Club Movement in Great Britain and Ireland*, (London: Longmans, 1950), pp.6-11, in which Hewitt puts forward that in the early twentieth century, business men and other '*members of the middle classes*' became involved in the Rotary Movement as a means of exercising '*service to humanity*'. The Rotary Club was another activity for the 'middle classes' that promoted education and '*good citizenship*'. See also Hugh Barty-King, *"Round Table" The Search for Fellowship 1927-1977*, (London: Heinemann, 1977).

society, the Craft giving a pathway to other, more secret orders, such as the Royal Arch, the Mark degree and the Knights Templar. The popularity of Freemasonry can be seen in its expansion during the latter half of the nineteenth century, and the next chapter will discuss why the up-and-coming professionals, industrialists and businessmen found the Craft so alluring.

Chapter 9

The flourishing of Freemasonry, Success and Expansion 1850-1930[512]

'Far off, most secret, and inviolate Rose,
Enfold me in my hour of hours; where those
Who sought thee in the Holy Sepulchre,
Or in the wine vat, dwell beyond the stir'
W.B. Yeats, *The Secret Rose*, 1899[513]

'The idea, or motif, of the design, in an artistic sense, is to present such a
combination of the architectural forms characteristic of the mediaeval ages, (which forms
owe, if not their invention, at least their development, to the combined labors of the
Travelling Masons of that period,) as naturally to suggest the most effective poetical and
historical associations connected with our Institution.'
The Freemasons' Monthly Magazine, 1864[514]

'Where Science, Art, and Labour have outpour'd
Their myriad horns of plenty at our feet.'
Alfred, Lord Tennyson, *Ode for the opening of the international exhibition,*
1862[515]

In the latter half of the nineteenth century, Freemasonry became so popular amongst the industrialists, businessmen and professionals that it quickly expanded, with membership increasing and new lodges being founded at a rapid rate. In Warrington for example, from having one lodge in 1865, by 1930, there were ten, all meeting regularly and all

---

[512] Part of the content of this chapter was presented as a paper at the Canonbury Masonic Research Centre 2009 conference on the 24th of October, 2009, entitled 'The Genesis of Freemasonry – a historiographical view'.

[513] W.B. Yeats, 'The Secret Rose' in R.K.R. Thornton, (ed.), *Poetry of the 'Nineties*, (Middlesex: Penguin, 1970), p.119.

[514] Charles W. Moore, Grand Secretary of The Grand Lodge of Massachusetts, 'Our New Masonic Temple', in *The Freemasons' Monthly Magazine*, Vol. XXIII, (Boston: printed by Hugh H. Tuttle, 1864), September 1, 1864, No. 11, p.321.

[515] Sir Herbert Warren, (ed.), *Poems of Alfred, Lord Tennyson 1830-1865*, (Oxford: Oxford University Press, 1929), p.590.

experiencing success.[516]   As discussed in previous chapters, with charismatic gentlemen joining various lodges, an influx of new industrialists and professionals joined Freemasonry during the 1850s and 1860s, such as Sir Gilbert Greenall who joined the Lodge of Lights in Warrington in 1850. He went on to found the Gilbert Greenall Lodge No. 1250 in 1869, and other new lodges followed, such as the Lodge of Charity No. 2651 and the aptly named Ashmole Lodge No. 5128. These charismatic gentlemen made their lodges interesting and alluring for the up-and-coming gentlemen of the town, Freemasonry becoming an attractive social scene which could offer an array of networking connections.

These charismatic personalities were not the only reason that Freemasonry became popular again, and after a period of public suspicion and mistrust in the first part of the nineteenth century, Masonic lodges became a perfect place for the aspiring Victorian men drawn from the 'High Street' businesses to learn the etiquette of circulating in high social circles, to gain confidence while in the presence of the aristocracy and Industrialists, and to learn about public speaking. Freemasonry could supply an education for a new era of social-climbing men; the new initiates could ascertain the whole Masonic experience, from learning the ritual and understanding the ethos of Freemasonry, to discovering about the dining decorum. They could then apply their new social skills to their business life, utilising their newly acquired Masonic contacts, and ultimately improving their social status. An example of this can be seen in The Merchants Lodge with Simon Jude, who became the first Liverpool Public accountant to pass the examination under the Charter of Incorporation when the Institute of Chartered Accountants was founded in 1880. He entered the lodge at the same time, and mixed with the local aristocracy within Freemasonry, such as the Earl of Latham, who served as Deputy Grand Master and Provincial Grand Master. Jude later entered into local politics, becoming a councillor in 1895 and an alderman in 1906. Jude also displayed his professional aptitude in the lodge, becoming Inner Guard in 1881, and quickly rose through the ranks to become Worship Master of the lodge in 1887, eventually being appointed Provincial Grand Director of Ceremonies.[517]

Reports of Masonic Banquets and Balls were a regular feature in the later nineteenth century publication *Freemasons Magazine and Masonic*

---

[516] Herbert Woods and James Armstrong, *A Short Historical Note of Freemasonry in Warrington*, (Warrington, 1938), pp.5-7.

[517] John Macnab, *History of the Merchants' Lodge No. 241*, p.74 and p.188.

Mirror, the social etiquette, dining decorum and the speakers of Masonic functions being discussed at length with their politeness and courtesy being commended. In a report dated January 1868 regarding the election of a new Provincial Grand Master of Ayrshire, the former Provincial Grand Master Brother Wylie was described as being held in high estimation among Edinburgh Masonic circles, and *'on several public occasions...amply sustained the dignity of his Masonic position'*. In the same issue, an article on Masonic Banquets was discussed, the writer endeavouring to put forward the correct dining etiquette:

> *The guests, unless the W.M. in the chair should intervene, which is rare, so far from being served first, are pretty generally served last.* [518]

As in Warrington, a similar Masonic expansion occurred in Liverpool; with many lodges being founded during the later part of the nineteenth century, such as the De Grey and Ripon Lodge No. 1356, founded in 1871. This lodge however changed its name to the Toxteth Lodge after Earl De Grey and Ripon, who had served as Deputy Grand Master from 1861, and Grand Master from May 1870 until September 1874, resigned from all Masonic offices after becoming a Catholic, an incident which suggests that even during this period, English Freemasonry was obstinately Protestant in its outlook, especially when it came down to its leadership.[519]   Other new Liverpool lodges included the Royal Victoria Lodge No. 1013, founded in 1864, being a daughter lodge of the older Merchants Lodge.

In the developing industrial towns of the north-west such as Runcorn in Cheshire, new lodges were also founded to accommodate the growth of Freemasonry in the area, such as the Ellesmere Lodge No. 758, which was founded in 1859 and whose brethren assisted in funding the building of a new Masonic Hall in the town in 1863. Because of the impact of the railways and the ever growing network of business contacts by individual Masons within these lodges, they began to attract more candidates from other areas; the Ellesmere Lodge for example began to appeal to men from various professions, such as solicitor William Jeffreys from St. Helens, the lodge attracting new Masons not only from the neighbouring industrial towns like Widnes, but from as far away as Birmingham and

---

[518] 'Masonic Banquets' in the *Freemasons Magazine and Masonic Mirror*, Vol. XVIII, January-June 1868, (London, Freemasons Magazine Company Limited), p.7.
[519] *Minutes of the Toxteth Lodge No. 1356, Liverpool, 1871-2009*. Not Listed.

Sheffield.[520] Freemasons could freely visit and join lodges in other areas, such as Thomas Domville, a builder who was a member of the Ancient Union Lodge in Liverpool and the Lodge of Lights in Warrington, joining both in 1866.[521]

Masonic Halls

Because of the ever growing number of lodges within towns and cities throughout the country during the later nineteenth century, Masonic Halls, like the one in Runcorn, became ever popular. Members of the lodges contributed funds for the specially constructed buildings, the foundation stones being laid with full Masonic pomp and public ceremony. Freemasonry flourished franticly, and unlike the early part of the nineteenth century, the Craft no longer had to hide in the shadows of the public houses of industrial towns or the cold corners of country taverns; Masonry could reside in magnificent Masonic Halls, many displaying symbolism prominently along with the architectural splendour of the society's ethos.[522] Unlike the lodges examined in the earlier part of the nineteenth century, an examination of the minutes of the lodges in the Victorian era reveal little trace of fines for swearing and drunkenness!

One such Masonic Hall was in Liverpool, where a committee was formed for the specific duty to purchase a property, a house in Hope Street being bought in 1857. The Masonic Hall was opened the following year after some alterations, but by 1872 the property was demolished and the corner stone of a new specially built Masonic Hall was laid on the 2nd of November with a full Masonic ceremony, with local Masonic dignitary Lord Skelmersdale doing the honours. The Hall was ready two years later, but had to be extended again by the 1920s, an indication of the growth of Freemasonry in the area. A strip of land next to the building was purchased and by 1932, the extension was completed. Some Masonic Halls had to move location as Freemasonry expanded in the area, such as in Manchester, where the beautifully decorative Freemasons

---

[520] Anon., The History of the Ellesmere Lodge No. 758, (Cheshire, 2009), pp.16-17.

[521] See *A List of the Members of the Ancient Union Lodge No. 203,19th of July, 1866, C.D. Rom: 139 GRA/ANT/UNI, The Library and Museum of Freemasonry, United Grand Lodge, Great Queen Street, London,* and *List of Members of the Lodge of Lights, No.148, Masonic Hall, Warrington, 31st of December, 1866.* Not listed.

[522] For a brief study of some of the Inns and Taverns in London where lodges met during the eighteenth century see Albert F. Calvert, 'Where Masons Used to Meet', in the *British Masonic Miscellany,* Compiled by George M. Martin, Vol.20, (Dundee: David Winter and Son, 1936), pp.95-98.

Hall was opened in Cooper Street in 1864, its foundation stone being laid by none other than Stephen Blair, the Provincial Grand Master of East Lancashire and member of the aforementioned Anchor and Hope Lodge. The Hall later moved to a larger art deco building at Bridge Street in 1929.[523] Freemasons Hall in Great Queens Street, London was also being rebuilt in a grand art deco style at this time, being opened in 1933. Charity still played a vital role within Freemasonry, an example being the founding of the Royal Masonic Hospital, which was opened by George V the same year as Freemasons Hall. The building was also meant to hold Masonic receptions and Masonic symbols can be found around the Hospital, including Zodiac signs on the etched glass windows.

The Warrington Masonic Hall was built in 1932, the foundation stone being laid by the Provincial Grand Master Arthur Foster, and was specially constructed to house the majority of the town's growing lodges. Like the Liverpool Masonic Hall, it became the focal point for Masonry in the town, being the centre for not only Lodge and Chapter meetings, but Masonic functions and dinners. Masonic Halls were being purposefully built and renovated in towns and cities all over the country, from York[524] to Penzance[525], from Hawarden[526] in North Wales to Swansea[527] in the south, all specially designed to accommodate a lodge room, ante-room, dining room and obligatory bar facilities, creating a more intimate Masonic experience for the Masonic gentlemen. The building of the Masonic Halls also testifies to the increasing popularity of the Craft, and like the Liverpool Masonic Hall in Hope Street and the York Masonic Hall at Duncombe Place, extensive improvements and extensions took place throughout the later nineteenth and early twentieth centuries to accommodate more lodges.[528]

Despite the fashion of building Masonic Halls in towns and cities, there were country lodges which still met in their local hotels or public

---

[523] Stephen Blair, the successful Bolton industrialist, was installed as Provincial Grand Master at the Royal Exchange in Manchester on the 24th of July, 1856.
[524] York Masonic Hall, in Duncombe Place, was built in 1862-3 by J Barton-Wilson and John Edwin Oates, and now houses the artifacts and archives of the 'York Grand Lodge'.
[525] In *Kelly's Directory of Cornwall, 1893*, under the heading of 'official establishments, local institutions &c.', the Masonic Hall at Penzance is listed as housing the Mount Sinai Lodge No. 121, as well as the Royal Arch Chapter and the Mark Masonry Lodge, see http://west-penwith.org.uk/pz293.htm [accessed 1st of May, 2009]
[526] Hawarden Masonic Hall was built in 1913.
[527] The Swansea Masonic Temple was built in 1923.
[528] See Robert Leslie Wood, *The Bi-centennial History of the York 'Union' Lodge No. 236 1777-1977*, (York: 1977), pp.62-63. The Masonic Hall at Duncombe Place in York was renovated in 1877 and again in 1899.

houses. With the introduction of the railways interconnecting villages to the towns and cities, the affluent and prosperous professional classes could move to the outlying villages, where they would found new lodges. An example of this is in the village of Lymm in Cheshire, where the Earl of Chester Lodge No. 1565 was consecrated in 1875, Lord De Tabley being one of the founders. By 1924, there were enough influential Freemasons residing in the village that another lodge, Domville Lodge No. 4647, was founded, one of the influential founders being local industrialist and politician Sir William Peter Rylands.[529] Another example of a country lodge was the Avon Lodge No.3569, which met at The Three Tuns in the small Worcestershire market town of Pershore. The lodge included the membership of local dignitaries such as General Sir Francis Davies, who was an extremely notable and charismatic Worcestershire Provincial Grand Master of the early 20th century. He became Deputy Grand Master of the United Grand Lodge of England and was responsible for consecrating over forty lodges; including the Worcestershire based Francis Davies Lodge No. 5053 which was named in his honor in 1928. General Sir Francis Davies was a popular figure in Worcestershire, being a war hero who had fought in the Boar War and in the First World War, being highly decorated.[530]

Some lodges that were founded during the later half of the nineteenth century seemed to purposefully locate themselves near to settings which had links to older Masonic associations, such as the lodge which met at the Canonbury Tavern, situated opposite the enigmatic Canonbury Tower near Islington in London. The Canonbury Tavern had in more recent times, been the location for the Islington Literary Society, which had been formed there in 1832.[531] Canonbury Tower had associations with the philosopher Sir Francis Bacon during the sixteenth century, and had also witnessed the annual feast of the 'Modern/Premier' Grand Lodge in 1797, but it was not until much later that a lodge would regularly meet at the Tavern.

The Canonbury Lodge No. 955 (now No. 657), was consecrated at the Tavern in February 1856, attended by the Deputy Provincial Grand

---

[529] See David Harrison, *Domville Lodge No. 4647, Lymm, Cheshire, The First 75 Years*, (Manchester, 1999), pp.1-6.

[530] The Avon Lodge No. 3569 was founded in 1911. See also 'Freemasonry's 270 years of Lodges in Worcestershire' in *Worcester News*, Saturday, 15th of June, 2002, http://archive.worcesternews.co.uk/2002/6/15/264560.html [accessed 1st of May, 2009] and the history of the Francis Davies Lodge No. 5035, http://www.francisdavieslodge.org.uk/LodgeHistory.htm [accessed 1st of May, 2009]

[531] Pieter Zwart, *Islington; A History and Guide*, (London: Eden Fisher, 1973), p.98.

Masters of Kent and Wiltshire, the lodge meeting there until a change of landlord forced them to move ten years later, after which the lodge met for a time at Freemasons Hall. The original landlord had been one Brother Todd, who was present at the consecration, and Masonic historian and scholar Matthew Cooke – who had the Cooke manuscript of the Old Charges named after him – was initiated into the lodge in 1857. Cooke was also a musician and songwriter, who actually wrote a song in the lodge's honour coincidently entitled 'Nine fifty five' after the original number of the lodge, in which he mentioned that the lodge met *Near the tow'r of Queen Bess'*. Cooke tried in vain to petition for the founding of a new lodge called The Elizabethan Tower Lodge in 1863, in obvious tribute to the Canonbury Tower over the road from the Tavern.

Another lodge which was founded in an area with older mystic traditions was The Pilgrims Lodge No. 1074 (now No. 772), which was consecrated at the George and Pilgrim Hotel, situated in the High Street of the market town of Glastonbury in 1859. Like The Canonbury Tavern, the George and Pilgrim Hotel was run by a Freemason at the time of the opening of the lodge, a certain Brother Bailey. A special train was put on from Bristol to take visiting brethren for the special occasion, and the consecration was attended by the Deputy Provincial Grand Master of Somerset Brother Randolph.[532] The George and Pilgrim was built in the late medieval period to house the ever growing visitors and pilgrims to the town, the supposed 'grave' of King Arthur and the sacred Holy Thorn being an attraction to Glastonbury Abbey even then, and like the Canonbury Lodge, the Pilgrims Lodge celebrated a connection to the ancient traditions of their town, with Freemason Frederick Bligh Bond excavating the Abbey using psychic mediums to assist him in 1908. Bligh Bond became convinced that the Abbey was a sacred place and had been built by the medieval stonemasons using sacred geometry.[533] Glastonbury had also been associated with the mystic John Dee, with the Freemason and alchemist Elias Ashmole reporting how Dee found a large quantity of the Elixir in the *'ruines of the Glastonbury-Abbey'*.[534]

---

[532] 'The Freemasons' Magazine and Masonic Mirror, (London: Published by Bro. Henry George Warren, 1859), p.52.

[533] See Frederick Bligh Bond, *Central Somerset Gazette Illustrated Guide to Glastonbury*, (Glastonbury: Avalon Press, 1927). Also see Frederick Bligh Bond, *The Gate of Remembrance, The story of the psychological experiment which resulted in the discovery of the Edgar Chapel at Glastonbury*, (Kessinger Publishing Co., 1999).

[534] Elias Ashmole, *Theatrum Chemicum Britannicum*, (London, 1652), pp.481-2. See also Arthur Dee, *Fasciculus Chemicus, Translated by Elias Ashmole*, (Edited by Lyndy Abraham), (London: Garland, 1997), p.xvi.

This celebration of local traditions within Freemasonry can also be seen with the Byron Lodge No. 4014, founded in 1920, which celebrated the Byron family's links to Freemasonry, the lodge meeting for an installation ceremony in 1923 at Newstead Abbey – the old seat of the Byron family.[535] The lodge still holds an annual church service in the chapel, which has a stained glass window revealing the building of Solomon's Temple in honour of Colonel Thomas Wildman, the one time provincial Grand Master of Nottinghamshire who purchased the Abbey from the cash-strapped poet Lord Byron in 1818. Wildman renovated the Abbey, constructing the Sussex Tower in honour of his friend, the Duke of Sussex who was Grand Master at the time.[536]

Masonic Expansion within Empire

Freemasonry also expanded rapidly throughout the British Empire during the nineteenth century, the Craft playing a role in the culture of colonization.[537] In India, an example of this can be seen with the Tyrell Leith Lodge No. 43 (formerly No. 2162 E.C.), which was consecrated by the then District Grand Master for Bombay Edward Tyrell Leith in 1886. This particular lodge attracted many distinguished members from the British Army and the civil service and also attracted the local elite, with two sons of Maharaja Sir Sayajirao Gaekwar joining the lodge. One of the Maharajas sons, Prince Dhairyashilarao S Gaekwar, actually served as Worshipful Master in 1924.[538] Lodges sprang up in other parts of the Empire such Canada and Australia, all assisting to provide a social network, the Masons striving to improve their local communities and establish contacts within their growing towns.

Canada had witnessed early Masonic activity during the later half of the eighteenth century when British forces organized various lodges when involved in the French and Indian War between 1754 and 1763, and Masonry was sometimes used to attract and secure the loyalty of certain members of the indigenous elite, bringing them closer to the British cause, such as in the case of Mohawk Joseph Brant. Brant became a favourite of Sir William Johnson, the British Superintendent for Northern

[535] See 'The Nottingham Journal', 14th of June, 1923.
[536] See David Harrison, *The Genesis of Freemasonry*, (Hersham: Lewis Masonic, 2009), pp.138-9.
[537] For a further analysis of the role of Freemasonry in building the British Empire, see Jessica Harland-Jacobs, *Builders of Empire: Freemasonry and British Imperialism 1717-1927*, (North Carolina: North Carolina Press, 2007).
[538] See the lodge website for a brief history http://www.lodge43.com/history.htm [accessed 11th of October, 2009]

Indian Affairs, who became close to the Mohawk people, and enlisted their allegiance in the French and Indian War. The young Brant took up arms for the British, and, after the war Brant found himself working as an interpreter for Johnson. He had worked as an interpreter before the war and had assisted in translating the prayer book and the Gospel of Mark into the Mohawk language, his other translations including the Acts of the Apostles and a short history of the Bible, Brant having converted to Christianity, a religion which he embraced.

Around 1775, after being appointed secretary to Sir William's successor, Guy Johnson, Brant received a Captain's commission in the British Army and set off for England, where he became a Freemason and confirmed his attachment to the British Crown, Brant's Masonic apron, according to legend, being presented to him by George III himself. On his return to America, Brant became a key figure in securing the loyalty of other Iroquois tribes in fighting for the British against the 'rebels' during the American War of Independence.

It was during the war that Brant entered into Masonic legend; after the surrender of the 'rebel' forces at the Battle of the Cedars on the St. Lawrence River in 1776, Brant famously saved the life of Captain John McKinstry, a member of Hudson Lodge No.13 of New York, who was about to be burned at the stake. McKinstry, remembering that Brant was a Freemason, gave him the Masonic sign of appeal which Brant recognized, an action which secured McKinstry's release and subsequent good treatment. McKinstry and Brant remained friends for life, and in 1805 he and Brant visited the Masonic Lodge in Hudson, New York, where Brant was given an excellent reception. Brant's portrait now hangs in the lodge. Another story relating to Brant during the war has another 'rebel' captive named Lieutenant Boyd giving Brant a Masonic sign, which secured him a reprieve from execution. However, on this occasion, Brant left his Masonic captive in the care of the British, who subsequently had Boyd tortured and executed.[539]

After the war Brant removed himself with his tribe to Canada, establishing the Grand River Reservation for the Mohawk Indians. Brant became affiliated with Lodge No. 11 at the Mohawk village at Grand River of which he was the first Master and he was later affiliated with Barton Lodge No.10 at Hamilton, Ontario. He returned to England in

---

[539] See Tim Fulford, *Romantic Indians: Native Americans, British Literature, and Transatlantic Culture 1756-1830*, (Oxford: Oxford University Press, 2006). Fulford discusses how Natuve North American Indians and British colonists had a closer relationship during this period and how they influenced each other in literature and culture.

1785 in an attempt to settle legal disputes on the Reservation lands, where he was again well received by George III and the Prince of Wales.[540]

Freemasonry subsequently spread throughout Canada and Grand Lodges were established in provinces such as Quebec and British Columbia, with Canada's first Prime Minister Sir John Alexander Macdonald being a Freemason. With the unification of the provinces, Freemasonry played a role in the development of communities throughout Canada, an example being the development of the North West Mounted Police Force, many of whom were Freemasons who founded the North-West Mounted Police Lodge No. 61 in 1894.[541]

In Australia, because of its early origins as a penal colony, Freemasonry seemed to have had a difficult start, especially during the opening years of the nineteenth century in the wake of the Unlawful Societies Act. Secret meetings were seen as suspicious, especially in a place where there were political prisoners and Masonic meetings without the Governor's permission were forbidden in Sydney in 1804. In other areas, Masonic lodges flourished, and an early example is of the unwarranted St. John's Lodge which operated on Norfolk Island, the site of another penal colony. The island is the site of the early Masonic grave of George Hales, the commander of the ship 'General Boyd', who, after falling ill on board ship, was brought ashore, but died shortly afterwards on the 16th of August, 1801. The grave, with its prominent Masonic symbolism of the square and compass set within an arch, and its skull and crossbones etched around the side, reveals how a Freemason could be buried many miles from home, and cared for in an isolated community by fellow Freemasons.[542] By the 1840s, Freemasonry was no longer met with

---

[540] Joseph Brant (1742-1807) was raised in Hiram's Cliftonian Lodge No. 814 in London, early in 1776, the lodge being been founded in 1771, and during Brant's visit, it had met at the Falcon in Princes Street, Soho. The lodge was erased in 1782. His association with the Johnson's may have been an influence in his links to Freemasonry; Guy Johnson had accompanied Brant on his visit to England, the Johnson family having Masonic links. See David Harrison, 'Joseph Brant A Masonic Legend', in *MQ*, Grand Lodge Publications, Issue 23, October 2007, http://www.mqmagazine.co.uk/issue-23/p-33.php [accessed 11th of October, 2009]. See also Anon., *The Life of Captain Joseph Brant with An Account of his Re-interment at Mohawk, 1850, and of the Corner Stone Ceremony in the Erection of the Brant Memorial, 1886*, (Ontario, Brantford: B.H. Rothwell, 1886).

[541] See Nelson King, 'The Mounties and Freemasonry', in *Freemasonry Today*, Issue 26, Autumn 2003, http://www.freemasonrytoday.com/26/p11.php [accessed 23rd of November, 2009]. Sir John Alexander Macdonald was initiated into Freemasonry in the St. John's Lodge No.5 in Kingston, Ontario, in 1844, and became the Grand Representative of the United Grand Lodge of England in his native Grand Lodge of Canada in the Province of Ontario.

[542] George Hales was made a Mason in 1789 in the Dundee Arms Lodge No. 9, which met in Wapping, London.

condemnation by the Australian authorities and it subsequently expanded rapidly. Each Australian State now has its own Grand Lodge, as does New Zealand.[543] Freemasonry also established itself in Hong Kong with the foundation of The Royal Sussex Lodge No. 501 in 1844.

In Southeast Asia, the Dutch were probably the first to set up organised lodges, but it was Sir Thomas Stamford Raffles, an employee of the East India Company, who played an important role in establishing Freemasonry there in the nineteenth century. Raffles was born on the 6th of July 1781, on the Ship *Ann*, off the harbour of Port Morant in Jamaica. He was the only surviving son of Benjamin Raffles, a captain trading in the West Indies. As a child Raffles was sent to an Academy at Hammersmith, then, at the age of 14 he became an employee of the East India Company, working as a clerk at East India House in London, an event which was to determine the rest of his relatively short life. He held high ambitions, and he gained the post of Assistant Secretary in Penang, and with a large increase in salary, he then married his first wife Olivia before setting out for Southeast Asia in 1805. Raffles had a passion for knowledge, and learned the Malayan language on the voyage.

This new position opened up a new world for Raffles and he entered into the sphere of colonial networking, finally joining Freemasonry in July 1812, in the Lodge Virtutis et Artis Amici, in Buitenzorg, Java, under the Grand Orient of the Netherlands. He was subsequently raised in the Lodge De Vriendschap in Surabaya, Java, in July 1813, serving as Worshipful Master the same year. His close friend and associate Thomas McQuoid was also a Freemason and a founder of the Lodge Neptune which was based in Penang and McQuoid was 'Perfected' with Raffles in Rose Croix Chapter La Vertueuse in Batavia in 1816. Thomas McQuoid became a long time friend and business partner of Raffles, supporting him in key decisions as his confidant.

His wife died in 1814, and certain charges had been made against him regarding mismanagement and improperly purchasing land. Raffles also succumbed to ill health – something which plagued him during his career in Southeast Asia - and forced him to leave Java and return to England on the 25th of March of 1816, just after his 'Perfection'.

Back in England, with his health recovered, he remarried; he was made a Fellow of the Royal Society, published his work *The History of Java* and

---

[543] The inauguration of the District Grand Lodge of Western Australia and the formation of the United Grand Lodge of New South Wales was mentioned in *AQC*, Vol. 1, (1888), p.191 and p.217. The AQC Transactions regularly discussed many Masonic events – not just within the British Empire - but in various countries.

was knighted, receiving support from Princess Charlotte, the daughter of the Price Regent – the future George IV, who had once served as Grand Master of the 'Moderns'. Raffles was celebrated while in London, the charges against him were dropped, and he was offered the position of Lieutenant General of Bencoolen. Raffles' reforms in Bencoolen were to later reflect his work in the administration of Singapore. From the lust of Empire building that was franticly taking place during the early nineteenth century, Raffles not only successfully established a British colony with Singapore, but he founded an international trading centre which became central to the expansion and control of the British Empire in Southeast Asia. He created churches and schools for the indigenous population, allowed local businesses to operate, outlawed slavery and cockfighting and influenced the planning of Singapore, drafting its constitution.[544]

Raffles is still renowned in Indonesia for his reforms[545] and he is still celebrated for helping to establish Freemasonry in Singapore and Java; with a local lodge still bearing his name and his coat of arms as their insignia. Freemasonry in Singapore officially began with the first 'mother' lodge, Lodge Zetland in the East No. 748 E.C. which was established and consecrated on the 8th of December 1845. The lodge attracted many leading members of the British community in Singapore; Sir Thomas Braddell, the first Attorney-General of Singapore, Robert Carr Woods the editor of The Straits Times, Admiral of the Fleet Sir Henry Keppel and Thomas Owen Crane, Justice of the Peace and trustee of the Raffles Institution – the ruling elite all becoming involved in local Freemasonry in the colony. Despite the lodges that operated there being mainly made up of the British community, there was an Asian presence, such as Edaljee Jamsetjee Khory, who had been initiated in England, but went on to join the Lodge of St. George No. 1152 E.C. in Singapore after arriving there in 1888 and founded a Mark Master Masons Lodge in 1891. Freemasonry continued to expand in Singapore and the Masonic Hall was built in 1879, and the Lodge of St. George still celebrates that it operates under the auspices of the United Grand Lodge of England.[546]

---

[544] Sir Thomas Stamford Raffles, *Statement of the Services of Sir Stamford Raffles*, (London: Cox and Baylie, Great Queen Street, 1824), pp.60-61.

[545] Ibid., pp.35-39. See also Sophia Raffles, *Memoir of the Life and Public Services of Sir Thomas Stamford Raffles FRS*, Vol. 1, (London: James Duncan, 1835).

[546] For a brief history of Freemasonry in Singapore see the official website of the Lodge of St. George No. 1152: http://www.stgeorge1152.sg/index.html [accessed 1st of April, 2010]

Freemasonry became important in establishing the trust, confidence and loyalty of the local elite in the colonies, the Craft – working as a society with secrets – being a sacred place in which the native leaders of the community were invited to share those secrets; in effect winning their hearts and minds and bringing them closer to the British establishment. Many of the countries once colonised under the Empire, Freemasonry is still extremely popular. If their respective Grand Lodges are recognised by the United Grand Lodge of England, their representatives are thus able to visit the English Grand Lodge, recognition providing an element of legitimacy and pride. To date, recognition by the United Grand Lodge is extended to the Grand Lodge of India, the Grand Lodges of the Australia States and New Zealand, Grand Lodges in Canada such as Quebec and British Columbia and Yukon, and Grand Lodges within the United States – along with the Prince Hall Grand Lodges. Certain Grand Lodges in Africa and Asia are also recognized. The former colonies obviously value their continued links with the United Grand Lodge of England (and indeed, in some cases, the Grand Lodge of Scotland) and equally value their historical and cultural heritage with Freemasonry; the regalia, the ritual, the administration – all providing a sense of identity and status within their communities.

The Continuation of the Ethos of Education and the Search for the Genesis of Freemasonry

The ethos of education within Freemasonry during the later nineteenth and early twentieth centuries was still vitally important, and this can be reflected in the foundation of many University Lodges catering specifically for graduates and students. An example of this can be seen with the University Lodge of Liverpool No. 4274, which became open for University graduates, staff and students alike, and was founded in 1921 by, amongst others, the 17th Earl of Derby who was the Chancellor of the University and Provincial Grand Master, the 1st Viscount Leverhulme, who was a benefactor and was the Chairman of the Liverpool School of Tropical Medicine, and R.J.M. Buchannan, who was the Professor of Forensic Medicine. The similar University of Manchester Lodge No. 5683 was also founded; some of the founders going on to form a University of Manchester Lodge of Mark Master

Masons in 1944, providing a further exclusive progression for its brethren.[547]

These University Lodges had followed the two original lodges attached to Universities; the Isaac Newton University Lodge No. 859, which was open to students and graduates of Cambridge University, and the equivalent lodge for Oxford University students and graduates called the Apollo University Lodge No. 357. The Apollo University Lodge first met in 1819, and boasts the past membership of Oscar Wilde, Cecil Rhodes, along with the membership of Royal brethren such as Albert Edward, Prince of Wales who was Worshipful Master in 1873 and Prince Leopold who served as Worshipful Master in 1876 - both being members while they were students at Oxford University.

The Isaac Newton University Lodge, along with the Oxford based Apollo University Lodge, publicise that they have the exclusive distinction of accepting members from under the age of 21 on the Provincial Grand Masters' judgment, though other University lodges, such as the University Lodge of Liverpool, can now also obtain special dispensations for undergraduates from the age of 18. Other University lodges include the Lodge of Fraternity No. 1418 in Durham, the University Lodge, Sheffield No. 3911 and the St. Augustine Lodge No. 972 in Canterbury – which was founded in 1863 with the assistance of the Provincial Grand Master Viscount Holmsdale MP. There were also many medical lodges and legal lodges being constituted from the nineteenth century onwards, all catering for professionals who wanted to join the Craft, creating a specialist and rather exclusive networking nexus of professional Masons throughout England and Wales.

The Masonic explosion of the later nineteenth century coincided with more published Masonic material, with new Masonic encyclopaedias such as Albert Mackey's *Encyclopedia of Freemasonry*,[548] new Masonic magazines such as *The Freemasons Magazine and Masonic Mirror*,[549] and, most

---

[547] Anon., *A Short History in Celebration of the Golden Jubilee of the University of Manchester Lodge of Mark Master Masons No. 1001*, (Published by the Lodge, 1994).
[548] See Albert Gallatin Mackey and H.L. Haywood, *Encyclopedia of Freemasonry Part 1*, (Montana: Kessinger, 1946), and Albert Gallatin Mackey, *A Lexicon of Freemasonry*, (London, 1869).
[549] 'The Freemasons Magazine and Masonic Mirror' was published from January 1856 until 1870. It was a combination of two previous magazines; the first being the 'Freemasons Monthly Magazine' which had gone through a number of name changes, its foundation being traced back to 1834 as the 'Freemasons Quarterly Review' by Masonic writer Dr. Robert Crucefix, the second magazine being the more independent 'Masonic Mirror' which was founded in 1854. These magazines can provide excellent material for any Masonic historian and include information on lodge meetings, social events, letters and reviews which give a revealing insight into nineteenth century Freemasonry. For a brief history of these magazines see Yasha Beresiner, 'Masonic

importantly, a modern focus on the origins of Masonry, examined in various new histories and in the new volumes of papers presented by the groundbreaking London based Quatuor Coronati Lodge. This Victorian period was certainly a time for Freemasons to be awakened and to eagerly seek the answers about their puzzling past.[550]

An example of this Victorian 'modern' historical examination of Freemasonry was Robert Freke Gould's famous *History of Freemasonry*, a vast work written in-between 1883-1887. Gould's *History* was an emblematic and highly respected bi-product of this era, presenting an 'official' antiquarian view of Masonry as seen through Victorian eyes. Gould had been an officer in the army and after becoming a Freemason in 1855, had visited numerous lodges throughout the British Empire; becoming involved in lodges as far away as Gibraltar and China. On leaving the army, he worked as a Barrister, his Masonic career developing accordingly, and by 1880 he was serving as Senior Grand Deacon for the Grand Lodge of England. His confidence as a writer and speaker is evident in his books and his many papers on Masonic history, his work becoming a trademark for Masonic study at the time.[551] Gould embraced an academic and thorough approach to his research and presentation, giving lectures on his work in countless lodges, and many other Freemasons followed his lead in searching for the origins of their society.[552]

It was exactly this drive and desire to research the early history of Freemasonry that inspired the founding of the London based Quatuor Coronati Lodge No. 2076 in 1884, where the members presented papers on all aspects of Masonic research which were published in their annual

---

Newspapers, Periodicals and Journals', in *Freemasonry Today*, Issue 17, Summer 2001, http://www.freemasonrytoday.com/17/p19.php [accessed 1st of September, 2009]

[550] See John L. Belton, 'Communication and Research versus Education' – the battle for a master mason's daily advance in Masonic knowledge', *AQC*, Vol. 118, (2006), pp.210-218.

[551] Gould was initiated in 1855 in the Royal Navy Lodge No. 621 (now 429), at Ramsgate, and was listed as a Lieutenant in the 31st Regiment. He then appears in lodges all over the British Empire as a Lieutenant in the 31st Regiment of Foot from 1855, though by 1863, he had been promoted to Captain, as he is listed as such on the register of Zion Chapter No. 570 in Shanghai. When he founded Quatuor Corinati Lodge No. 2076 in 1884 he was listed as a Barrister of Vale Lodge, Hampstead on the petition. In 1875 he had joined Moira Chapter No. 92, in London, where he was described as a Barrister on the register. In 1910 he founded King Solomon's Temple Lodge No. 3464 in Chester and was described as a Barrister of Woking on the petition. He was also described on the 1881 Census as being a Barrister; see 1881 Census, London, Middlesex. Library Ref: RG11/0156/61.

[552] Gould lectured in many lodges during his career, his visits being celebrated in many lodge histories, such as his visit to the York 'Union' Lodge No. 236 in 1890, see Wood, *History of the York 'Union' Lodge*, p.60.

Transactions, of which Gould and many others, such as Golden Dawn founders Dr. William Wynn Westcott and the Rev. A.F.A. Woodford contributed to. Both Westcott and Woodford predictably produced very esoterically themed papers for the first Volume of the *Transactions* published in 1888, Westcott discussing the Kabbalah and Woodford talking about Hermeticism.[553]

Gould was a founder of the lodge and published a paper in the first volume which echoed his own search for hidden knowledge entitled *English Freemasonry Before the Era of Grand Lodge*.[554] He went on to publish many varied papers in the *Transactions* – searching for the origins of Freemasonry, Gould becoming one of the leading Masonic historians during the late Victorian period. Other founders of the Quatuor Coronati Lodge included the writer and founder member of the Authors' Club Sir Walter Besant, the explorer and archaeologist Sir Charles Warren and George William Speth. On Speth's motion to form a Literary Society under the guidance and protection of the lodge, a Quatuor Coronati Correspondence Circle was created, which promoted the work done by the lodge, and ensured a wider reading of the *Transactions* and an increased attendance within the lodge meetings.[555]

The Victorian period experienced continued interest in the research of Solomon's Temple, and one particular Freemason who became personally involved in excavating a section underneath the Temple Mount was Sir Charles Warren – now more famous perhaps for his involvement in the Jack the Ripper case when working as Commissioner of the Police.[556] Warren excavated underneath the Temple Mount and surveyed Herod's Temple in 1867 as an agent of the Palestine Exploration Fund, his work paving the way for a new modern approach to Biblical archaeology. Warren went on to present a paper concerning the *Orientation of Temples* to the Quatuor Coronati Lodge in 1887, a paper which also went on to be published in the first Volume of the *Transactions* the following year.[557]

---

[553] See Rev. A.F.A Woodford, 'Freemasonry and Hermeticisim', and W.W. Westcott, 'The Religion of Freemasonry illuminated by the Kabbalah', in *AQC*, Vol. 1, (1888), pp.28-36 and pp.55-59.

[554] R.F. Gould, 'English Freemasonry Before the Era of Grand Lodge', in *AQC*, Vol. 1, (1888), pp.67-74.

[555] See Robert A. Gilbert, 'Masonic Education: Leading the way', in *MQ, Grand Lodge Publications, Issue 11, October, 2004*.

[556] Sir Charles Warren was initiated into Freemasonry in 1859, and became the elected Founding Master of the Quatuor Coronati Lodge No. 2076 in 1884, but due to his departure to Africa, the lodge did not meet until his return at the end of 1885.

[557] See Sir Charles Warren, 'On the Orientation of Temples', in *AQC*, Vol. 1, (1888), pp.36-50. For more information on modern interpretations of Solomon's Temple see Leroy Waterman, 'The

The interest in using supposed stones from Solomon's Temple for inclusion in modern Cathedrals became more commonplace – especially as more modern research in Biblical archaeology developed during the later nineteenth century, with stones excavated from the Temple being placed within St. Paul's Cathedral in London by archaeologist James Fergusson.[558] Fergusson's views on the Temple brought him into direct conflict with Freemason Sir Charles Warren, their differing opinions on the Temple causing some conflict in archaeological circles. Even in the USA, in the Washington National Cathedral, the high alter was made from stone which was quarried from Solomon's Quarry – which supposedly supplied the stone for the Temple. The building of the beautiful gothic Washington National Cathedral commenced in 1907 when Freemason Theodore Roosevelt laid the foundation stone.

Another important Masonic historian from this period was Dr. Wilhelm Begemann, a German Freemason, who was a prolific contributor of the Quatuor Coronati Lodge *Transactions*, writing various papers on aspects of the origins of Freemasonry, and, like Gould, was deeply fascinated by the history of the Craft. Begemann's thorough study and classification of the 'Old Charges' became widely celebrated, his paper entitled *An Attempt to Classify the "Old Charges" of the British Masons*, appearing in Volume 1 of the Quatuor Coronati Lodge *Transactions*, becoming a distinguished paper which dealt with the categorisation of the of the 'Old Charges' into 'family' groups.[559]

Unlike Gould however, Begemann was never a fully elected member of the Quatuor Coronati Lodge, and his meticulous work *Antecedents and Beginnings of Freemasonry in England* published in 1910, was followed by a work focussing on Ireland in 1911, and a volume focusing on Scotland in 1914, all written in Begemann's native German language.[560] On

---

Damaged "Blueprints" of the Temple of Solomon', in the *Journal of Near Eastern Studies*, Vol. 2, No. 4. (The University of Chicago Press, October, 1943), pp.284-294.

[558] A photograph of one of the 'Temple' stones can be seen in Harrison, *The Genesis of Freemasonry*.

[559] Dr. W. Begemann, 'An Attempt to Classify the "Old Charges" of the British Masons', in *AQC*, Vol. 1, (1888), pp.152-167.

[560] See Alain Bernheim, 'Dr. Wilhelm Begemann vs. The English Masonic History Establishment: A Love-Hate Story', in *Heredom*, Vol. 7, (1998), http://www.srmason-sj.org/web/heredom-files/volume7/dr-wilhelm-begemann.htm [accessed 1st of September 2009]. Bernheim also mentions how the views of Masonic historian Henry Sadler in his *Masonic Facts and Fictions* published in 1887, clashed with the more 'official' views of Gould, regarding the use of the term 'schismatics' to describe the founders of the 'Antient' Grand Lodge. Sadler put forward that the term was inappropriate as the founders of the 'Antients' were not members of the 'Premier/Modern' Grand Lodge as Gould had indicated. Bernheim suggests that this contradiction of Gould's work was responsible for Sadler having to wait until 1903 before becoming a full member of the Quatuor Coronati Lodge.

Begemann's death in 1914, the same year of the outbreak of the Great War, plans by AQC to translate this work into English were announced, but these plans seemed to have been quickly put on hold, with only a partial translation taking place.

Begemann's volume concerning the history of Freemasonry in England was translated into English by Lionel Vibert in 1913, but remains unpublished. Apart from some editing and the writing of an introduction, the volumes concerning the history of Freemasonry in Ireland and Scotland still awaits full translation into English. The unpublished English translation can be found in the library of the United Grand Lodge of England. Begemann's work can be compared now to Gould's *History* for sheer attention to documentation and the thorough approach to his research, though a modern study of his original work and a new translation is perhaps long overdue.[561]

The Masonic research presented by the Quatuor Coronati Lodge inspired other lodges to be founded along the same lines, such as the Leicester Lodge of Masonic Research No. 2429 in 1889. Another research lodge was the Minerva Lodge No. 2433, based in Birkenhead and founded in 1892; one of the founders being the Masonic historian John Armstrong who had joined the Warrington based Lodge of Lights in 1873.[562] Armstrong was an Engineer who had ventured into Masonic research with vigour, publishing a number of books and papers, mainly concerning the history of Freemasonry in Cheshire and Lancashire, his mammoth work *A History of Freemasonry in Cheshire* being an austere Victorian assemblage of lodge histories and personal views on early Freemasonry in Chester.[563]

Armstrong, like Gould, became a member of many different lodges and chapters, mainly in the north-western industrial towns of Warrington, Birkenhead and Liverpool, where he later settled. He died in July 1902,[564] leaving behind a number of works on early Freemasonry and having

---

[561] The volumes of Begemann's *Antecedents and Beginnings of Freemasonry* can be found in the library of the United Grand Lodge of England; *Vorgeschite und Anfäfnge der Freimaurerei in England* (Berlin: Ernst Siegfried Mittler und Sohn, 1909), translation by Lionel Vibert (Ms.) c.1913. United Grand Lodge of England, Great Queen Street, London; Class mark BE 50 BEG.

[562] John Armstrong, *A History of Freemasonry in Cheshire*, (London: Kenning, 1901), pp.394-395. See also *List of Members of the Lodge of Lights, No.148, Masonic Hall, Warrington, 27th of October, 1873*. Not listed.

[563] Ibid.

[564] Death Registration for John Armstrong, Toxteth Park, Liverpool, July 1902, reference; 8b, 140. Armstrong remained a member of the Lodge of Lights No. 148 in Warrington until his death.

served in the Cheshire Provincial Grand Lodge.[565] Armstrong's northern location and his work probably stopped him from travelling to London on a regular basis to become involved in the Quatuor Coronati Lodge, but as a Masonic historian, his work on early Chester lodges is extremely valuable, Armstrong having painstakingly transcribed many now lost minutes, accounts, newspaper reports and notes on these long extinct lodges of the early eighteenth century.[566]

Other 'literary' and 'research' lodges followed in the wake of the Quatuor Coronati Lodge, such as the aforementioned Authors Lodge and the Manchester Lodge for Masonic Research No.5502, all exploring the developing interests in Masonic history and expressing the ethos of education within the Craft. Freemasons had started to search more intensively for their lost origins, and having more opportunities to write and publish different aspects of their society's history, more publications appeared and even more professional historians began to peel away the deep layers of mystery surrounding the genesis of Freemasonry.

This self searching and highly disciplined academic approach into the origins of Freemasonry continued into the twentieth century, with mainly English Masonic historians such as Gould, influencing researchers such as Douglas Knoop, a Mason and a Professor of Economics at the University of Sheffield, who, along with non-Mason G.P. Jones, who was a lecturer in Economic History also at the University of Sheffield, wrote many joint papers for the Quatuor Coronati Lodge *Transactions* and published many books – all examining the early origins of the Craft, such as *The Medieval Mason* in 1933, which examined the medieval stone mason's trade guilds in England, and *The Genesis of Freemasonry* in 1947, which attempted to put forward the 'transition' from operative to speculative Freemasonry.[567]

---

[565] John Armstrong had also joined the Warrington based Gilbert Greenall Lodge No.1250 in 1874, and the Bootle based Fermor Hesketh Lodge No 1350 in 1889, as well as a number of Chapters, such as the Liverpool based Sefton Chapter No. 680 in 1875, and the De Tabley Chapter No. 605 in Birkenhead in 1881. He served as Provincial Grand Warden for the Provincial Grand Lodge of Cheshire.

[566] See John Armstrong, *Chester Lodges*, (Chester, 1900), a paper read before the Cestrian Lodge No. 425 on the 15th of November, 1900.

[567] See Douglas Knoop, and G.P. Jones, *The Medieval Mason*, (Manchester: University of Manchester Press, 1933), and Douglas Knoop, and G.P. Jones, *Genesis of Freemasonry: An Account of the Rise and Development of Freemasonry in its Operative, Accepted and Early Speculative Phases*, (Manchester: University of Manchester Press, 1947). See also Douglass Knoop, and G.P. Jones, *A Short History of Freemasonry To 1730*, (Manchester: University of Manchester Press, 1940), and Douglas Knoop, and G.P. Jones, (ed.), *Early Masonic Pamphlets*, (Manchester: University of Manchester Press, 1945).

Knoop was deeply involved in Freemasonry; becoming a senior ranking officer within the Province of West Yorkshire and becoming Master of the Quatuor Coronati Lodge in 1935. His work expanded the research into the origins of Freemasonry and shifted the focus into the medieval period – charting the development of the stone mason's guilds and examining the links between them and the appearance of what he termed 'speculative' Freemasonry.[568] His work however, being mostly published by the University of Manchester Press, and with both Knoop and Jones being under the employ of the University of Sheffield, gained academic credibility, their books being placed on the University library shelves.[569]

The historians of the Quatuor Coronati Lodge were somewhat restrained by their Masonic membership, the official and austere attitudes presented in some of the papers making for dry reading. Despite this, these Masonic historians searched with vigour to find the true origins of their society, and as the Freemason, mystic and writer Arthur Edward Waite put it:

'There are some of us who have searched these records with reverent and anxious care and who are acquainted substantially with all that has been said concerning them. On my own part I remember Gould with affection for his open and unbiased mind. I have gone over the Regius MS. line by line, with his script on the subject in my hands, but have failed to discover the Speculative and Symbolic Elements which he contrived to trace therein'.[570]

The mysterious origins of the Craft and its symbolic ritual fascinated these Freemasons, with Gould being more grounded in his approach to practical research, while other Masonic writers and historians such as Waite searched for more esoteric meaning within the ritual and symbolism. This explosion of Masonic research was part of the Masonic expansion of the later Victorian era; the mysterious origins of Freemasonry stirred the imaginations of the educated professional classes

---

[568] Douglas Knoop, *On The Connection Between Operative & Speculative Masonry*, The Inaugural Address delivered to the Quatuor Coronati Lodge, No. 2076, London, on his Installation as Master, 8th of November, 1935.

[569] Douglas Knoop was to have the building which housed the Centre for Research into Freemasonry and Fraternalism at the University of Sheffield named after him. Knoop's work was distributed to many University libraries and can still be found on their shelves.

[570] Arthur Edward Waite, *Secret Tradition in Freemasonry*, (Kessinger Publishing Co., 1997), p.39. The 'Regius MS. is the oldest of the 'Old Charges' which contain the rules and traditions of medieval 'operative' Masonry and has been dated to c.1390 by Masonic historian Douglas Knoop.

and stimulated their minds. This brought a whole new dimension to the symbolic theme of the search for lost knowledge, which was applied as these Masonic Scholars endeavoured to find their lost origins. This search for the genesis of Freemasonry became somewhat of an obsession, with many of the Masonic Scholars focusing on the mysterious beginnings of the Craft and the cryptic nature of Freemasonry, a search which still goes on today.[571]

This expansion of Freemasonry was down to popular interest by the new up-and-coming industrialist and professional classes, all wanting to get involved in the Craft, which offered an education of social etiquette, a networking nexus, an access to a maze of mysterious secret orders, and an intricate web of association. Freemasonry presented a mysterious and highly fashionable secret society with an exclusive and elitist membership; Royalty and members of the aristocracy were involved, along with a host of fashionable writers and politicians, and even at local level, high ranking military officers, industrialists and professionals were included on the membership lists of the lodges. Obsessed with its own history and self disciplined in its self promotion, Freemasonry truly transformed itself in the later nineteenth century, becoming fashionable and almost essential to the up-and-coming aspiring gentleman.

---

[571] See Andrew Prescott, 'Freemasonry and the Problem of Britain', the Inaugural Lecture to mark the launch of the University of Sheffield's Centre for Research into Freemasonry, 5th of March, 2001, http://www.southchurch.mesh4us.org.uk/pdf/contemporary/freemasons-problem-sheffield.pdf [accessed 3rd of August, 2009], in which Prescott discusses how the work of Masonic Scholars have been seen as baffling and confusing for historians, especially the work produced by the Quatuor Coronati Lodge, of which, as Prescott puts forward, has tended to concentrate on elaborating theories of the origins of Freemasonry which range from the over-pragmatic to the over-fantastical. Prescott also mentioned how this focus on the early period could lead to a neglect of Masonic research in the nineteenth and twentieth centuries – a period which has a wealth of documentation.

Conclusion

Freemasonry went through a metamorphosis as a society during the nineteenth century, being forced to adapt after the Unlawful Society Act in 1799, changing its character as the Industrial era progressed. This change can best be seen in the local lodges, where they provide a clearer picture of how Freemasonry reacted to the social changes of the period, especially in the developing Industrial areas of England. Freemasonry also influenced the local community in many ways; through the promotion and funding of education by certain Freemasons, and by charity. Localised Freemasonry actively supported and assisted in developing a cultural identity within the embryonic Industrial towns.

Education and Charity

Local education in Warrington was certainly influenced by active Freemasons. For example a local Freemason was involved in setting up the Warrington Circulating Library in 1758, and two leading tutors from the Dissenting Academy in the town were prominent Freemasons. The central Masonic ideals of education, and charity, were deeply reflected in the Academy. Dr. Joseph Priestley, though not a Freemason, was, like John Reihnold Forster, a Fellow of the Royal Society, and two of Priestley's close friends, Dr. Richard Price and Benjamin Franklin, were Freemasons and also Fellows of the Royal Society. Joseph Banks was also a Mason, and was President of the Royal Society, and it was their interest in science and discovery that linked these very diverse and influential men together.

Different men have in the past used Freemasonry for different means; natural philosophers like Forster using it for networking contacts and access to ambitious new positions, while Banks seemed to represent the strong principles of political and religious harmony. A strong link between many of the Freemasons discussed in this work is the yearning for lost knowledge, and an awareness of the need for education.

Freemasonry and the Royal Society had been entwined since the later part of the seventeenth century, and the philosophy of Freemasonry seemed to appeal to the scientific minds of the period, with early leading Freemasons such as Dr. John Theophilus Desaguliers and Martin Folkes being Fellows of the Royal Society. The political climate of the time created an almost fashionable atmosphere for radical thinkers, such as Dr. Richard Price, to become involved with new Revolution Societies and to mix in radical circles, which attracted other prominent free thinking figures, such as Priestley and Paine. It was inevitable that, with so many free thinking radicals involved within Freemasonry, that the Craft would become entwined with radicalism and Revolution, and educational centres such as the Warrington Academy was also associated with radicalism.

Status and elitism also played a part in Freemasonry, and this is shown in the ambition displayed by Forster, a man who would stop at nothing to achieve scientific and academic recognition. The advantages of being a member of any fashionable society during this period were to have influential contacts and to find an avenue for their ambition. Priestley, Franklin, Price, Banks, and Forster, were all leading men in their field, and they all contributed to science with the discovery of new ideas. The Academy became famous because of the links to this new cultural movement, and with the backdrop of revolution in America and France, a radical political dimension was always present, a dimension that was also reflected in the secrecy of Freemasonry, something which certainly worried the paranoid government of Pitt the Younger. The education values of Freemasonry are evident throughout this period, not only with the Academy and the many schoolmasters and printers that entered the Lodge of Lights, but in the lectures that took place within the lodge itself.

The self help elements seen in the Academy and in the Lodge of Lights also reflected the development of a local cultural identity, the Academy being self reliant and the lodge providing self support, as seen in its claims for relief, especially during the early nineteenth century. The shaping of a cultural identity can certainly be seen later on in the nineteenth century in Warrington when leading Freemasons became involved in local educational societies and openly celebrated the town as the 'Athens of the North', venerating the history of the Academy and the achievements of it's tutors and students throughout the world.

Charitable connections to the local Bluecoat School are evident as well as the support given by individual Freemasons in funding civic buildings and places of worship, and later, links to the many learned societies also suggest a strong bond between education, charity and the Craft. Again, the civic pride which developed among Warrington's Freemasons during the early nineteenth century and the many societies that commemorated the Academy mirror these educational and charitable values. Indeed, in other industrial areas such as Sheffield, Liverpool, Bolton and

Manchester, involvement in, and promotion of local charity by local Freemasons was also very much apparent.

Labouring men within lodges

The Terror in France, the rise of Napoleon and growing anti French sentiment resulted in the passing of the Unlawful Societies Act in 1799, casting a shadow of suspicion on Freemasonry. Many local gentlemen distanced themselves from the lodges in Warrington and other industrial towns, the empty seats of the lodges being filled by labouring tradesmen, such as weavers, joiners, fustian cutters and mill workers. The lodge, like every other English lodge, began to submit a list of members in compliance to the Act, the influx of membership of labouring tradesmen reflected a lodge in transition, the lodge struggling to survive, accepting new members from the growing industrial town.

In 1813, the two Grand Lodges of the 'Moderns' and the 'Antients' came together, the ritual was revised and the new United Grand Lodge of England re-organised, while the localised self-help social and benevolent features of Freemasonry began to be played down as the administration became more centralised under one Grand Lodge. This transition seemed to have taken a few decades to be fully implemented, the labouring tradesmen still joining the lodges situated in industrial towns, and claims for relief still being made. It was only natural for existing members to have been stuck in their ways, and it was not until the older generation of members gave way to the new, that changes occur. By the later 1840s, less labouring tradesmen appear in the records, and the lodges became closer to its Victorian image of a 'gentlemen's dining club'. This change coincides with the success of the IOR, Oddfellows and Foresters, societies which were more Friendly Society-based, and attracted 'working class' members. Legal Trade Unionism also flourished during this period, and the political climate began to change as the fear of riot and revolution gradually subsided as the nineteenth century progressed.

Trade Unions and Friendly Societies may have lured labouring tradesmen men away from Freemasonry, and certain lodges may have wanted to distance themselves from these more radical and 'working-class' movements. Freemasonry ultimately directed itself, through the new United Grand Lodge of England, towards a new future, one that catered for the new aspiring industrialists, businessmen and professionals, as issues of class became more redefined, especially after the Reform Act of 1832. A very public Freemasonry still had similarities to Trade Unionism and other Friendly Societies like the Oddfellows and the Foresters; the regalia of these societies were very similar, from the banners and marches of Trade Unions, to the aprons, medals and sashes of the Oddfellows. Similarly, oaths were taken and the societies shared certain ritualistic contents. Freemasonry also had Royal connections and an ancient mysterious history, all helping Masonry to become a very attractive society for the professional classes to join, the society presenting a vast networking opportunity.

The Lodge of Lights struggled to survive during the early decades of the nineteenth century, and the influx of working men into the lodge certainly reminds one of Eric Hobsbawm's suggestion of how tradesmen during this period adopted Masonic ceremonial content, words, signs and grips for their own 'societies'. A secret society culture was very evident, with working men being extremely careful to meet and discuss problems, taking the utmost care in combining together. Due to the labouring men entering the Lodge of Lights during this period, it survived and, in the later nineteenth century, ultimately expanded.

Certainly a cultural identity can be seen being forged through the interaction of Freemasonry and the local community with the occurrence of the Liverpool Masonic Rebellion and the subsequent development of the Wigan Grand Lodge, where a group of Freemasons – mainly local tradesmen - bonded together to form an independent Grand Lodge which was, overall, a localised incident. The Grand Lodge of Wigan also had an element of self support with its own burial and sickness fund, ensuring its members, all from the locality, were looked after. Freemasonry during this period certainly followed local patterns, and overall, became important to the culture of the local community.

Professionals, Industrialists and Expansion
As the nineteenth century progressed, the Lodge of Lights became very exclusive, and the local industrial giants became involved, such as the Greenall and Rylands families. Joseph Stubs, a local tool maker had been a member from 1830, and became Mayor in 1852[572], but had been well known for his friendliness and generosity towards his workers and their

---

[572] G.A. Carter, *Warrington Hundred*, Warrington, list of Mayors of Warrington, 1847-1947, (Warrington, 1947), pp.65-69.

families[573]. His brother George was also a Mason[574], and these industrialists seemed to relish in their Masonic membership, the networking qualities of the society being evident. A similar pattern could also be seen in the other lodges that were studied, such as the Lodge of Friendship in Oldham, the Lodge of St. John in Stockport and lodges in Wigan and Liverpool.

However, the changes in the lodge makeup that the Lodge of Lights seemed to have experienced can not be seen as a true reflection of what was happening in Freemasonry in general during the early nineteenth century. In Chester for example, the lodges had a very different makeup, and retained the local gentry, having little trace of a working class element. Chester was traditionally the provincial centre for Cheshire, and would have been closer to Grand Lodge. However, the Chester lodges still suffered from the low attendance and financial difficulties that plagued the lodges in intense industrial areas such as the Lodge of Lights and the Lodge of St. John, resulting in neglect and closure for some of them. Other lodges situated in the more industrial outskirts of the province, such as in Nantwich, also had working class members during this time, and may point to a more localised cultural influence.

The later half of the nineteenth century witnessed the Craft becoming *'respectable'* once more, the membership of the lodges swelled with professionals, businessmen and industrialists, Freemasonry becoming in essence a Victorian 'gentleman's dining club'. Indeed, the gentlemen's clubs of London society also boasted the membership of certain prominent Freemasons; politicians, natural philosophers, writers and poets, all being involved in an intricate nexus of influential societies. Thus Freemasonry, in attracting affluent and influential gentlemen, ultimately became important in the establishment of colonies, and throughout the British Empire, in areas such as Southeast Asia, India, Australia and Canada, Masonic lodges were operating. In certain colonies such as in Canada and India, lodges displayed membership of the local indigenous population, Masonry providing a space in which the cultures of Britain and the native population could potentially mix, creating opportunities to work together to develop the local community.

Freemasonry certainly inspired the genesis of other ritualistic societies, such as the Hermetic Order of the Golden Dawn and the United Ancient Order of Druids, the obvious similarities in certain symbols and regalia

---

[573] E. Surrey Dane, *Peter Stubs and the Lancashire Hand Tool Industry*, (Sherratt & Sons Ltd., 1973), p.32.
[574] *List of Members of the Lodge of Lights no.148, Warrington, 1765-1981.* Not listed.

being apparent. More lodges were founded and as transport improved, networking within Freemasonry became easier, with Freemasons able to visit and join other lodges in other areas more freely and frequently. Other Orders within Freemasonry became appealing to the up-and-coming professionals and industrialists, such as Mark Master degree, Freemasonry offering a progression of further 'degrees' and Orders to whet the appetite for the further search of lost knowledge and to increase their networking potential within Masonry.

The Future of Freemasonry

English Freemasonry expanded immensely after World War II, but certainly since the last few decades of the twentieth century, the society has suffered with loss of membership; with certain lodges struggling to get new initiates and subsequently closing as existing members leave or die. Some writers have suggested that Freemasonry is simply adjusting itself after the massive expansion it went through after World War II,[575] though it has been put forward recently by Masonic historian John Belton that *the popularity of Freemasonry, measured as a percentage of the base male population over the age of twenty, was lower after World War II than World War I*.[576] Others have pointed to the change in society; the introduction of more golf clubs and gyms, or the 'bowling alone' condition,[577] new social pursuits like the increase in television, the internet, and change in work patterns or even the counter culture of the 1960s.

Anti-Freemasonry has developed through the internet, with websites and fringe writers linking Freemasonry to all kinds of world domination theories, Freemasons supposedly pulling the strings of government decisions and some writers linking Freemasonry to Devil worship. These

---

[575] See Leon Zeldis, 'The Future of Freemasonry: Challenges and Responses', a paper delivered to the Regular Meeting No. 19 of Montefiore Lodge, Tel Aviv, on the 29th of December, 2002, http://www.freemasons-freemasonry.com/zeldis05.html [accessed 28th of December, 2009]
[576] John L. Belton, 'Masonic Membership Myths Debunked', in *Heredom*, Vol. 9, (Washington DC: Scottish Rite Research Society, 2001), pp.9-32, http://www.lodgehope337.org.uk/lectures/belton%20L2.pdf [accessed 28th of December, 2009]. In his paper Belton argues that the reasons put forward by Putnam in relation to declining social organisations need further examination in respect to Freemasonry.
[577] See Robert D. Putnam, *Bowling Alone: The Collapse and Revival of American Community*, (New York: Simon & Schuster, 2000). Putnam explores how since 1950, the USA has experienced the decline of 'social capital', with a decline of all forms of social intercourse, giving examples of falling membership of traditional organisations, and also discusses a growing distrust in government and people becoming less tied to religious organisations. Also see Robert D. Putnam, 'Bowling Alone: America's Declining Social Capital', in *Journal of Democracy*, Volume 6, Number 1, (Baltimore, Maryland, USA: Johns Hopkins University Press, January 1995), pp.65-78.

accusations are nothing new, in the eighteenth century for example Freemasons were accused of raising the Devil[578] and the previously discussed Unlawful Societies Act of 1799 testifies to how the government of Pitt the Younger felt very insecure about societies meeting behind closed doors during the war with France.

Putnam's work *Bowling Alone* puts forward how, since the 1960s, various scandals within the American government such as Watergate, the stigma of Vietnam and various assassinations have led people to develop a *'disgust for politics and government'* and Freemasonry, as a somewhat traditional society, may have been subjected to similar feelings by a disgruntled public that increasingly prefers to 'bowl alone'.[579] Certainly in this respect, England can be seen in a similar light, and the thriving social scene of the gentlemen's clubs and Freemasonry in the nineteenth century has been affected by changing social attitudes. The public may have distanced itself from traditional societies in recent decades, which they see has having connections with members of the establishment.[580] According to Putnam, the public have increasingly shunned conventional forms of social interaction for new forms of entertainment and social pursuits.

In Britain, the public's distrust of government has recently gained momentum with the MP's expenses scandal in 2009 and the inquest into the Labour government's decision to invade Iraq, and this certainly supports the arguments presented by Putnam; Freemasonry being a secretive society, filled mostly with professional males who toast the monarch, and whose current Grand Master is a member of the Royal Family is perhaps seen as being too close to an establishment which has lost the trust of many of its people. Changes in religious trends and attitudes in Britain have also developed over the last few decades, and like the growing distrust of politics and government, this change would certainly produce another challenge for Freemasonry. Putnam also presents how *'religious sentiment in America seems to be becoming somewhat less*

---

[578] Harrison, *The Genesis of Freemasonry*, p.50.

[579] Putnam, 'Bowling Alone: America's Declining Social Capital', *Journal of Democracy*, p.68.

[580] Some Gentlemen's Clubs have also suffered from a decline in membership, and, like the re-founded Crockford's, have closed in recent decades. Some of the traditional London based Clubs, like the Reform Club, the Carlton Club and the Athenaeum Club, have recently accepted women members, the Carlton Club still being popular amongst politicians from the Conservative Party. The Reform Club however, due to the decline of the Liberal Party in the mid-twentieth century, started to draw membership from the Treasury in the Civil Service, and became one of the early established London Clubs to accept women members. The Manchester Reform Club however, despite merging with the Engineers Club, closed in 1987, see the Manchester Reform Club Archive, The John Rylands University Library, Manchester, reference; GB 133 MRC.

tied to institutions and more self-defined,[581] a view which can be supported by
Grace Davie's book *Religion in Britain Since 1945: Believing Without Belonging*,
in which Davie puts forward how an increasing number of people have a
religious belief of some kind, but do not actually attend a Church.[582] This
self defined religious belief could pose a challenge to Freemasonry,
especially as Freemasonry currently insists on a belief in God to join. As
an increasing number of the public have a self defined view of God and
religion, and as Britain becomes more multi-cultural, then Freemasonry
may have to adapt to the swift changes in society.

This is what Freemasonry had constantly done; it had transformed the
way it had operated on many occasions. It had adapted after the
Unlawful Societies Act of 1799, and certain lodges in certain industrial
areas underwent changes in the make-up of their membership, changes
which ensured the survival of these lodges during a period in the early
nineteenth century when gentlemen and professionals distanced
themselves from Masonry. Freemasonry formed a Union in 1813
between the main rival Grand Lodges – the 'Moderns' and the 'Antients'
– and a major transformation within the Craft followed; with changes in
ritual, changes in administration and changes in the rules of the society.
These changes ultimately caused a rebellion in Liverpool and in other
parts of Lancashire, and in other parts of the country, such as in
Gloucestershire, rules were challenged when a member of the local gentry
imposed himself as Provincial Grand Master. In the later half of the
nineteenth century Freemasonry seemed to undergo another change; with
an influx of professionals and businessmen joining the Craft, a change
which, especially in relation to the lodges studied, followed the
introduction of local charismatic individuals extracted from the
professional classes. As the nineteenth century progressed, Freemasonry
in Britain expanded rapidly, with an ever increasing number of lodges
being founded and a large number of Masonic Halls being constructed.
Freemasonry can change its character again, just like it has many times in
the past.

---

581 Putnam, 'Bowling Alone: America's Declining Social Capital', *Journal of Democracy*, p.69.
582 See Grace Davie, *Religion in Britain Since 1945: Believing Without Belonging*, (Oxford: Wiley-Blackwell, 1994), p.4-5.

Appendix I

Lodge membership lists and cross referencing

The lodge membership lists that have been analysed for this paper vary from UGLE membership returns (which have been copied and are now available on CD-ROM at the UGLE library and archive) to local lodge histories which compiled the membership from the individual lodge Minutes and documents. Where possible the available membership lists of the lodges have been used, such as the Warrington based Lodge of Lights and the Oldham based Lodge of Friendship. There are difficulties with all types of membership lists, for example, names are sometimes entered without complete dates, ages, occupations or addresses, and in the case of the copied UGLE lodge returns the writing is sometimes of poor quality and lacks continuity. Different lists also contain contrasting membership information, so a study of all available lists is necessary to determine the most accurate analysis. For example the lists held by UGLE could be compared with the lists held by the individual lodge in question.

During the pre-census period, the documentation available to cross reference the information supplied by the lodge lists can present its own difficulties, with sources such as church records, early Trade Directories, local newspapers, and in some cases, Wills, probate inventories, Court records, gravestones and private letters, all creating their own pitfalls in research, especially if the name of the person is a relatively common one. The British Census, which began to list names, addresses, ages, occupation and place of birth from 1841, and subsequently took place every ten years after, supplied more accurate information in relation to cross referencing.

The occupations presented in the membership lists can also be ambiguous, with certain occupations being misleading, for example, certain cotton manufacturers or cotton merchants are commonly listed at the time as 'cotton-spinner', which can be confusing as the same term was also sometimes used for the labouring cotton mill workers. This can be seen in the Leigh based Marquis of Lorne Lodge, founded in 1871, where a founding member, Thomas Joseph Lancashire J.P., who served as the first Worshipful Master of the lodge, listed his occupation as 'cotton-spinner' when he was in fact a cotton manufacturer. He was also listed as a 'cotton-spinner' in the 1881 Census, living in an affluent area with his family and four servants.[583] In the same year, the same lodge also lists Thomas Travers Hayes J.P as a 'cotton-spinner' but like Thomas Joseph Lancashire, he was also a local cotton manufacturer.[584]

The Manchester builder and business man David Bellhouse for example ventured into owning cotton mills and was listed as a 'cotton-spinner' in the Manchester directories. Other members of the Bellhouse family, such as mill owner James Bellhouse, were also listed as 'cotton-spinners'.[585] Another example is Thomas Eskrigge, who, when he entered the Lodge of Lights in 1830, his occupation was given as 'cotton manufacturer', though in the Warrington Trade Directory of 1824, his occupation was given as 'cotton-spinner'.[586] However, the term 'cotton-spinner' was also used when describing John Doherty who was secretary to the 'Grand General Union of the United Kingdom' in 1829 in Manchester and was a mill worker.[587]

The occupations of some Freemasons listed also change suddenly, giving a confusing picture, an example being James Butterworth, who entered the Oldham based Lodge of Friendship as a weaver in 1790, but soon changed his occupation to teacher, bookshop owner and writer. Much has been written on Butterworth in relation to local history in Oldham, and his changing career has been well documented, but despite this information, there were two men with the name James Butterworth who entered the same lodge; the other being a soldier who was initiated in 1793, thus creating confusion when 'James Butterworth' was discussed in the minutes of the lodge.[588]

An example of what I have termed 'labouring tradesmen' within Freemasonry during the early nineteenth century can be seen with Henry Harrison of the Warrington based Lodge of Lights, who was listed a weaver in the membership lists, and was a worker in a mill, family papers

[583] *Lists of Members from the Marquis of Lorne Lodge no.1354, Leigh, 1871-1971, Leigh Masonic Hall.* Not Listed. Also see Thomas Joseph Lancashire in the *1881 Census for Stretford, Lancashire, PRO reference RG11, Piece: 3886, Folio: 104, Page: 30.*

[584] *Lists of Members from the Marquis of Lorne Lodge no.1354, Leigh, 1871-1971, Leigh Masonic Hall.* Not Listed. See also P.G. Monk and F. Bent, *A History of the Marquis of Lorne Lodge No. 1354,* (Leigh: P.T.H. Brooks Ltd., 1971), p.37.

[585] *The Cotton Spinners' and Manufacturers' Directory and Engineers' and Machine Makers' Advertiser,* (Oldham: J. Worrall, 1882).

[586] Anon., *Warrington in 1824,* (Warrington: Mackie & Co. Ld., Guardian Office, 1906), p.43. See also *List of Members of the Lodge of Lights, No.148, Masonic Hall, Warrington, 29th of March, 1830.* Not listed.

[587] P.W. Kingsford, *Engineers, Inventors and Workers,* (London: Edward Arnold, 1973), pp.91-92.

[588] *Minutes of the Lodge of Friendship, No.277, Masonic Hall, Oldham, James Butterworth, weaver, initiated on the 28th of April, 1790, and James Butterworth, soldier, initiated on the 13th of November, 1793.* Not listed.

confirming his status as a labouring tradesman.[589] Harrison's marriage also appears in the local Church records for St. Elphin's in Warrington, where he reveals himself as educated as he had signed the marriage banns with confidence[590] and was listed on the 1841 Census as an 'independent', being 66 years of age, living as a boarder in rented accommodation.[591] William Bullough, another weaver who joined the Lodge of Lights in 1830, was listed on the 1841 Census in Warrington as a 'warehouseman' aged 50, and like his fellow Mason Henry Harrison, was living in a poorer 'working class' area in the town.[592] Both Harrison and Bullough are buried in St. Elphin's churchyard with Masonic gravestones.[593] John Latham who joined the Lodge of Lights the same time as Henry Harrison in 1820, was a fustian cutter, and was listed in the 1841 Census, still working as a fustian cutter and, like Harrison and Bullough, was living in a poorer area in Warrington.[594] Joshua Wood, a weaver who joined the Wigan based Lodge of Antiquity in 1803, was also listed on the 1841 Census, still working as a weaver aged 65, and living in a poorer area of Wigan.[595]

It is possible in some circumstances to cross reference the information with local Trade Directories, family papers, church records, gravestones and the Census returns to give a more accurate picture. In the above cases, as examples of 'labouring tradesmen' entering the lodges, these can be cross referenced and their 'working class' status confirmed using the 1841 Census and information from the local libraries (maps and photographs of the local area determining the quality of housing). Equally the 'industrialist' status of Thomas Kirkland Glazebrook, who entered the Lodge of Lights in 1802 as a glass manufacturer, can be confirmed by using the Warrington Trade Directory of 1824, where he was still listed as being a glass manufacturer and living in an affluent area

---

[589] *Family papers of Henry Harrison.* Private collection. Not Listed.

[590] *The marriage of Henry Harrison and Martha Forshaw,* 16th of October, 1791, St. Elphin's Parish Church, Warrington, Lancashire. Warrington Library. Ref: MS35, Reel 3, Vol. 17, marriages 1784-1802.

[591] Henry Harrison in the *1841 Census for Warrington, Lancashire, PRO reference RG: HO107, Piece: 521, Folio: 10/16, Page: 25.*

[592] William Bullough in the *1841 Census for Warrington, Lancashire, PRO reference RG: HO107, Piece: 521, Folio: 12/40, Page 23.*

[593] Photographs of the Masonic gravestones of Henry Harrison and William Bullough are featured in David Harrison *The Genesis of Freemasonry,* (Lewis Masonic, 2009).

[594] John Latham in the *1841 Census for Warrington, Lancashire, PRO reference RG: HO107, Piece: 521, Folio: 5/39, Page 23.*

[595] Joshua Wood in the *1841 Census for Wigan, Lancashire, PRO reference RG: HO107, Piece: 521, Folio: 8/19, Page: 31.*

of the town.[596]   Joseph Stubs, the file manufacturer who entered the Lodge of Lights in 1830 is also listed in the 1824 Warrington Trade Directory as living in School Brow, an affluent area of the town.[597]

---

[596] Anon., *Warrington in 1824*, (Warrington: Mackie & Co. Ld., Guardian Office, 1906), p.44.
[597] Ibid., p.50.

Appendix II

Lodge Numbering

Lodges formed prior to 1886 will have had several numbers during their history. Between 1751 and 1813 both Grand Lodges had their own numberings. 'Modern' Lodges renumbered lodges in 1770, 1780 and 1792 while the 'Antients' did not follow the practice. There was a mass renumbering of all lodges following the merger and subsequent further re-numberings in 1832, 1863 and 1886. These were not due to the failure of lodges in England but rather to lodges in the colonies, or ex-colonies in the case of the USA, transferring their allegiance to newly formed Grand Lodges locally. This renumbering can cause confusion and in all cases we have stuck to those of the last renumbering of 1886.

Indeed the situation got so confusing that John Lane in 1886 published his *Masonic Records 1717–1886*. This lists all the known lodges, including those without numbers, and all their meeting places from formation until 1886 can be seen online: http://www.freemasonry.dept.shef.ac.uk/lane

Appendix III

Lodge of St John 104 Membership Data Analysis

It has been the practice of many Masonic lodges to keep records of all men who join the lodge, either to become a mason, or join from another lodge. The date of becoming a member or Worshipful Master was also considered important, subject to the assiduity of the various secretaries. Thus it is possible to know how and when men became Masons and to a variable extent the occupation and place of residence of the new member.

The historian of the Lodge of St John has recently combed the minutes of the lodge and added data for the leaving of each member whether resignation, exclusion for non-payment of dues or death. This enables a more detailed analysis of membership to be undertaken. Total membership of any lodge is a composite total rising or falling over any year according to the numbers who join or depart from the lodge, and does not distinguish between those who joined decades ago or merely last year. The number that joined is of course of interest but also the average duration of membership or the time to become master of the lodge. By taking a five year cohort graph system it is thus possible to see how that and each successive cohort behaves and to compare that over the period of a couple of centuries.

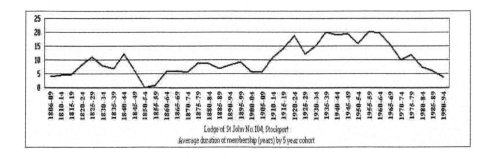

Lodge of St John No.104, Stockport
Average duration of membership (years) by 5 year cohort

Period	No.New Members	New Av Age (yrs)	No. Joining members	No. Died	No. Left	No. WM	Av years to leaving	Av years to Master
1806-09	30		19	3	29	10	4.1	2.7
1810-14	25		6	2	20	5	4.5	8.6
1815-19	23	32.5	6	1	23	0	4.8	
1820-24	10	36.4	6	3	13	2	8.5	17
1825-29	12	27.3	4	4	12	5	11.1	3.5
1830-34	18	27.7	0	3	15	1	7.9	20.0
1835-39	24	31.9	3	4	10	0	7.1	
1840-44	7	36.5	2	3	6	1	12.2	9.0
1845-49	5	31.8	1	1		1	6.3	3.0
1850-54	0		0	0	0	0		
1855-59	1	35.0	0	0	1	0	1	-
1860-64	52	31.7	6	3	56	6	5.8	3.5
1865-69	64	35.3	3	4	57	8	6.1	7.5
1870-74	76	33.0	2	5	73	4	5.7	7.2
1875-79	39	32.0	5	12	28	6	9.1	7.7
1880-84	22	33.0	5	1	20	5	8.8	8.2
1885-89	17	33.8	5	3	14	2	6.9	9.0
1890-94	14	38.9	2	7	7	5	8.2	7.2
1895-99	10	31.3	2	2	9	4	9.4	6.5
1900-04	21	32.8	4	6	16	3	5.7	7.0
1905-09	13	38.0	2	7	6	5	5.8	6.4
1910-14	20	43.5	2	13	7	12	11.0	10.1
1915-19	30	36.4	2	14	16	10	14.3	15.5
1920-24	23	39.1	1	13	11	4	18.8	18.2
1925-29	19	37.1	0	9	9	4	12.2	15.5
1930-34	13	44.3	0	9	4	3	15.0	13.3
1935-39	11	39.2	1	3	3	4	20.1	11.5
1940-44	18	39.4	0	4	14	7	19.1	11.0
1945-49	14	45.3	3	10	5	5	19.6	10.4
1950-54	16	45.6	6	12	6	3	16.0	11.0
1955-59	15	40.0	2	7	6	7	20.3	10.0
1960-64	14	44.4	1	4	8	5	19.9	11.0

1965-69	15	38.4	2	4	10	4	15.5	10.0
1970-74	12	46.8	1	2	10	2	10.2	7.7
1975-79	13	40.3	1	2	7	4	12.1	8.5
1980-84	5	48.6	0	0	4	2	7.5	6.5
1985-89	8	41.0	0	0	4	4	6.3	
1990-94	9	41.9	3	0	4	1	3.7	

Notes:-

1. The number of men becoming masons shows great variation by year during the 19th century and stabilises much more during the 20th century. Taking a 5 year cohort does of course smooth out any annual variation. The drop on the second half of the 20th century is typical of that shown in many other fraternal and society based organisations. Quite how this compares during the industrial revolution is not known.

2. Age at becoming a Mason. The 19th century gives a typical range of 28-33 years of age, but this changes around the turn of the century to 38-46.

3. Joining members. These are Masons who either changed lodges within the area or moved into the area from elsewhere.

4. Death.

5. Left the lodge. This includes those members who left the lodge either by resignation or exclusion (for non-payment of dues) and specifically excluded deaths. It is unusual for Masonic data sets to have information for its members leaving lodges although all this data is recorded in the minutes of meetings.

6. WM (Worshipful Master). This records the number of members from the cohort who became master of the lodge. While it is now the custom that the master changes once a year it was the custom prior to the middle of the nineteenth century to have two masters per year who were installed in July and December and also that a popular master could be re-elected repeatedly either straight after a term of office or at a later date.

Appendix IV

Some relevant Masonic terminology

Given the potential confusion it is worth providing a brief explanation of some of the terms used. The first Grand Lodge was formed in London in 1717 by four lodges, although there were earlier and pre-existing lodges prior to that date in various parts of the England. There are separate Grand Lodges in both Ireland (1725) and Scotland (1736).

The 'Antient' Grand Lodge was formed in 1751, the Grand Lodge having strong Irish links. They claimed that the original 'Premier' Grand Lodge had changed the ritual, modernised it, and dubbed their opponents the 'Moderns'. Both titles have stuck to this day. In 1813 as a result of both internal and external political pressures the two Grand Lodges joined together to become 'The United Grand Lodge of England' (which includes Wales as well). For further information see David Harrison *The Genesis of Freemasonry*, (Lewis Masonic, 2009).

Bibliography

Primary Source Material

Art School Documents: including the Annual Report 1854, Minute Books 1853-1893, and Account Books 1875-1893, Warrington Library, reference B3536.

Church records for St. Peter's, Church Street, Liverpool 1815-1826. Liverpool Library. Ref: 283PET.

Church records for St. Nicholas, Liverpool, 1817-1842. Liverpool Library. Ref: 283NIC3/12.

Family papers of James Broadhurst. Private collection. Not listed.

Family papers of John Eltonhead. Private collection. Not listed.

Family papers of Hargreaves Hope, complied by John Hope. Private collection. Not listed.

Foresters Laws & Regulations, Warrington, 1842, Warrington Library, reference p1423.

List of Members of the Lodge of Lights No.148, Warrington, 1765-1981, Warrington Masonic Hall. Not listed.

List of the Members of Lodge No. 428 (Merchants Lodge), 1789. Liverpool Masonic Hall, Hope Street, Liverpool. Not listed.

List of Members & Minutes of the Lodge of Friendship, No.277, Oldham Masonic Hall, 1789-1900. Not listed.

Minutes from the Amicable Club, 1788-1803, Warrington Library, reference MS13.

Minutes from the Eagle & Child Club, 1781-1785, Warrington Library, reference MS14.

The Minute Books for the Mechanics Institute, 1838-1855, Warrington Library, reference MS235.

Minutes of the Lodge of Lights No.148, 1850-1900, Warrington Masonic Hall. Not listed.

Minutes of General Meetings of the Natural History Society, 1837-1853, Warrington Library, reference MS22.

Minutes of the Ancient Union Lodge no. 203, 1795-1835, Garston Masonic Hall, Liverpool. Not listed.

Minutes of the Lodge of Harmony no. 220, 1822-1835, Garston Masonic Hall, Liverpool. Not listed.

Minutes of the Toxteth Lodge No. 1356, Liverpool, 1871-2009. Held by the Lodge. Not listed.

Oddfellows Contribution Book, Loyal Orange Lodge no.143, 1835-42, Warrington Library, reference MS280.

Patten Deeds, Warrington Library, reference MS1216.

Reminiscences of an Unrecognized Lodge, namely Old Sincerity Lodge No. 486 by James Miller. Many thanks to the Rev. Neville Cryer who supplied the memoirs of James Miller. Not listed.

Various Collected Newspaper Reports of Provincial Grand Lodge Meetings, Warrington Masonic Hall, 1867 & 1869. Not listed.

Warrington Musical Society Documents: including the secretaries books, accounts, and list of members and subscribers 1833-1995, Warrington Library, reference MS2847.

Warrington School of Science Minute Book 1878-1884, Warrington Library, reference MS239.

1851 Census for Liverpool, Lancashire. Liverpool Library. Ref: 153/2183.

1861 Census for Liverpool, Lancashire. Liverpool Library. Ref: 18/2681.

Published Source Material

Anderson, James, *The Constitutions of The Free-Masons*, (London: Senex, 1723).

Anon., *The Life of Captain Joseph Brant with An Account of his Re-interment at Mohawk, 1850, and of the Corner Stone Ceremony in the Erection of the Brant Memorial, 1886*, (Ontario, Brantford: B.H. Rothwell, 1886).

Anon., 'The Manchester and Liverpool Rail-Road' in the *Monthly Supplement of The Penny Magazine of The Society for the Diffusion of Useful Knowledge*, March 31 to April 30, 1833.

Anon., *Liverpool & Slavery by a Genuine Dicky Sam*, (Newcastle on Tyne: F. Graham, 1969 Edition).

Ashmole, Elias, *Theatrum Chemicum Britannicum*, (London, 1652).

Barbauld, Anna Laetitia, *Poems by Anna Laetitia Barbauld*, (Boston: Wells and Lilly, 1820).

Barbauld, Anna Laetitia, *The Works of Anna Laetitia Barbauld With a Memoir by Lucy Aikin*, (Boston: David Reed, 1826).

Bligh Bond, Frederick, *Central Somerset Gazette Illustrated Guide to Glastonbury*, (Glastonbury: Avalon Press, 1927).

Bligh Bond, Frederick, *The Gate of Remembrance, The story of the psychological experiment which resulted in the discovery of the Edgar Chapel at Glastonbury*, (Kessinger Publishing Co., 1999).

Boswell, James, *Boswell's Life of Johnson*, (London: John Murray, 1847).

Burke, Edmund, 'Reflections on the Revolution in France, and on the proceedings in certain societies in London relative to that event: In a letter intended to have been sent to a gentleman in Paris', in *The Works of*

The Right Honorable Edmund Burke, Revised Edition, Vol. III, (Boston: Little, Brown, and Company, 1865).

Conan Doyle, Arthur, *The History of Spiritualism*, (Teddington: Echo Library, 2006).

Conan Doyle, Arthur, *The Coming of the Fairies*, (Forgotten Books, 2007).

Coustos, John, *The Sufferings of John Coustos for Free-Masonry And For His Refusing to Turn Roman Catholic in the Inquisition at Lisbon*, (London: W. Strahan, 1746).

Craig, R., & Jarvis, R., *Liverpool Registry of Merchant Ships*, Vol. 15, (Manchester: Chatham Society, 1967).

Crow, Hugh, *Memoirs of the late Captain Hugh Crow of Liverpool*, (Liverpool: Longman, Rees, Orme, Brown & Green, and G. & J. Robinson, 1830).

Cunningham, Peter, *Hand-Book of London, past and present*, (London: J. Murray, 1850).

Davies, J. A., (ed.), *The Letters of Goronwy Owen (1723-1769)*, (Cardiff: William Lewis Ltd, 1924).

Desaguliers, J.T., *A Dissertation Concerning the Figure of the Earth*, The Royal Society Library, London, (1724).

Dickens, Charles, Jr, *Dictionary Of London: An Unconventional Handbook*, (London: Charles Dickens and Evans, 1879).

Duncan, Malcolm C., *Duncan's Masonic Ritual and Monitor*, (Forgotten Books, 2008).

Fatout, Paul, *Mark Twain Speaking*, (Iowa: University of Iowa Press, 1978).

Fenn, Thomas, The Prince of Wales's Lodge No. 259: list of members from the time of its constitution, (London: Jarrold & Sons Ltd., Revised ed. 1938).

Forster, George, *A Voyage Round The World, Vol. I & II*, (White, Robson, Elunsley & Rhodes, 1777).

Franklin, Benjamin, *The Autobiography of Benjamin Franklin*, (New York: Courier Dover Publications, 1996).

The Freemasons' Magazine: And Cabinet of Universal Literature For January 1796.

Garnett, Robert, J.P., 'What I Saw in Palestine', in *Proceedings of the Warrington Literary & Philosophical Society*, (Warrington: Printed at the Guardian Office, 1892), pp.1-81.

Gaskell, Elizabeth, *North And South*, (London: Penguin, 1994).

Gore's Liverpool Trade Directory, 1825, Liverpool Library. Ref: H942.7215.

Gronow, Captain R.H., *Celebrities of London and Paris*, (London: Smith, Elder & Co., 1865).

Gronow, Captain R.H., *Reminiscences of Captain Gronow*, (London: Smith, Elder & Co., 1862).

Hunt, Leigh, *The Poetical Works of Leigh Hunt and edited by his son Thornton Hunt*, (London: George Routledge and Sons, 1860).

Hunt, Leigh, *The Town*, (Oxford: Oxford University Press, 1907).

Idzerda, Stanley J., (ed.), *Lafayette in the Age of the American Revolution: Selected Letters and Papers 1776-1790*, Vol.I, December 7, 1776-March 30, 1778, (New York: Cornell University Press, 1983).

Jupp, P., (ed.), *The Letter-Journal of George Canning, 1793-1795*, Royal Historical Society, Camden Fourth Series, Volume 41, (London, 1991).

Kipling, Rudyard, *Many Inventions*, (Kessinger Publishing Reprint, 2005).

Malthus, Thomas, An Essay on the Principle of Population as it Affects the Future Improvement of Society, (London: Printed for J. Johnson, 1798).

Moore, Charles W., Grand Secretary of The Grand Lodge of Massachusetts, *The Freemasons' Monthly Magazine*, Vol. XXIII, (Boston: printed by Hugh H. Tuttle, 1864).

Morgan, Owain, *Pabell Dofydd Eglurhad ar anianyddiaeth grefyddol yr hen dderwyddon Cymreig*, (Caerdydd: argraffwyd gan Daniel owen d'I ywmni, 1889).

Moss, W., *The Liverpool Guide*, (Printed for and sold by Crane and Jones, Castle Street, sold by Vernor and Hood, London, 1796).

Oliver, George, *A Dictionary of Symbolic Masonry including The Royal Arch Degree*, (London: Richard Spencer, 1853).

Oliver, George, *Origin of the Royal Arch Degree*, The American Freemason Magazine, (New York, 1859).

Oliver, George, *The Historical Landmarks and other Evidences of Freemasonry: Explained in a Series of Practical Lectures*, (New York: Masonic Publishing and Manufacturing Co., 1867).

Oliver, George, *The Origin of the Royal Arch Order of Masonry*, (London: Bro. Richard Spencer, 1867).

Paine, Thomas, *Origin of Free Masonry*, in *The Works of Thomas Paine*, (New York: E. Haskell, 1854).

Paine, Thomas, *Rights of Man: Being An Answer to Mr. Burke's Attack on The French Revolution*, (London: Holyoake and Co., 1856).

Paine, Thomas, 'African Slavery in America' (1775), in Micheline Ishay, (ed.), *The human rights reader: major political writings, essays, speeches, and documents from the Bible to the present*, (Routledge, 1997).

Percival, Thomas, *Medical Ethics; or, A Code of Institutes and Precepts adapted to the Professional Conduct of Physicians and Surgeons*, (Oxford: John Henry Parker, mdcccxlix).

Pike, Albert, *Morals and Dogma of the Ancient and Accepted Scottish Rite of Freemasonry*, (NuVision Publications LLC, 2007).

Polidori, William John, *The Vampyre*, (London: Sherwood, Neely and Jones, 1819).

Price, Richard, 'Additional Observations on the Nature and Value of Civil Liberty, and the War with America', (1777), in David Oswald Thomas, (ed.), *Political Writings by Richard Price*, (Cambridge: Cambridge University Press, 1991).

Priestley, Joseph, *The History and Present State of Electricity*, (London: Printed for J. Dodsley, J. Johnson and T. Cadell, 1767).

Priestley, Joseph, *Lectures on History and General Policy*, (Dublin: P. Byrne, 1788).

Priestley, Joseph, *The Memoirs of Joseph Priestley*, (Allenson, 1904).

Raffles, Sir Thomas Stamford, *Statement of the Services of Sir Stamford Raffles*, (London: Cox and Baylie, Great Queen Street, 1824).

Raffles, Sophia, *Memoir of the Life and Public Services of Sir Thomas Stamford Raffles FRS*, Vol. 1, (London: James Duncan, 1835).

Stukeley, William, *Stonehenge a temple restor'd to the British Druids*, (W. Innys and R. Manby, 1740).

Viscount Leverhulme by his son, (London: Allen & Unwin Ltd., 1928).

Walesby, F.P., (ed.), *The Works of Samuel Johnson*, (Oxford: Talboys and Wheeler, 1825).

Wallis Budge, Ernest A., *The Mummy, Funeral Rites & Customs in Ancient Egypt*, (Guernsey: Senate Press, 1995).

Walsh, Robert, (ed.), *Select Speeches of the Right Honourable George Canning with a Preliminary Biographical Sketch, and an Appendix of Extracts From His Writings and Speeches*, (Philadelphia: Crissy & Markley, 1850).

Warren, Sir Herbert, (ed.), *Poems of Alfred, Lord Tennyson 1830-1865*, (Oxford: Oxford University Press, 1929).

Warrington Trade Directories, 1792-1855, Warrington Library, reference S10121.

Warrington Examiner, 2nd of December, 1916.   Private collection.   Not Listed.

Warrington Guardian, 22nd of September, 1855. Private collection.   Not Listed.

Wilde, Oscar, *The Complete Works*, (London: Magpie, 1993).

Yeats, W.B., 'The Secret Rose' in R.K.R. Thornton, (ed.), *Poetry of the Nineties*, (Middlesex: Penguin, 1970).

Secondary Works

Anon, *Duke of Athol Lodge Bi-Centenary*, published by the Lodge, (1995).

Anon., The History of the Ellesmere Lodge No. 758, (Cheshire, 2009).

Armstrong, J., *A History of Freemasonry in Cheshire*, (London: Kenning, 1901).

Armstrong, J., *History of the Lodge of Lights, no. 148,* (Warrington, 1898).

Arrowsmith, P., *Stockport - a History*, (Stockport MBC, 1997).

Barrow, G., *Celtic Bards, Chiefs and Kings*, (London: John Murray, 1928).

Barty-King, Hugh, *"Round Table" The Search for Fellowship 1927-1977*, (London: Heinemann, 1977).

Beesley, E.B., *The History of the Wigan Grand Lodge*, (Leeds: Manchester Association for Masonic Research, 1920).

Begemann, Wilhelm, *Vorgeschite und Anfäfnge der Freimaurerei in England* (Berlin: Ernst Siegfried Mittler und Sohn, 1909).

Bennet, A., *A Glance at some old Warrington Societies*, (Warrington: Mackie & Co. Ltd, 1906).

Blocker, Jack S., Fahey, David M., and Tyrrell, Ian R., *Alcohol and Temperance in Modern History*, (ABC-CLIO Ltd., 2003).

Bullock, S.C., *Revolutionary Brotherhood*, (North Carolina: University of North Carolina Press, 1996).

Calvert, Albert F., 'Where Masons Used to Meet', in the *British Masonic Miscellany*, Compiled by George M. Martin, Vol.20, (Dundee: David Winter and Son, 1936), pp.95-98.

Carter, G.A., *Warrington Hundred*, (Warrington, 1947).

Crowe, A.M., *Warrington, Ancient and Modern*, (Warrington: Beamont Press, 1947).

Davie, Grace, *Religion in Britain Since 1945: Believing Without Belonging*, (Oxford: Wiley-Blackwell, 1994).

Debo, Angie, *The Road to Disappearance, A History of the Creek Indians*, (Oklahoma: The University of Oklahoma Press, 1941).

Evans, E. J., *The Forging of the Modern State: Early Industrial Britain 1783-1870*, (London: Longman, 1992).

Faulks, Philippa and Cooper, Robert L.D., *The Masonic Magician; The Life and Death of Count Cagliostro and his Egyptian Rite*, (London: Watkins, 2008).

Fort Newton, Joseph, *The Builders*, (London: Unwin Brothers Limited, 1924).

Gee, B., *History of the Lodge of Friendship no.277*, (Oldham, 1989).

Gosden, P.H.J.H., *The Friendly Societies In England 1815-1875*, (Manchester: Manchester University Press, 1961).
Gould, R.F., *The History of Freemasonry, Vol. I-VI*, (London, 1884-7).

Greer, Mary K., *Women of the Golden Dawn; Rebels and Priestesses*, (Rochester, Vermont: Park Street Press, 1995).

Haakonssen, Lisbeth, *Medicine and Morals in the Enlightenment: John Gregory, Thomas Percival and Benjamin Rush*, (Amsterdam: Rodopi, 1997).

Harland-Jacobs, Jessica, *Builders of Empire: Freemasonry and British Imperialism 1717-1927*, (North Carolina: North Carolina Press, 2007).

Harrison, David, *Domville Lodge No. 4647, Lymm, Cheshire, The First 75 Years*, (Manchester, 1999).

Harrison, David, *The Genesis of Freemasonry*, (Hersham: Lewis Masonic, 2009).

Hewitt, C.R., *Towards My Neighbour: The Social Influence of the Rotary Club Movement in Great Britain and Ireland*, (London: Longmans, 1950).

Hobsbawm, E. J., *Labouring Men*, (London: Weidenfeld and Nicolson, 1986).

Hoffmann, Stefan-Ludwig, *The Politics of Sociability: Freemasonry and German Civil Society, 1840-1918*, Translated by Tom Lampert, (University of Michigan Press, 2007).

Hyneman, Leon, *Freemasonry in England from 1567 to 1813*, (Montana: Kessinger Publishing, 2003).

Kelly, T., *A History of Adult Education in Great Britain*, (Liverpool: Liverpool University Press, 1970).

Kingsford, P.W., *Engineers, Inventors and Workers*, (London: Edward Arnold, 1973).

Longmate, N., *The Hungry Mills*, (London: Temple Smith, 1978).

Lovett, T., *Adult Education Community Development & The Working Class*, (Department of Adult Ed., University of Nottingham, 1982).
Mackey, Albert Gallatin, *A Lexicon of Freemasonry*, (London, 1869).

Mackey Albert Gallatin, and Haywood, H.L., *Encyclopedia of Freemasonry Part 1*, (Montana: Kessinger, 1946).

Macnab, John, History of The Merchants Lodge, No. 241, Liverpool, 1780-2004, Second Edition, (Liverpool, 2004).

McLachlen, H., *Warrington Academy, Its History and Influence*, (Manchester: The Chetham Society, 1968).

Moran, Maureen, *Victorian Literature and Culture*, (New York: Continuum, 2006).

Nulty, G., *Guardian Country 1853-1978*, (Cheshire County Newspapers Ltd, 1978).

O'Brien, P., *Warrington Academy, 1757-86, Its Predecessors & Successors*, (Owl Books, 1989).

O'Brien, P., *Eyres' Press, 1756-1803, An Embryo University Press*, (Owl Books, 1993).

O'Brien, P., M.D., *Debate Aborted: Burke, Priestley, Paine & The Revolution in France 1789-91*, (Durham: Pentland Press, 1996).

Oxford, A.W., *No. 4 an introduction to the History of the Royal Somerset House and Inverness Lodge*, (London: Bernard Quaritch Ltd., 1928).

Picton, J. A., *Memorials of Liverpool*, Vol. I, (London: Longmans, 1875).

Putnam, R.D., *Bowling Alone: The Collapse and Revival of American Community*, (New York: Simon & Schuster, 2000).

Putnam, R.D., *Democracies in Flux: The Evolution of Social Capital in Contemporary Society*, (New York: Oxford University Press 2002).

Roberts, Allen E., *House Undivided: The Story of Freemasonry and the Civil War*, (Missouri, USA: Missouri Lodge of Research, 1961).

Rule, J., (ed.), *British Trade Unionism 1750 - 1850: The Formative Years*, (Longman, 1988).

Sandbach, R.S.E., *Priest and Freemason: The Life of George Oliver*, (Northamptonshire: The Aquarian Press, 1988).

Saxelby, C. H., (ed.), *Bolton Survey (County History Reprints)*, (Bolton: SR Publishers, 1971).

Scholes, J. C., *History of Bolton*, (Bolton: The Daily Chronicle Office, 1892).

Stephens, W.B., *Adult Education And Society In An Industrial Town: Warrington 1800-1900*, (University of Exeter, 1980).

Surrey Dane, E., *Peter Stubs and the Lancashire Hand Tool Industry*, (John Sherratt and Son Ltd, 1973).

Tait, A., *History of the Oldham Lyceum 1839-1897*, (Oldham: H.C. Lee, 1897).

Thomas, H., *The Slave Trade*, (New York: Simon & Schuster Inc., 1997).

Thompson, E.P., *The Making of the English Working Class*, (Pelican, 1970).

Turner, W., *The Warrington Academy*, (Warrington: The Guardian Press 1957).

Williams, Gomer, *History of the Privateers and Slave Trade of Liverpool*, (Liverpool: Edward Howell, 1906).

Willey, B., *The Eighteenth Century Background*, (Chatto & Windus, 1946).

Wood, Robert Leslie, *York Lodge No. 236, formerly The Union Lodge, the becentennial history 1777-1977*, (York, 1977).

Woodford, A.F.A., *Kennings Cyclopaedia of Freemasonry*, (London: Kenning, 1878).

Woods, Herbert, and Armstrong, James, *A Short Historical Note of Freemasonry in Warrington*, (Warrington, 1938).

Journals

Alexander, Jennifer S., 'The Introduction and Use of Masons' Marks in Romanesque Buildings in England', in *Medieval Archaeology*, 51, (2007), pp.63-81.

Ashworth, William J., 'Memory, Efficiency, and Symbolic Analysis: Charles Babbage, John Herschel, and the Industrial Mind', *ISIS*, Vol.87, No.4, USA, (1996), pp.629-653.

Belton, John L., 'Masonic Membership Myths Debunked', in *Heredom*, Vol. 9, (Washington DC: Scottish Rite Research Society, 2001), pp.9-32.

Belton, John L., 'Communication and Research versus Education' – the battle for a master mason's daily advance in Masonic knowledge', *AQC*, Vol. 118, (2006), pp.210-218.

Begemann, W., 'An Attempt to Classify the "Old Charges" of the British Masons', in *AQC*, Vol. 1, (1888), pp.152-167.

Burt, Roger, 'Industrial Relations In The British Non-Ferrous Mining Industry in the Nineteenth Century', in *Labour History Review*, Vol. 71, No. 1, (April 2006), pp.57-79.

Durr, Andy, 'Chicken and Egg – the Emblem Book and Freemasonry: the Visual and Material Culture of Associated Life', in *AQC*, Vol. 118, (2006), pp.20-36.

Gould, R.F., 'English Freemasonry Before the Era of Grand Lodge', in *AQC*, Vol. 1, (1888), pp.67-74.

Halstead, J., and Prescott, A., 'Breaking The Barriers: Masonry, Fraternity And Labour', *Labour History Review*, Vol. 71, No. 1, (April 2006), pp.3-8.

Harrison, David, 'Freemasonry, Industry and Charity: The Local Community and the Working Man'. *The Journal of the Institute of Volunteering Research*, Volume 5, Number 1, (Winter 2002), pp.33-45.

Harrison, David and Belton, John, 'Society in Flux' in *Researching British Freemasonry 1717-2017: The Journal for the Centre of Research into Freemasonry and Fraternalism*, Vol. 3, (Sheffield: University of Sheffield, 2010), pp.71-99.

Jupp, P., (ed.), *The Letter-Journal of George Canning, 1793-1795*, Royal Historical Society, Camden Fourth Series, Volume 41, (London, 1991).

Klein, Lawrence, 'The Third Earl of Shaftesbury and the Progress of Politeness', *Eighteenth-Century Studies*, Vol. 18, No. 2, (Winter, 1984-1985), pp.186-214.

Klein, Lawrence E., 'Liberty, Manners, and Politeness in Early Eighteenth-Century England', *The Historical Journal*, Vol. 32, No. 3, (September, 1989), pp.583-605.

Mill, John S., 'The Corn Laws', in *The Westminster Review*, Vol. 3, (April 1825).

Money, John, 'The Masonic Moment; Or Ritual, Replica, and Credit: John Wilkes, the Macaroni Parson, and the Making of the Middle-Class Mind', in *The Journal of British Studies*, Vol. 32, No. 4, (October, 1993), pp.358-95.

Porter, George R., 'Free Trade', in *The Edinburgh Review*, Vol. 90, (July 1849).

Putnam, R.D., 'Bowling Alone: America's Declining Social Capital', in *Journal of Democracy*, Volume 6, Number 1, (Baltimore, Maryland, USA: Johns Hopkins University Press, January 1995).

Read, Will, 'The Spurious Lodge and Chapter at Barnsley', in *AQC*, Vol. 90, (1978), pp.1-36.

Sandbach, R.S.E., 'Robert Thomas Crucefix, 1788-1850', in *AQC*, Vol. 102, (1990), pp.134-163.

Seemungal, L.A., 'The Rise of Additional Degrees' in *AQC*, Vol. 84, (1971), pp.307-312.

Spurr, Michael J., 'The Liverpool Rebellion', in *AQC*, Vol. 85, (1972), pp.29-60.

Starr, Martin P., 'Aleister Crowley: Freemason!', in *AQC*, Vol. 108, (1995), pp.150-161.

Warren, Sir Charles, 'On the Orientation of Temples', in *AQC*, Vol. 1, (1888), pp.36-50.

Westcott, W.W., 'The Religion of Freemasonry illuminated by the Kabbalah', in *AQC*, Vol. 1, (1888), pp.55-59.

Woodford, A.F.A., 'Freemasonry and Hermeticisim', in *AQC*, Vol. 1, (1888), pp.28-36.

Vatcher, S., 'John Coustos and the Portuguese Inquisition', *AQC*, Vol. 81, (1968), pp.50-51.

Websites

Some Websites used in the Research

John Lane's Masonic Records of England and Wales 1717-1894
online: http://www.freemasonry.dept.shef.ac.uk/lane
[accessed 1st of April, 2010]

University of Wisconsin-Milwaukee special collection under the section titled 'Unitarians and Other Dissenters':
http://www.uwm.edu/Library/special/exhibits/18thcent/18thcent_un itarians2.htm [accessed 10th of August, 2009]

http://www.liverpoolmuseums.org.uk/ladylever/collections/masonicapro n.asp [accessed 6th of April, 2009]

The official website of the Lodge of St. George No. 1152:
http://www.stgeorge1152.sg/index.html [accessed 1st of April, 2010]

The official website of The Tyrell Leith Lodge No. 43:
http://www.lodge43.com/history.htm [accessed 11th of October, 2009]

The history of the Fredericksburg Lodge No. 4:
http://masoniclodge4.org/ [accessed 11th of January, 2010]

The history of the Cumberland and Westmorland Province:
http://www.cumbwestmasons.co.uk/main/history.shtml [accessed 3rd of
May, 2009]

The official website for the Travellers Club:
http://www.thetravellersclub.org.uk [accessed 16th of April, 2009]

The official website for the Army and Navy Club:
http://www.armynavyclub.co.uk/the-club/index.php [accessed 16th of
April, 2009]

The official website for the Reform Club:
http://www.reformclub.com [accessed 16th of April, 2009]

The official website for The Athenaeum Club:
http://www.athenaeumclub.co.uk/ [accessed 16th of April]

'Freemasonry's 270 years of Lodges in Worcestershire' in *Worcester News*,
Saturday, 15th of June, 2002,
http://archive.worcesternews.co.uk/2002/6/15/264560.html [accessed
1st of May, 2009]

The history of the Francis Davies Lodge No. 5035,
http://www.francisdavieslodge.org.uk/LodgeHistory.htm [accessed 1st
of May, 2009]

'The history of the Indefatigable Lodge No. 237'
http://www.province.org.uk/Lodges/237.htm [accessed 1st of May,
2009]

The Freemasonry Today Magazine official website:
http://www.freemasonrytoday.com [accessed 1st of April, 2010]

The MQ Magazine official website: http://www.mqmagazine.co.uk

[accessed 1st of April, 2010]

Jennifer S. Alexander, 'The Introduction and Use of Masons' Marks in Romanesque Buildings in England', in *Medieval Archaeology*, 51, (2007), pp.63-81. http://www2.warwick.ac.uk/fac/arts/arthistory/research/staffinterests/ja/med51-alexander.pdf [accessed 25th of July, 2009]

John L. Belton, 'Masonic Membership Myths Debunked', in *Heredom*, Vol. 9, (Washington DC: Scottish Rite Research Society, 2001), pp.9-32, http://www.lodgehope337.org.uk/lectures/belton%20L2.pdf [accessed 28th of December, 2009]

Alain Bernheim, 'Dr. Wilhelm Begemann vs. The English Masonic History Establishment: A Love-Hate Story', in *Heredom*, Vol. 7, (1998), http://www.srmason-sj.org/web/heredom-files/volume7/dr-wilhelm-begemann.htm [accessed 1st of September 2009]

Robert Currie, *Early Royal Arch Chapters in the South of Scotland*, http://www.lodgehope337.org.uk/lectures/rcurrie%20L1.PDF [accessed 15th of March, 2009]

Pam Davies, 'Sir Josiah John Guest and the Merthyr Radicals: A Symbiotic Relationship', *CRF*, University of Sheffield, Seminars (2001-2007), http://freemasonry.dept.shef.ac.uk/index.php?lang=0&type=blog&level0=242&level1=263&level2=367&op=261 [accessed 15th of May, 2009]

Andrew Prescott, 'Freemasonry and the Problem of Britain', the Inaugural Lecture to mark the launch of the University of Sheffield's Centre for Research into Freemasonry, 5th of March, 2001, http://www.southchurch.mesh4us.org.uk/pdf/contemporary/freemasons-problem-sheffield.pdf [accessed 3rd of August, 2009]

Andrew Prescott, 'The Spirit of Association: Freemasonry and Early Trade Unions', A Paper Presented at the Canonbury Masonic Research Centre, 30 May 2001, *CRF*, University of Sheffield, http://freemasonry.dept.shef.ac.uk/index.php?lang=0&type=page&level 0=243&level1=387&level2=394&op=387 [accessed 15th of May, 2009]

Andrew Prescott, "THE VOICE CONVENTIONAL' Druidic Myths and Freemasonry', a paper given to the Kirkcaldy Masonic Research Conference, May 2001, and at the Fourth International Conference of the Canonbury Masonic Research Centre, November 2002, http://www.lodgehope337.org.uk/lectures/prescott%20S01.PDF [accessed 20th of August, 2009]

Joannes A.M. Snoek, *The Evolution of the Hiramic Legend in England and France,* (2003), http://www.scottishrite.org/what/educ/heredom/articles/vol11-snoek.pdf [accessed 8th of June, 2009]

F. H. W. Sheppard (General Editor), 'St. James's Street, East Side', in *Survey of London: volumes 29 and 30: St James Westminster, Part 1* (1960), pp.433-458.http://www.british-history.ac.uk/report.aspx?compid=40621 [accessed 16th of April, 2009]

Leon Zeldis, 'The Future of Freemasonry: Challenges and Responses', a paper delivered to the Regular Meeting No. 19 of Montefiore Lodge, Tel Aviv, on the 29th of December, 2002, http://www.freemasons-freemasonry.com/zeldis05.html [accessed 28th of December, 2009]

Index

CPSIA information can be obtained at www.ICGtesting.com
Printed in the USA
LVOW04s1724130815

450005LV00008B/88/P